Healthy Dining

in Los Angeles

Second Edition

Restaurant Nutrition Guide

Featuring Healthy Entrees from
91 of Los Angeles' Best Restaurants

Including:

✓✓ **Calories**   ✓✓ **Cholesterol**
✓✓ **Fat**   ✓✓ **Sodium**

Diabetic Food Exchanges and Other Information

by

Accents On Health, Inc.

Authors:

Anita Jones, M.P.H.
Esther Hill, Ph.D.
Erica Bohm, M.S.

Healthy Dining
in Los Angeles
Second Edition

Restaurant Nutrition Guide
by
Accents On Health, Inc.

<u>Authors:</u>

Anita Jones, M.P.H., Esther Hill, Ph.D., and Erica Bohm, M.S.

Restaurant and Nutrition Information:

Accents On Health, Inc., 4945 Mercury St., San Diego, CA 92111
(619) 541-2049

Book Publication and Sales:

Hill & Hill Publishing, P.O. Box 927215, San Diego, CA 92192-7215
(619) 453-3814 or (800) 953-DINE

Cover Design by Patricia Mattison, Logo by Ramon Hutson
Photos by Rachael Kutras (619) 558-7238

Library of Congress Cataloging in Publication Data
Jones, Anita
Healthy Dining in Los Angeles
1, Nutrition. 2, Diet. 3, Restaurant Food,
I. Title   II. Hill, Esther   III. Bohm, Erica
91-71724
ISBN 1-879754-21-5

About Accents On Health:

Accents On Health is a health and wellness organization incorporated in 1988. They specialize in corporate and individual lifestyle-enhancement programs including nutrition, fitness, smoking cessation and stress management. The Accents On Health advisory board consists of physicians, registered dietitians, fitness specialists, a health educator and health promotion specialist. A major focus has been working with local physicians to help patients enhance their health status and reduce health risks through positive lifestyle changes. The staff has expertise in analyzing diets and foods for nutrition content.

About the Authors:

Anita Jones earned a Master's Degree in Public Health from San Diego State University. As director of Accents On Health, she works extensively in the field of nutrition, both with individuals and in group education and support sessions. Her goal has been to help people achieve healthier lifestyles through better diet, exercise, stress reduction and stop-smoking programs. Anita directs *Healthy Dining*, develops the text material for the books, and supervises the nutritional analysis of the recipes.

Esther Hill, a physiologist with a Ph.D. in Biomathematics, has worked for over 15 years in medical research at the University of California at San Diego and published over 30 scientific articles. Her motivation for being involved in this project comes largely from dealing with her 13-year old son's unstable diabetes. Her family has found restaurant dining difficult because of her son's dietary limitations. Dr. Hill understands how important restaurant nutrition information is to those with dietary restrictions. She assists in the development of the books and directs editing, typesetting and publishing.

Erica Bohm earned her Master's Degree in Community Health Science from New York City's Hunter College and has experience in nutrition education, cholesterol reduction, weight control and smoking cessation. She has worked for the American Red Cross, the American Health Foundation, other health organizations, hospitals, and businesses. Erica's roles in *Healthy Dining* include contacting restaurant owners, consulting with the chefs to choose appropriate entrees, networking with community and health organizations to support the project, and promoting the book.

Acknowledgements:

Susan Goldstein strengthens the *Healthy Dining* team with her degree from Cornell University in Human Development and Family Studies, her diverse business background, and her work with voluntary health organizations. Her *Healthy Dining* activities include contacting restaurant owners, managers and chefs, and working with them to select appropriate entrees. She also contributes to the program through marketing, publicity, promotion and community relations. Susan's experience and genuine enthusiasm help continue the growth and success of *Healthy Dining*.

Cindy Maynard, R.D., M.S. serves as a consulting dietitian for *Healthy Dining*. She works at Mesa Vista Hospital in San Diego and also has her own private practice, specializing in nutrition counseling, sports nutrition and eating disorders.

We extend our sincerest appreciation to the following respected professionals who acted as reviewers of this book:

John Campbell, M.D., Pathologist
Charlotte Crucean, Ph.D., Clinical Psychologist
Marci Daniels, J.D.
Mila De Los Reyes, M.A., R.D., Clinical Nutritionist, Mercy Hospital & Medical Center
Mary Donkersloot, R.D., Private Nutrition Counselor for Personal Nutrition Management
    and author of "Fast Food Diet: Quick & Healthy Eating at Home and on the Go"
Michele Edwards, Assist. Dir. Public Education, Am. Cancer Society, San Diego Unit
Therese A. Eyre, M.S., R.D., Obesity Treatment Team Manager, Tri-City Medical Center
    and Past President of the San Diego Dietetics Association
Betsy Horton-La Forge, R.D., M.P.H., Director of Wellness Center, Grossmont Hospital
Anita Johnson, M.S., UCSD Cancer Center
Jeanne Jones, Author of 20 cookbooks and internationally syndicated columnist
Dale Kooistra, M.D.
Ralph La Forge, Director of Health Promotion, San Diego Cardiac Center Medical Group
Cindy Maynard, M.S., R.D., Chief Clinical Dietitian, Mesa Vista Hospital
Margaret Miller, R.D., Scripps Clinic and Research Foundation
Wayne I. Newton, M.D., Cardiovascular Surgeon
Susan Plese, Marketing and Communications
Patricia Porter, Cardiopulmonary Technologist
Susan Slaughter, Jazzercise and "Know More Diet" Instructor
Cindy Stack-Keer, R.D., Health Education, Kaiser Permanente
Jamie Steele, President of Fitness West, Inc., Steele Bodies, Island Fitness
Patti Tveit-Milligan, M.S., R.D.
Suzanne Weeks, R.D., Consulting Nutritionist, Scripps Center for Executive Health
Margaret Wing-Peterson, M.S., R.D., Dietitian for San Diego Cardiac Center

And finally, we especially wish to thank the participating restaurants for the effort they put into preparing this information --- and all health-conscious diners who are supporting **Healthy Dining**. Thanks for your enthusiasm and best wishes for a healthy year of dining out!

iv

Table of Contents

Disclaimer:

The purpose of this book is to provide nutrition information for selected menu items from restaurants that have chosen to participate in the *Healthy Dining* program. It should be noted that the items listed in this book are not necessarily appropriate or healthy for all individuals. Some people may need to be more careful about certain items such as salt or sugar, or have food allergies which put additional restrictions on their food choices. Each individual is responsible, in cooperation with his or her physician, dietitian or other health consultant, for making personal dietary decisions.

Please note that we have not included all the restaurants that serve healthy food, nor are we recommending all entrees from restaurants that are included in this book.

It is also important to note that the numerical values for the nutrition information included in this book are approximations only, and the categories "Very Low" and "Low" are a better indication of the nutrition content of the menu items.

The nutrition information provided is based on the United States Department of Agriculture (USDA) nutrition information database, the source most commonly used for estimating nutritional content of foods. Participating restaurants supplied their recipes for the computerized analysis. The analyses were completed using the Nutritionist IV Computer program developed by N-Squared Computing in Oregon. Research shows the Nutritionist program to be one of the most current and reliable nutrition analysis programs available. If values for recipe ingredients were not available from the USDA data base, the manufacturer was contacted for the nutrition information. If the manufacturer did not have nutrition information, ingredients were closely matched to a similar product's nutrition information. Data were rounded to the nearest whole number and nearest 1/4 for diabetic exchanges.

All information contained in this book has been carefully compiled and reviewed by qualified health professionals. Nutrition information is based on recipes supplied by the restaurants. Participating restaurants have agreed to prepare food according to the recipes submitted for a period of one year, or to clearly notify customers otherwise.

The authors are not responsible for maintaining quality control over the food that is prepared by the restaurants. The restaurants are ultimately responsible for the quality of the food they serve.

Los Angeles County
Medical
Association

Leadership and Excellence in Health Care

1925
Wilshire
Boulevard

Los Angeles,
California
90057-3691

Mailing Address:

P.O. Box 3465

Los Angeles,
California
90051-1465

Telephone:
(213) 483-1581

Fax:
(213) 483-4560

Preface

Healthy Dining in Los Angeles is truly a book for everyone. Whether you are a fitness enthusiast, health-conscious or following a special diet prescribed by your physician, this book is invaluable. **Healthy Dining in Los Angeles** gives you the information you need to avoid excess fat, calories, cholesterol and sodium when eating in restaurants.

Only a small percentage of restaurant meals meet nutritional guidelines recommended by the U.S. Surgeon General and health professionals. Fortunately, the *Healthy Dining* team has consulted with many talented chefs in the Los Angeles basin to provide you with a wide selection of healthy entrees to choose when dining out. **Healthy Dining in Los Angeles** is a vital reference guide for restaurants dedicated to your health goals.

Sound nutrition is the foundation upon which good health rests. We at the Los Angeles County Medical Association commend you for your interest in good nutrition and wish you many hours of satisfying and healthy dining.

Sincerely yours,

Robert M. Karns, M.D.
President

Healthy Dining in <u>Orange County</u>

Second Edition

Participating restaurants:

The Alley Restaurant
Amelia's
Anaheim Marriott Hotel - La Plaza
Angie's
Antonello Ristorante
Back Bay Rowing & Running Club
Bamboo Terrace
Bistango
Black Sheep Bistro
Brazilian Tropical Cafe
Brio
Cafe Nordstrom
The Cannery
Carl's Jr.
Cathay Newport
Cedar Creek Inn
Chinatown
Chin's Chinese Kitchen
Ciao
Claes Seafood, Etc. - Hotel Laguna
Classic Q
COCO'S
Crocodile Cafe
Dana Point Resort - Watercolors Restaurant
Dimitri's
Disneyland Hotel - Shipyard Inn
El Cholo
El Pollo Loco
Farmers Market at Atrium Court
Ferdussi Taste of Persia
Fisherman's Restaurant
Forty Carrots
Four Seasons Hotel - Pavilion Restaurant
Gandhi Indian Cuisine
Garden Bistro
Gen Kai
The Healthy Gourmet
Heidelberg Bistro
Hotel Laguna - Claes Seafood, Etc.
Hyatt Newporter - Jamboree Cafe
Hyatt Regency Irvine - Le Cafe
Il Fornaio
Indian Paradise
Jack in the Box
Jamboree Cafe - Hyatt Newporter
JW's Calif. Grill - Newport Beach Marriott

La Plaza - Anaheim Marriott
Le Cafe - Hyatt Regency Irvine
Magic Pan
Mandarin Gourmet
Marco Polo
Mezzanine at the Towers
Mon Chateau
Mother's Market & Kitchen
Muldoon's Irish Pub & Restaurant
Natraj Cuisine of India
Newport Beach Marriott - JW's Calif. Grill
Nieuport 17
Oysters
Pasta Mesa
Pavilion Chinese Restaurant
Pavilion Restaurant - Four Seasons Hotel
Pick Up Stix
Ralphs Grocery Chef Express
Randell's
Red Lion Hotel - Maxi's Grille
Renaissance Cafe
Renato
Ritz Carlton Hotel - The Terrace
Rosalynn's
Royal Khyber
Royal Thai
Ruby's Diner
Rutabegorz
Scampi
Scott's Seafood Grill & Bar
Shelly's
Shipyard Inn - Disneyland Hotel
Sizzler
Skinny Haven
The Stuft Noodle
TGI Friday's
The Terrace - Ritz Carlton Hotel
Thai Kitchen
Trattoria Ciao
Tutto Mare
Villa Nova
The Village Farmer
Watercolors Restaurant - Dana Pt. Resort
Wendy's
Wolfgang Puck Cafe
Z Pizza

Second edition: 160 pages and over $200 worth of coupons, $14.95.
To order, call (619) 453-3814 or 1-800-953-DINE

Healthy Dining in <u>San Diego</u>

Third Edition

Participating restaurants:

Anthony's
Bali Hai
Blue Crab
Bully's
Cafe 6TH & K - Clarion Hotel Bay View
Cafe California - at the Broadway
Cafe Greentree
Cafe India
Cafe Nordstrom
Cafe on Park
Cafe Pacifica
Cafe San Diego - Doubletree Hotel
Carmel Highland Doubletree - Terraces Cafe
Carrows
Casa de Bandini
Casa de Pico
Casady's Whole Foods
Chang Cuisine of China
ChickeNest
Chilango's Mexico City Grill
Chili's
Clarion Hotel Bay View - Cafe 6TH & K
COCO'S
CrazyBurro
Croce's
Daily's
Daniel's Market
DiMille's
D'Lish
Doubletree - Cafe San Diego
The Eggcry
El Indio
El Pollo Loco
Fifth & Hawthorne
Fish Merchant
French Gourmet
French Pastry Shop
Gentleman's Choice
Great Harvest Bread Co.
Hungry Hunter
Il Fornaio
Ingrid's Wild West Cafe
Jack in the Box
Jimbo's.....Naturally!

KC's Tandoor
Kabul West
Kirby's Cafe
Kung Food Vegetarian Restaurant
La Gran Tapa
La Salsa
Le Meridien Hotel - L'Escale Restaurant
Lino's
Los Cabos
Marina Sea Grill - San Diego Marriott
Montanas American Grill
Mucho Gusto
Nicolosi's
Pacifica Del Mar
Panda Panda
Papachinos
Pasta Experience
Peking Wok
Pick Up Stix
Pizza Nova
Pizzeria Uno
Poseidon
Rainwater's
Ralphs Grocery Chef Express
Rancho el Nopal
Rancho Valencia Resort Restaurant
Royal Thai Cuisine
Ruby's Diner
Salmon House
SandCrab Cafe
Second Nature Vegetarian Cafe
Sheik Cafe
Sheraton Grande Torrey Pines - Torreyana Grill
Sizzler
St. Germain's Cafe
Star of India
T.D. Hays
Terraces Cafe - Carmel Highland Doubletree
T.G.I. Friday's
Thai Chada
Tom Ham's Lighthouse
Torreyana Grill - Sheraton Grande Torrey Pines
Welk Resort Center Restaurant
Wendy's

Third edition: 168 pages and over $200 worth of coupons, $14.95.
To order, call (619) 453-3814 or 1-800-953-DINE

Foreword

The surprising truth about dining out

You think you are health conscious. You pick chicken or fish from restaurant menus and believe you'll be safe by doing so. Read on!

Accents On Health has analyzed thousands of restaurant recipes and found lots of surprises. Menu descriptions just aren't enough, and you rarely know what you're getting!

But <u>now you can be sure</u>. The menus that appear within these pages have passed the closest scrutiny. You'll find great tasting food here that's also <u>good for you</u>! As you can see, these participating restaurants have demonstrated their interest in your health.

You, who are watching your diet, counting calories, and eating less cholesterol --- you win! If you have a heart problem and severe restrictions --- you can dine out too. Watching your sodium (salt)? --- come along! Even those with diabetes can safely leave home and venture into the wonderful, romantic world of dining out, because diabetic food exchange values are printed with every menu entree.

Hooray for the restaurants that are making this possible, and for everyone who is health conscious --- all of you! The information you need is here. Read this guide to the restaurants that proudly display their nutrition information in the *Healthy Dining* menus. Pick a restaurant from <u>this book</u>, not by chance!

David G. Daniels, M.D.

P.S. Please tell everyone in your restaurant --- the manager, the hostess, the waiting staff --- tell everyone why you are there. <u>Your business and your requests for the "Healthy Dining" menus are the strongest motivations for them to continue with the Healthy Dining program.</u> They need to hear from you, their customers, that it was worthwhile. So...

> Please ask for the <u>*"Healthy Dining"*</u> menus in the restaurants and let them know that you appreciate the healthy menu choices.

A Fund-Raiser with Good Taste!

Looking for an exciting, effective and innovative way to raise funds for your organization?

Healthy Dining in Los Angeles is your answer.

<u>**Healthy Dining** is a great way to raise money</u>:

• distinguishes your group from others selling the "usual" products
• high monetary return to your organization
• priced right
• easy to sell, especially with the valuable restaurant coupons
• informative and useful - has genuine health/educational value
• a unique, attractive, trend-setting book
• wide appeal for:
>   - the weight-conscious
>   - those with healthy, active lifestyles
>   - those with high cholesterol, high blood pressure, etc.
>   - everyone who enjoys dining out

For more information, please contact
Healthy Dining at (619) 453-3814

People are talking about *Healthy Dining...*

"I encourage patients to use the book whenever they dine out.
It's great that there is finally a "nutrition label" for restaurant dining.
That's exactly what Healthy Dining provides for health-conscious Americans."
- *Mary Felando, M.S., R.D., Preventive & Rehab. Cardiac Center,*
Cedars-Sanai Medical Center

"*Healthy Dining* is an invaluable book for those concerned about their health."
- *Elmer Dills, KABC Talk Radio*

"It is a rewarding challenge to please our customers with healthy, innovative
and creative dishes which are not loaded with butter and fat."
- *Joachim Splichal, chef & proprietor of Patina Restaurant & Pinot Bistro*

"The *Healthy Dining* book is a great addition to our Fat Loss Program - the members
love it and the book helps our members get true results and maintain them."
- *April Morgan, Fitness & Aerobics Director, The Sports Club Company*

"I always applaud any effort to bring nutritional information to the
community. You've done an outstanding job."
- *Jeanne Jones, cookbook author and internationally syndicated columnist*

"*Healthy Dining* makes healthy low-calorie restaurant dining easy.
It's a wonderful tool that allows people the freedom and
enjoyment of restaurant dining without guilt and anxiety."
- *Linda Trozzolino, Ph.D., writer and director of*
weight control programs for 17 years in West LA

"*Healthy Dining in San Diego* is an effective tool to help members
identify foods lower in fat when dining out."
- *Cathy Perry, Kaiser Permanente Cholesterol Treatment Center*

"The American Heart Association applauds the participating restaurants
for accommodating the customer of the 90's, the customer that
cares about good health... This book enables the consumer
to make healthy choices. <u>It's a very useful tool.</u>"
- *Patricia Lozada-Santone, M.P.H., American Heart Association volunteer*

People are talking about *Healthy Dining...*

"I didn't realize until I read this book that I <u>have</u> been avoiding
eating in restaurants in an effort to stay healthy and slim.
Armed with this book, I'm eager to dine out again!"
- *Michele Edwards, Public Education, American Cancer Society*

"*Healthy Dining*...is as valuable for the generally health conscious as...
for those with special dietary needs. Having eaten at many of the
restaurants listed, I was delighted to find detailed information...that will
enable me to continue enjoying 'fine dining' and not sacrifice my health!"
- *Renee LaBriola, M.A., R.D., Kaiser Permanente*

"This healthy eater's guide to dining out will help you achieve
your goals without limiting you to a dinner salad."
- *Carol LeBeau, KGTV News*

"I have searched far and wide for a restaurant guide that finds
not only good food, but delicious HEALTHY food. My prayers
have been answered with the *Healthy Dining* series!"
- *Victor Ettinger, M.D., Medical Director, Bone Diagnostic & Treatment Centres*

"The guidelines developed in this book closely correspond to those I've
used in my book and with my clients. This resource will make my job
as a nutrition counselor much easier and more effective."
- *Mary Donkersloot, R.D., Dietitian and author of*
"Fast Food Diet: Quick and Healthy Eating at Home and On the Go"

"A fantastic reference for both health educators and their students.
It's like having your own personal dietitian with you while dining out."
- *Robert Abelson, Ph.D., Certified Health & Fitness Instructor and*
Health Instructor, UCLA Extension

"This is opening up restaurant dining to...people who have
been concerned about it, maybe even fearful about it..."
- *Roger Hedgecock, former mayor of San Diego*

"A road map gets you where you want to go when you travel.
Healthy Dining does the same thing when you dine
out and do not want to do yourself in."
- *Annette Globits, R.D., Nutritional education & counseling*

An Important Message
from the Authors

Welcome to the *Healthy Dining* "family." This program has grown from San Diego to Orange County to Los Angeles. More than 1000 individuals have participated in this effort, including restaurant chefs and management, health professionals, and members of community organizations. You, the *Healthy Dining* reader, play an essential role in this as well.

Why? Because restaurants respond to their customers. Most of the restaurants joined *Healthy Dining* on a trial basis. They need to hear from <u>you</u> that health-conscious menu items and nutrition information are important to you.

Please Help! Here's how you can help *Healthy Dining* to grow in your community:

1. Eat at the restaurants listed in the book, and tell the restaurant staff and/or the owner that you appreciate and value their participation in *Healthy Dining*. Also, ask for the *Healthy Dining* menus (available at participating restaurants) and use the discount coupons.

2. Tell friends, family and business contacts about *Healthy Dining*.

3. Tell other restaurants about *Healthy Dining* and recommend that they participate next year.

4. Give *Healthy Dining* books as gifts for birthdays, holidays, etc.

5. Consider using *Healthy Dining* as a fund-raiser (see page xi).

6. Please call us with your suggestions and feedback (619) 453-3814.

Thanks! We appreciate your support.

How to Use This Book

This introduction summarizes how to interpret the nutrition information for the restaurant menu items. Part I of the book provides more in-depth information to help you become an informed and health-conscious diner. Part II contains menu information about 91 restaurants at over 300 locations in the greater Los Angeles area.

The Check Mark System - An easy way to find entrees to fit your goals

First, we should define "healthy entree." In this book, a healthy entree is one with high-quality, nutritious calories. In general, these are low or very low in fat, cholesterol, calories and sodium. Because many entrees are not low in all areas, the check mark system will help you easily and quickly identify which entrees best fit your individual dietary goals.

Nutritional guidelines are difficult to set. Each individual has different nutritional needs, and we recognize that. For example, caloric needs vary according to age, gender, activity level, body weight and health goals (e.g., reducing body fat, gaining weight, etc.). Nevertheless, we've provided some general guidelines to make the menu information easy to interpret. These guidelines are based on recommendations by the Surgeon General's Office and the American Heart Association. Details about how the values were chosen are included in Chapters 3 through 6, but here's a quick summary of what the check marks mean:

ENTREE GUIDELINES

Calories	✓✓ Very Low = 0 to 350 calories/entree ✓ Low = 350 to 600 calories/entree
Fat	✓✓ Very Low = 0 to 10 grams (g)/entree ✓ Low = 10 to 20 grams (g)/entree
Cholesterol	✓✓ Very Low = 0 to 100 milligrams (mg)/entree ✓ Low = 100 to 200 milligrams (mg)/entree
Sodium	✓✓ Very Low = 0 to 300 milligrams (mg)/entree ✓ Low = 300 to 600 milligrams (mg)/entree

Although the "Low" and "Very Low" designations may not be as strict as some would like to see, they represent fairly high standards for restaurant entrees and are realistic goals for most diners. We've also compromised between a relatively easy-to-read format that will meet most people's needs vs. including very extensive nutrition information that may be necessary for some individuals. Diabetic food exchanges are included, as well as footnotes (*) to designate which items contain primarily unsaturated fat.

We occasionally include a menu item that is described as "moderate" in one of the nutrient categories. "Moderate" means that the item does not meet the guidelines for "low," but it is less than twice the cut-off value for "low." Some items are listed as "high" in sodium (meaning above 1000 mg. sodium per entree) and are not recommended for those watching sodium intake but may be acceptable for others.

Please note that these are general guidelines developed for the general public. You, your physician and your dietitian are responsible for setting individual nutritional guidelines, according to your particular health needs, so...

Depending on your particular dietary goals...

If you are health-conscious and looking for better ways to eat and enhance your overall health, this book will provide an easy way to choose entrees that don't have the hidden calories, fat, cholesterol and sodium you'd rather avoid.

If you are trying to lose weight, you'll be especially interested in the calorie and fat categories. Choose items that are very low (✓✓) or low (✓) in these areas.

If you're trying to reduce your blood cholesterol level, look for items that are very low (✓✓) or low (✓) in both cholesterol and fat. For reducing sodium in your diet, select items very low (✓✓) or low (✓) in sodium and request no added salt.

If your physician or dietitian has given you daily limits in terms of sodium, cholesterol, etc., by all means note the numerical values as well as the check marks, and be sure they fit your restrictions. You may need to ask for additional modifications to your meal.

We've included brief entree descriptions, but they are not complete ingredient lists. Therefore, if you have food allergies or sensitivities, be sure to emphasize this to the restaurant personnel so they will understand how important it is to prepare your meal according to your specifications.

Comments about serving sizes, dressings and sauces, and side dishes

It's important to remember that the nutrition information is based on the FULL SERVING (unless stated). If you eat only 2/3 of the entree, you're only consuming 2/3 of the calories, fat, cholesterol, sodium, etc. So if you're craving an item that is a little higher in a particular area, order it, eat only part, and save the rest for tomorrow.

In some cases the nutrition analysis includes dressings or sauces, and in other cases it does not. We often recommend that you order sauces or dressings on the side and use them only sparingly. Dressings and sauces often contain 5 to 10 grams of fat (45 to 90 calories) per tablespoon. Depending on your goals, you may choose to completely avoid them, or order them on the side and limit the amount you use. You will likely be served more than one tablespoon, so don't assume you can pour it all on your meal. You can measure out the amount you want using your teaspoon, since 3 teaspoons is equivalent to one tablespoon (Tbs.) or ½ ounce (oz.).

The check mark system and guidelines listed on the previous page apply to main entrees only. In some cases, we've included selected side dishes, appetizers, and desserts, and have set the guidelines for calories, fat, cholesterol and sodium equal to 1/3 of the entree guidelines. Items such as breads and vegetables are not generally shown because the nutrition values are generally standard.

<u>GUIDELINES *for* SIDE DISHES *and* APPETIZERS</u>†

Calories	✓✓	Very Low = 0 to 117 calories/serving
	✓	Low = 117 to 200 calories/serving
Fat	✓✓	Very Low = 0 to 3 grams (g)/serving
	✓	Low = 3 to 7 grams (g)/serving
Cholesterol	✓✓	Very Low = 0 to 33 milligrams (mg)/serving
	✓	Low = 33 to 67 milligrams (mg)/serving
Sodium	✓✓	Very Low = 0 to 100 milligrams (mg)/serving
	✓	Low = 100 to 200 milligrams (mg)/serving

<u>FOOTNOTES - *Summary of what they mean*</u>

† Side dish guidelines are 1/3 of entree guidelines
* Primarily unsaturated fat (see Chapter 4 for more details)
** If you request no added salt (see Chapter 6 for more details)

<u>OTHER SYMBOLS</u>

Symbols at the end of the introductory paragraph for each restaurant represent the following information as provided by the restaurant:

$ - inexpensive, average cost of entree is under $10
$$ - moderate, average cost of entree is $10 to $20
$$$ - expensive, average cost of entree is over $20

How were restaurants selected to be included in this book?

Our goal was to include a wide variety of restaurants. We did not just look for restaurants that specialize in serving "health food," but for a selection of popular restaurants that have a sincere interest in providing healthy foods and nutrition information. If you want organic and natural foods, we have included restaurants that cater to those preferences as well. Vegetarian dishes are available at many of the restaurants. A good clue for vegetarian dishes is to look for items with no cholesterol (no animal products) or very low values, which may indicate small quantities of cheese or dairy products. You may, of course, double check with the restaurant personnel before ordering.

Restaurants participating in this book have a sincere interest in preparing healthy food. They paid a fee for the nutritional analysis, and they have signed an agreement with Accents On Health to prepare the selected entrees in accordance with the recipes they submitted or clearly notify customers otherwise. We highly respect the restaurants included in this book for their interest and commitment to serving healthy entrees. We purposely included many different types of cuisines with a wide price range and feel this will have the greatest impact in encouraging all restaurants to offer healthy, delicious choices.

How were entrees selected?

When a restaurant agreed to participate in the **Healthy Dining** Program, our staff of qualified health professionals worked with the chef to select recipes low in fat, cholesterol, calories and sodium.

Our first choice was to find items already on the menu, without making any modifications. This would be the easiest for you and for the restaurant. However, in some cases the recipe analysis didn't meet the **Healthy Dining** guidelines. So we worked with the chef to develop a "Special Request" version of the dish which contains less calories, fat, cholesterol and/or sodium than the original dishes served at the restaurant (see Chapter 2). The analyses listed in this book for the "Special Request" items correspond to the lower calorie, fat, etc. content that you will be served <u>if and only if you make the special request</u>. Otherwise you will probably be served a much meal with considerably higher fat and higher calorie values. See page 17 for examples.

We need your help!

The restaurants in this book have devoted time, money and effort to participate. In many cases the restaurants have modified recipes to meet your needs. Now they need to hear from you that this nutrition information is important to you and that you appreciate their participation in **Healthy Dining**.

We have provided **Healthy Dining** menus for customers' use at each of the participating restaurants. We encourage the restaurants to hand out one menu per table. Many restaurants, however, do not hand them out - *you must ask for the Healthy Dining menu.* And please do! The more that restaurants hear customers asking for the nutrition information and ordering "Special Request" versions, the more they will realize how important healthy dining is to many people.

So if this information is important to you, if you want to have the choice to "order healthy," **PLEASE tell the restaurants!** Please tell other restaurants that you'd like them to participate. This will enable us to include more restaurants and an even greater variety of healthy choices in the next edition of **Healthy Dining in Los Angeles**.

We welcome your ideas

This program is still growing, and we welcome your ideas on how we can enhance it. Please feel free to write to us with your ideas. We hope to update this publication yearly with more restaurants, more healthy entrees, and more nutrition information.

Part I

Healthy Dining Tips:

Realistic Guidelines and Practical Information

> "If you don't smoke, what you eat may be
> the biggest factor influencing your health."
>
> - U.S. Surgeon General

CHAPTER 1

Health, Lifestyle, Diet,
Misconceptions & ...
Dining Out

In 1988, the Surgeon General made a startling announcement to the American public:

"If you don't smoke, what you eat may be
the biggest factor influencing your health."

We've come a long way...

Diet has always strongly influenced health and disease. Until the early decades of this century, our country suffered from problems of _undernutrition_. Rickets, pellagra, scurvy, beriberi and goiter plagued our nation. Fortunately, in the United States, the advances in medicine, fortification of foods, and successful cures virtually eliminated the vicious diseases caused by a lack of essential nutrients.

Currently, we've reached a whole new perspective in health and disease. A large body of medical research shows that lifestyle greatly influences health status. It is well recognized that daily health habits - what we eat and drink, whether or not we smoke, how much exercise we get and how effectively we manage stress - contribute to _how long and how well_ we live.

The 1988 Surgeon General's Report on Nutrition and Health outlines the substantial impact of dietary practices on health. Five of the ten leading causes of death (heart disease, cancer, stroke, diabetes, and atherosclerosis), which together account for over 2/3 of all deaths in the U.S., are directly related to diet. The report's main conclusion is:

"_Overconsumption_ of certain dietary components is now a major concern for Americans. While many food factors are involved, chief among them is the disproportionate consumption of foods high in fats, often at the expense of foods high in complex carbohydrates and fiber that may be more conducive to health."

-- 1988 Surgeon General's Report on Nutrition and Health --

Clearly, a priority for Americans is to reduce intake of total fat, especially saturated fat, because of the relationship between excess dietary fat and the development of many leading chronic disease conditions.

Dietary guidelines for Americans:

Based on extensive scientific evidence, the following recommendations were developed by the Surgeon General's Office and the American Heart Association:

1. Reduce overall consumption of fat, especially saturated fat. The American Heart Association recommends that <u>no more than 30%</u> of total calories come from fat (the average American diet contains approximately 35% fat). Saturated fat should comprise no more than 10% of the daily diet. Choose foods low in fat such as vegetables, fruits, whole grain foods, fish, lean meats and non-fat dairy products. Use food preparation methods that add little or no fat.

2. Reduce cholesterol consumption to under 300 mg. per day, as recommended by the American Heart Association. The average American consumes about 400 - 600 mg. daily.

3. Reduce intake of sodium by choosing foods relatively low in sodium and limiting the amount of salt in food preparation and at the table. The American Heart Association recommends fewer than 3,000 mg. per day. The average American consumes about 4,000 - 6,000 mg. daily.

4. Achieve and maintain a desirable body weight. To do so, choose a balanced diet in which energy (caloric) intake is consistent with energy expenditure. To reduce caloric intake, limit consumption of foods relatively high in calories, fat, and sugar, and minimize alcohol consumption. Increase energy expenditure through regular exercise.

5. Increase consumption of complex carbohydrates and fiber, such as whole grain foods, cereals, vegetables, fruits, dried beans, peas, and lentils.

Americans are catching on!

We're watching what we eat. Learning more about what we eat. Making healthier choices. We're beginning to cherish our health for its influence on all other aspects of our lives. For top performance, we're eating more high-quality fuel - more fruits, vegetables and whole grains - and less beef, butter, whole milk and other foods high in saturated fat.

Since the mid-1970's, consumption of saturated fats has decreased significantly. In addition, U.S. death rates from heart disease have fallen dramatically, close to 25 percent in the last decade. Leading health organizations attribute some of this decline to better medical care but give most of the credit to healthier diets and lifestyles.

Food manufacturers are catching on, but...

Marketing efforts toward our increasingly health-conscious society have intensified in the past several years. Close to 30% of food advertising includes some type of health message. Although this spiraling emphasis on healthy eating from food makers is encouraging, it's also very misleading. Milk flaunts a 2% fat label (meaning 2% of the milk's <u>weight</u> is fat), but 35% of total <u>calories</u> come from fat. Similarly, lunchmeats brag about a 96% lean composition. Again, this means that only 4% of the meat's <u>weight</u> is fat, not 4% of the calories (a high percentage of the weight is water, thus decreasing the percentage weight from fat). Cookies, crackers and chips leap out from shelves with bright "NO CHOLESTEROL" banners, although the amount of total fat or saturated fat seems to be of no concern (at least to the manufacturer). Recently fat-free and cholesterol-free cakes and cookies made their debut into society - with so much sugar, there's definitely not much room for fat and cholesterol.

Reading between the lines

Until recently, deciphering food labels was a difficult task. Nutrition information on labels was often misleading, confusing and incomplete. Terms such as "low-fat," "light," "natural," and "healthy" had virtually no enforced meaning and could be added to any package, regardless of contents.

Fortunately, since May 1994, the Food and Drug Administration (FDA) has required almost all food packages to display a universal nutrition information label. These new labels are designed to help you easily identify important nutrition information. The FDA has also developed strict guidelines for several nutritional claims commonly used by food manufacturers. For example, any food package stating the product is "low-fat" must now have less than 3 grams of fat per serving. A "low-calorie" food must now contain less than 40 calories per serving. A food package promoting the product as "light" (e.g., light mayonnaise) must now contain 50% less fat or one-third fewer calories than the food with which it is being compared (e.g., regular mayonnaise). If the original product contains more than 50% calories from fat, the fat must be reduced by at least 50% in the "light" product.

It is important to note that the guidelines set by the FDA for food packages are significantly different from the *Healthy Dining* guidelines because the *Healthy Dining* guidelines are designed to represent the better part of a full meal, whereas the FDA guidelines are designed for a single product or serving.

A crusader for healthier fast foods

In April 1990, Phil Sokolof and his non-profit organization, The National Heart Savers Association, attacked American fast food restaurants with full-page ads in large newspapers accusing them of "poisoning" Americans with foods high in saturated fat. A Gallup poll showed that almost 40% of those that saw the ads immediately decreased their visits to fast food restaurants. Just three weeks later, McDonald's responded by removing beef tallow from their french fries. Other fast food chains quickly followed. Sokolof points out that his major goal was to stop fast food from being a *"fast track to a heart attack."*

With Sokolof paving the way, consumers began demanding to know - just what are we getting in fast food meals? In response, several fast food restaurants now provide nutrition information for menu items. At last, the fast American favorites have exposed their "fat facts."

Some fat facts

A McDonald's Big Mac has 560 calories, 32 grams of fat and 950 milligrams (mg.) of sodium. The Filet of Fish is almost as fat-laden with 440 calories, 26 grams of fat and 1,030 mg. sodium. Add french fries and a shake, and you're drowning in fat and sodium.

Three pieces of Kentucky Fried Chicken contain a whopping 762 calories, 53 grams of fat and 1549 milligrams of sodium. Add coleslaw, mashed potatoes with gravy and a biscuit, and you get a total of 1184 calories, 74 grams of fat and 2627 mg. of sodium. That's over a full day's recommended allowance for both fat and sodium in just one meal, and 56% of the total calories come from fat!

Salads are usually considered a safe choice. However, many salads have close to 1000 calories, over 50 grams of fat, and over 1000 milligrams (mg.) of sodium. Sometimes salads are higher in calories and fat than many other items on the menu.

Improvements in fast foods

In response to their new "fat visibility," most fast food restaurants quickly added items which look much better on the nutritional charts.

McDonald's added a Chunky Chicken Salad and a Garden Salad, both under 150 calories and 7 grams of fat. Low-calorie salad dressing is available. In addition, they've added their McLean burger, non-fat muffins, low-fat milk and yogurt to their menu.

Carls Jr.'s Lite Menu offers a Charbroiled BBQ Chicken Sandwich with just 400 calories and 7 grams of fat. The Lite Menu also includes a Lite Potato, Garden Salad and Chicken Salad with reduced-calorie salad dressing.

Jack In the Box serves a Chicken Fajita Pita with fewer than 300 calories and 8 grams of fat. They recently added a Chicken Teriyaki Bowl containing lots of rice, which is very filling and very low in fat (1½ grams). They also serve low-fat milk and provide a reduced-calorie salad dressing.

Arby's has introduced a new "light" menu that includes salads and sandwiches with fewer than 300 calories. El Pollo Loco specializes in healthy, broiled chicken that contains no added fat.

Consumer power

As a result of health-conscious consumers speaking out, we're now beginning to have the choice to "order healthy" at fast food restaurants. "The public does not realize the dramatic power it wields," Sokolof emphasizes. "The consumer's wish is big business' command."

But what about dining out in restaurants?

What's healthy and what's not?

If dining out were only for special occasions, the rich and creamy dishes could be wonderful treats. An occasional splurge might not be so bad. But as restaurant dining for business, pleasure and convenience becomes more common, it is important to find healthier choices.

That's what *Healthy Dining in Los Angeles* is all about. It's the first book of its kind. Never before has so much comprehensive information been available for restaurant menu items. Each restaurant has its own unique recipes, prepared in its own special way. So nutrition information must be compiled restaurant by restaurant, recipe by recipe. And that's a lot of work.

There are books which give general information for dining out. They list common entrees to avoid and those which are probably best to order. However, as restaurants become more specialized and creative, "common" entrees are not so common, so it's hard to follow those guidelines.

You can learn how to order healthy entrees by asking the right kinds of questions. *Healthy Dining* will make the process of ordering healthy food much easier, however.

As you read on about what we've discovered with our research, you'll find that often you can't tell what you're getting by the menu description. It may portray a healthy item, but many times there are hidden ingredients and the method of preparation is not specified. Without complete nutrition information, you don't know what you're getting, and that can be dangerous!

Goals of *Healthy Dining in Los Angeles:*

1. To guide you in choosing healthy entrees served at many favorite Los Angeles restaurants.

2. To provide you with specific nutrition information for the selected menu items.

3. To give you straight-forward information enabling you to interpret and apply the nutrition information.

4. To initiate a trend encouraging restaurants to prepare and serve healthy entrees.

CHAPTER 2

Is Restaurant Food
Fattening and Unhealthy?

It can be if you're not careful! But it doesn't have to be.

Many restaurants smother meals with excess fat, sodium, cholesterol and calories. Butter, oil, cream, cheese and salt are frequently added to achieve the taste and texture that the average American expects. To make matters worse, many restaurant diners have the habit of adding "extras" such as salad dressing, sour cream, and butter (which push up the calorie and fat count even more). Let's take a shocking look at a favorite restaurant dinner:

Chicken Breast
Topped with a Creamy Parmesan Sauce
Served with Dinner Salad, Baked Potato and Sauteed Vegetables

	Calories	Fat (g)	Cholest. (mg)	Sodium (mg)
Dinner Salad	32	0	0	53
Blue Cheese Dressing (4 Tbs.)	308	32	36	668
Chicken Breast with Sauce	1312	91	481	1517
Baked Potato	220	0	0	16
Butter (2 Tbs.)	200	23	61	232
Sour Cream (2 Tbs.)	62	6	13	15
Sauteed Vegetables	117	11	0	207
Meal Total	2251	163	591	2708

Calories: Close to a FULL day's recommended calories <u>in one meal</u>.
Fat: <u>Almost three times</u> the recommended fat intake for a FULL Day.
Cholesterol: <u>Almost twice</u> the recommended cholesterol intake for a FULL Day.
Sodium: <u>Almost the entire</u> recommended sodium intake for a FULL Day.

Other fat-filled favorites:

	Calories	Fat (g)	Cholest. (mg)	Sodium (mg)
Italian manicotti with garlic bread	1393	79	411	2330
Beef & cheese enchiladas, rice & refried beans	1510	88	210	3516
Chicken fried steak with fries	1119	77	205	1895
Ultimate cheeseburger with fries & shake	1625	96	165	1708
Chicken sandwich with onion rings & shake	1282	68	82	2290
Seafood platter - fried - with tarter sauce	1195	70	97	1780
Salmon - smothered in a cream sauce	1024	76	283	1017
Fried chicken - with potato salad & cole slaw	1124	71	239	2552
Stir fry chicken with rice & egg rolls	1213	62	99	2907
Lasagna with garlic bread & salad	1538	77	194	2805
Omelet with hashbrowns	850	53	892	852
Pizza - sausage & mushroom	1290	48	84	1656
Chimichanga with sour cream & cheese	922	68	205	2125
Salad bar - with potato & tuna salad, dressing, and muffins with butter	1715	89	310	2954

Does dining out have to be so destructive to our health?

Some say, "Order grilled fish, salads or vegetarian dishes. By avoiding red meat, fried foods and creamy sauces, you can dine out and stay on your diet."

Be careful! We analyzed hundreds of apparently "healthy" entrees and found that many were diet disasters. Frequently, "healthy" dishes are laced with unhealthy, hidden ingredients. The menu descriptions portray a healthy item, but when we looked into the preparation methods, we found the items contained too much of certain unhealthy ingredients.

Surprising nutrition information about apparently "healthy" meals:

Grilled Swordfish - *Marinated in herbs and olive oil.*

884 Calories	
71 Fat (g)	Over a full day's recommended fat intake.
115 Cholesterol (mg)	Too much olive oil used in the preparation!
846 Sodium (mg)	

Vegetarian Pasta Primavera - *Fresh vegetables and garlic sauteed in a vegetable broth. Served over fettucini noodles and tossed with Parmesan cheese.*

816 Calories	The menu description didn't mention that the
45 Fat (g)	pasta was heavily tossed with oil, and the
139 Cholesterol (mg)	vegetables were sauteed in both broth *and*
892 Sodium (mg)	*butter.* This brings the fat total to 75% of
	a FULL day's recommended fat intake.

The "Healthy" Sandwich - *Avocado, tomato & cheese on whole wheat bread.*

746	Calories	
50	Fat (g)	This is a healthy sandwich?
66	Cholesterol (mg)	Avocado, cheese, and mayonnaise add
958	Sodium (mg)	up to too much fat and sodium.

Cobb Salad - *Crispy greens topped with chicken, avocado, bacon, tomato, hard-boiled egg and blue cheese crumbles. Served with a generous portion of your favorite dressing.*

1296	Calories	
102	Fat (g)	Very unhealthy. Much too high in fat,
647	Cholesterol (mg)	cholesterol, sodium and calories.
2553	Sodium (mg)	

Shrimp Stirfry - *Shrimp and assorted vegetables with chow mein noodles.*

866	Calories	Too much fat, calories, cholesterol and sodium.
64	Fat (g)	1 oz. oil to saute (27 g fat), butter/cream
392	Cholesterol (mg)	sauce (25 g fat), and the chow mein noodles
668	Sodium (mg)	(9 g fat) quickly add up.

Tostada - *Mexican beans, guacamole, lettuce, tomato and cheese.*

1416	Calories	
77	Fat (g)	The cheese alone contributes 519 calories,
288	Cholesterol (mg)	43 grams of fat, 137 mg cholesterol and
2010	Sodium (mg)	802 mg sodium.

We also found other items labeled "Light" or "Light-Fare" that included potato skins (deep fried), vegetables with cheese sauce, a hamburger patty and cottage cheese (too much saturated fat), cheese quesadillas (there's that saturated fat in the cheese again) and deep fried fish tacos.

Remember: It's all in the preparation

You can't tell enough about menu items by just reading the menu description. The preparation method also determines how healthy an entree is. If you're concerned about what goes into your body, you must rely on complete nutrition information, not just a menu description.

WARNING:

The ♥ used on menus has absolutely nothing to do with the American Heart Association, and those concerned about health should not depend on the ♥ when choosing entrees.

What you don't know <u>CAN</u> hurt you!

If you rely on the ♥ listed on restaurant menus to guide you in choosing healthy entrees, you may be gambling with your health. It's commonly assumed that these entrees are approved by the American Heart Association (AHA), and they must be low in fat, cholesterol and sodium. However, this symbol is simply an indication that <u>the restaurant</u> considers it a healthy choice. Unfortunately, in almost all cases, these items have never been nutritionally analyzed.

Any restaurant which claims its menu items have been approved or endorsed by the American Heart Association is making a false claim. The AHA does not regulate, monitor or endorse restaurant items. When Accents On Health analyzed entrees with a ♥ next to them, we discovered that many were too high in fat. Here are just a few examples:

??? Heart Healthy Entrees ???

♥	Eggplant Salad	34 grams fat - 86% of calories from fat
♥	Pasta with Tomatoes & Garlic	42 grams fat - 50% of calories from fat
♥	Greens Topped with Grilled Ahi	26 grams fat - 73% of calories from fat
♥	Grilled Halibut	64 grams fat - 75% of calories from fat

Is all restaurant food fattening & unhealthy?

NO! Many restaurants in the Los Angeles area are preparing delightfully delicious entrees which are wonderfully good for you! Instead of smothering foods with excessive amounts of unhealthy ingredients, they've creatively used herbs, spices, small amounts of unsaturated oils and healthy preparation methods. They have your health <u>and</u> your tastebuds in mind.

Some scrumptious and healthy examples:

Il Fornaio (Pasadena & Beverly Hills)
PIZZA VEGETARIANA (½ PIZZA)
Tomato sauce, tomatoes, red onions, sweet peppers, artichokes, and zucchini (no cheese).
✓✓ CALORIES: Very Low (300)   ✓✓ CHOLESTEROL: None (0 mg)
✓✓ FAT: Very Low* (9 g)   ✓ SODIUM: Low (549 mg) **

Jimmy's (Beverly Hills)
HAWAIIAN AHI TUNA GRILLED, WITH TROPICAL FRUIT SALSA
✓ CALORIES: Low (554)   ✓✓ CHOLESTEROL: Very Low (98 mg)
✓ FAT: Low* (18 g)   ✓✓ SODIUM: Very Low (121 mg) **

Hugo's (West Hollywood)
PUMPKIN PANCAKES (3 PANCAKES)
Golden pancakes made with spiced pumpkin puree.
✓✓ CALORIES: Very Low (193)   ✓✓ CHOLESTEROL: Very Low (3 mg)
✓✓ FAT: Very Low* (1 g)   ✓ SODIUM: Low (500 mg)

* Primarily unsaturated fat
** If you request no added salt

JW's Restaurant & Lounge (at Century City Marriott)
SEARED PACIFIC TUNA WITH LIME PEPPER CRUST & ORANGE MINT SALSA
Served with Japanese rice and steamed vegetables (included in analysis).
✓ CALORIES: Low (391) ✓✓ CHOLESTEROL: Very Low (76 mg)
✓✓ FAT: Very Low* (8 g) ✓✓ SODIUM: Very Low (226 mg) **

Border Grill (Santa Monica)
GRIDDLED FISH TACOS
Our homemade corn tortillas with sea bass, avocado, & cucumber relish. Analysis is for 2 tacos.
✓✓ CALORIES: Very Low (211) ✓✓ CHOLESTEROL: Very Low (30 mg)
✓✓ FAT: Very Low* (4 g) ✓✓ SODIUM: Very Low (167 mg) **

Wok Spirit (Woodland Hills)
CHINESE GARDEN (½ SERVING) - REQUEST WOK SMART
Steamed fresh broccoli, carrots, peppers, mushrooms, pea pods, bok choy and water chestnuts.
✓ CALORIES: Low (364) ✓✓ CHOLESTEROL: None (0 mg)
✓✓ FAT: Very Low* (1 g) ✓✓ SODIUM: Very Low (40 mg)

La Luna (Hollywood)
BAKED ORANGE ROUGHY
baked with zucchini and fresh tomato.
✓✓ CALORIES: Very Low (230) ✓✓ CHOLESTEROL: Very Low (40 mg)
✓✓ FAT: Very Low* (9 g) ✓✓ SODIUM: Very Low (170 mg) **

El Pollo Loco (nearly 100 Southern California locations)
CHICKEN TACO
✓✓ CALORIES: Very Low (170) ✓✓ CHOLESTEROL: Very Low (25 mg)
✓✓ FAT: Very Low (5 g) ✓ SODIUM: Low (400 mg) **

Carrows (24 locations in Los Angeles county)
FRESH VEGETABLE PLATTER
A medley of seasonal fresh vegetables with low-cal dressing, with seasoned new potatoes.
✓✓ CALORIES: Very Low (323) ✓✓ CHOLESTEROL: Very Low (16 mg)
✓✓ FAT: Very Low (7 g) ✓✓ SODIUM: Very Low (152 mg) **

Clearwater Cafe (Pasadena)
MIXED GRILL OF VEGETABLES WITH CREAMY POLENTA
✓✓ CALORIES: Very Low (300) ✓✓ CHOLESTEROL: None (0 mg)
✓✓ FAT: Very Low* (8 g) ✓ SODIUM: Low (390 mg) **

* Primarily unsaturated fat
** If you request no added salt

"Special Requests"

In some cases, after we analyzed the restaurant recipes, we found the dish contained too much fat, cholesterol or sodium. So we asked the chef to modify the dish to meet the *Healthy Dining* guidelines. We noted these dishes as "Special Requests." A "Special Request" may include less oil or butter, salad dressing served on the side, less cheese, etc. When you order, <u>you must ask for the "Special Request"</u> to make it correspond to the published nutrition information. See the examples below to find out how many calories and grams of fat you save by ordering some of the "Special Requests."

Examples of "Special Requests:"

Sisley Italian Kitchen (West Los Angeles & Valencia)
DIJON MUSTARD BOWTIE PASTA - SPECIAL REQUEST
Chicken, garlic, mushrooms, and onions with a Dijon - white wine sauce over bowtie pasta.
<u>Request light oil</u> (½ oz instead of 2 oz). This request saves 357 calories and 41 grams of fat!

Sabor (Santa Monica)
CHICKEN BREAST - SPECIAL REQUEST
Grilled and served on a bed of angel hair pasta with basil, tomatoes, pasilla chile, olive oil and anejo cheese.
<u>Request light oil in sauce</u> (1 Tbs.) <u>and skinless chicken</u>. This request saves 283 calories and 32 grams of fat.

Da Pasquale (Beverly Hills)
LINGUINE CON ARAGOSTA - SPECIAL REQUEST
Baby lobster tail, garlic, parsley and tomatoes. <u>Request light oil</u>
(1 Tbs. rather than 4 Tbs.) and save 357 calories and 41 grams of fat!

Spago (West Hollywood)
GRILLED LOUISIANA SHRIMP - SPECIAL REQUEST
with spicy fettucini and curried summer vegetables. <u>Request light butter and oil</u>
(½ Tbs. each) <u>and parmesan cheese served on the side</u>. This request saves
706 calories, 68 grams of fat, 90 mg cholesterol, and 1229 mg sodium!

Earth, Wind & Flour (Encino, Santa Monica & Westwood)
PIZZA ALTOBELLO - REQUEST EASY CHEESE (½ PIZZA)
Extra thin crusted. Mushrooms, eggplant, basil, cilantro with mozzarella, white cheddar and parmesan.
<u>Request easy cheese</u> (½ portion of cheese). This request saves 178 calories and 14 grams of fat.

Louise's Trattoria (at 13 L.A. area locations)
RIGATONI WITH GRILLED VEGETABLES - SPECIAL REQUEST
Tossed in extra virgin olive oil. <u>Request light oil</u> (½ oz). This request saves 595 calories and 68 grams of fat!

Some great tasting dessert ideas

We've even included a few desserts that taste great, are prepared with healthy ingredients, and help keep your calorie, fat, cholesterol and sodium totals down. As explained on page 3, the guidelines for the side dishes and desserts are 1/3 of the entree guidelines, so the categories for low (✓) and very low (✓✓) are different from the entrees.

Examples:

McCormick & Schmick's (Downtown, Pasadena & Beverly Hills)
FRUIT COBBLER†

✓ CALORIES: Low (184) ✓✓ CHOLESTEROL: Very Low (9 mg)
✓✓ FAT: Very Low (3 g) ✓✓ SODIUM: Very Low (82 mg)

Gratis (Brentwood)
TRIPLE LAYER CHOCOLATE CAKE†

CALORIES: Moderate (206) ✓✓ CHOLESTEROL: Very Low (1 mg)
✓✓ FAT: Very Low* (1 g) SODIUM: High (730 mg)

VANILLA BEAN CHEESECAKE†

CALORIES: Moderate (299) ✓✓ CHOLESTEROL: Very Low (18 mg)
✓✓ FAT: Very Low* (<1 g) SODIUM: High (837 mg)

Andree's Oven & Catering (Malibu)
PEACH AND BLUEBERRY COBBLER†

✓ CALORIES: Low (190) ✓✓ CHOLESTEROL: Very Low (1 mg)
✓✓ FAT: Very Low (1 g) SODIUM: Moderate (215 mg)

Jimmy's (Beverly Hills)
BAKED BANANAS WITH ORANGE SAUCE†

CALORIES: Moderate (321) ✓✓ CHOLESTEROL: Very Low (10 mg)
✓ FAT: Low* (5 g) ✓✓ SODIUM: Very Low (42 mg)

The menu items above and in the following chapters are just a taste of the wonderful entrees served at the restaurants participating in *Healthy Dining in Los Angeles*. We invite you to visit the restaurants featured in this book. You'll discover a whole new world of menu items that are marvelously delicious and so good for you!

---

* Primarily unsaturated fat
† Side dish guidelines are 1/3 of entree guidelines

CHAPTER 3

Do Your Calories Have a Purpose?

Calories have a bad reputation in our society. We're counting calories and cutting calories, as though we've forgotten that calories are what keep us alive. Food and water fuel our bodies to do the miraculous tasks we perform each day. Instead of focusing on just cutting calories, we need to look at the _quality_ of the calories we consume.

Just what are you getting from your calories?

Calories add up from the amounts of protein, carbohydrate and fat in foods. Each type of calorie has a very different function in the body. The following chapters explain the functions in more detail, but briefly:

Protein calories help the body to build and restore.

Carbohydrate calories are the body's main energy source.

Fat calories turn to fat -- _easily_.

In general, protein and carbohydrate calories supply our bodies with nutrients necessary to function optimally. We need a very small amount of fat each day, but because fat is very easy to get, most Americans suffer from an excess of dietary fat, not a deficiency.

We should strive to eat foods with high-quality, nutritious calories. Recommendations vary according to individual needs, but generally 50% to 65% of total daily calories should come from carbohydrates, 10% to 20% from protein, and 15% to 30% from fat. Because most Americans get enough protein and too much fat, the best way to determine the quality of your calories is to determine the percentage of calories from fat, and keep it under 30%.

Percentage of calories from fat

It's important to note that the 30% fat recommendation is the suggested average for the whole day. Over the day, some foods will add little, if any, fat to your diet, while other foods may supply a big chunk of the fat for the day. Of course, it's best to avoid (or use sparingly) foods which have a high percentage of fat (e.g. butter, margarine, oils, sour cream, cheese, cream cheese, etc.).

A fattening example:

Salmon - *Smothered in a cream sauce*
    Total Calories: 1024
    Protein   77 grams
    Carbohydrate   8 grams
    Fat   76 grams

How to calculate the percentage of calories from fat:

Each gram of fat has nine calories. Using this information, you can calculate the percent of calories from fat as shown in the following example. For the **Salmon with Cream Sauce** listed above:

1. Multiply the number of grams of fat by 9 (the number of calories per gram of fat):
    76 grams x 9 cals/gram = 684 calories from fat

2. Divide by total calories and multiply by 100 to get the percentage:
    684 calories ÷ 1024 calories x 100 = 67%

67% of calories from this dish come from fat!

Carbohydrates and protein percentages can be calculated in a similar way, except that the number of grams of each is multiplied by 4 rather than 9, because carbohydrates and proteins have 4 calories per gram. The division step is the same. For this example, these calculations show that 3% of calories come from carbohydrate and 30% from protein. Cholesterol and sodium do not contribute to calories.

The small percentage of carbohydrates is common for meat, poultry, and fish entrees, but a nutritious entree should contain less fat. In this example, most of the fat comes from the cream and butter used in the sauce; however, it's not necessary to add excess fat to get a delicious tasting entree.

Let's look at a healthier salmon dish:

Poached Salmon with a Cucumber Dill Sauce (Tower Restaurant - Downtown)
Calculations below are for salmon & sauce; asparagus & potatoes not included.

    Total Calories: 533
    Protein   70 grams
    Carbohydrates   23 grams
    Fat   18 grams

To calculate the percentage of calories from fat:

1. Multiply grams of fat by 9 calories per gram:
    18 grams x 9 cals/gram = 162 calories from fat

2. Divide by total calories and multiply by 100 to get a percentage:
162 calories ÷ 533 calories x 100 = 30.3

30% of calories from this dish come from fat.

Remember, the guideline of 30% or fewer calories from fat applies to the entire day, not just one entree. Restaurants differ greatly in the ways meals and side dishes are presented. If you order a lean meat or fish entree, it consists mainly of protein and fat, and the percentage of fat will generally appear to be high. By themselves, many lean meats and fish contain 30% to 40% fat. Even soybeans contain about 40% of their calories from fat. But generally these high-protein entrees are not eaten by themselves. If you choose quality carbohydrate side dishes such as vegetables, grains, breads, and fruits, the percentage of fat for the overall meal will be significantly less. Entrees which are made up largely of carbohydrates (such as pasta or rice dishes) will generally have a lower percentage of calories from fat.

As an example of how the side dishes change the overall percentage fat, let's include the asparagus and red potatoes that are served with this meal:

	Calories	Fat (g)
Poached Salmon with Cucumber Dill Sauce	533	18
Steamed Asparagus	25	0
Steamed Red Potatoes	105	0
Totals	663	18

To calculate percentage of calories from fat:

18 grams of fat x 9 cals/gram = 162 calories from fat
162 calories from fat ÷ 663 total calories x 100 = 24%

Only 24% of total calories from this meal come from fat, which is well within the recommended guidelines and significantly less than the percentage of fat calculated for only the entree by itself.

This example of the salmon demonstrates how a healthy entree, although near the 30% fat limit, can still be an excellent choice. It's protein-rich, and it also contains the "good" type of unsaturated fat. Remember that a meal like this one will probably be the largest of your day, and your choices for the remainder of the day can also bring the overall percentage of fat down.

Grams of fat vs. percentage calories from fat

We list grams of fat for each of the dishes on the menu pages rather than percentage of calories from fat. The example above illustrates how calculating percentage calories from fat for only a single menu item does not adequately reflect values for the entire meal or the entire day. Instead, if you total the grams of fat for each meal, you can more accurately determine your daily fat intake. Chapter 4 discusses in more detail how to choose guidelines for fat intake that are appropriate for you.

How the check mark guidelines for calories were set:

We set the guidelines assuming an average intake of 2,000 calories per day. Next, we assumed that the restaurant meal probably accounts for the largest of the day's meals, or at least 1/3 of the daily total calories. So 600 calories for the main entree would fit into the calorie budget. Thus, 600 calories is labeled as "Low" in calories. The "Very Low" value of 350 calories represents a proportionately lower level, corresponding to about 1200 calories per day. Side dishes are marked with a † footnote and use guidelines that are 1/3 of the entree guidelines.

Glance through the restaurant pages and use the quick, easy check mark system to see the wide variety of entrees which contain high-quality, nutritious calories and are low (✓) or very low (✓✓) in total calories.

CHAPTER 4

Fat - How Much and What Type?

Fat - clogging our arteries and building up around the stomach, thighs and buttocks. Too much body fat, almost always caused by <u>too much fat in our diet</u> and <u>too little exercise</u> in our day, increases the risks of high blood pressure, elevated blood fats (triglycerides and cholesterol), heart disease, stroke, diabetes, cancer and other health problems.

How much is too much?

The guidelines recommended by the American Heart Association and the Surgeon General's Office (see Chapter 1) suggest that fat should contribute no more than 30% of total calories. Chapter 3 showed examples of calculating percentage fat from calories. This section deals with counting grams of fat. If we assume a daily intake of 2000 calories, then no more than 600 calories per day (30%) should come from fat. Since each gram of fat contributes nine calories (see Chapter 3), then about 66 grams of fat (600 ÷ 9) would be the suggested upper limit of fat intake per day. If you're not careful, it's very easy to go way over that with just one meal!

So what is a reasonable limit per meal or per entree? If we divide the day's allotment (66 grams) into three equal meals, then a <u>reasonable limit per meal is 22 grams of fat</u>. Main entrees usually contribute the largest amount of fat to the meal (unless you load your side dishes with too much fat, as discussed below), so we set a guideline of

    ✓ "Low" = 10 to 20 grams/entree
    ✓✓ "Very Low" = 0 to 10 grams/entree

If you're an athlete and eat more calories per day, then a higher limit would be appropriate. If you're on a <u>weight loss diet</u> or <u>very low fat diet</u>, then the <u>"Very Low" guideline of up to 10 grams</u> of fat per entree is probably more appropriate.

Notice that these recommended guidelines represent an average intake for an average meal. Don't be overly concerned about the arbitrary cutoff between our designations of "Low" and "Very Low." Unless you're on a very restricted diet, the difference between an entree with 11 grams of fat (which would receive one check mark) and one with 9 grams of fat (two check marks) is probably not worth worrying about. An occasional meal with somewhat more fat (but don't overdo it!) can be fairly easily compensated for by reducing fat intake during other meals.

Be aware of portion sizes. Some people remember food labels on products which list only 2 or 3 grams of fat, and so they consider 9 or 10 grams of fat unthinkable! However those 2 or 3 grams of fat may be for only a one-ounce serving size. The entrees listed in this book often correspond to 6 - 10 ounces of a <u>very filling</u>, protein-rich meal. Even 20 grams of fat is <u>much</u>

lower than most other restaurant meals (see Chapter 2) and will probably still fit into your daily limit. You may also choose to eat a smaller serving and save some for later.

Types of fat:

Together with protein, fats form the structures in our bodies, including muscles, nerves, membranes and blood vessels. However, we need very little fat to perform these functions, and only *unsaturated* sources of fat aid in these processes. The fat we eat is saturated and unsaturated. These terms refer to the chemical structure of the fat molecules.

<u>Saturated Fats</u>. Saturated fats are the <u>*very unhealthy*</u> fats which raise blood cholesterol levels. Excess saturated fat is related to an increased risk of cardiovascular disease. Foods that contain saturated fats are usually hard at room temperature. Saturated fat is found mostly in animal products (beef, chicken, butter, ice cream, cheese), processed and fast foods and some vegetable oils (palm oil, coconut oil, partially hydrogenated oils).

<u>Unsaturated Fats - Monounsaturated, Polyunsaturated</u>. These are the *"good"* types of fat. A <u>low total fat intake</u>, with the majority of fat from unsaturated sources, appears to lower blood cholesterol levels. The best sources for these "good" fats are natural grains, seeds and nuts, and fish. Many oils are primarily unsaturated, such as olive, canola, peanut, corn, safflower, sesame, cottonseed and soybean. Once again, these fats are "good" only in very small amounts! Look for menu items with the * for dishes that contain primarily unsaturated fat.

<u>Hydrogenated Fats</u>. The vegetable oils found in many packaged or processed foods are hydrogenated. The process of hydrogenation changes the chemical structure of unsaturated fats by adding hydrogen atoms to make the fats more saturated. Manufacturers use the hydrogenation process because it increases product stability and shelf life. Thus, a larger quantity can be produced at one time, saving the manufacturer money. Unfortunately, this money-saving process contributes to elevated blood cholesterol levels and increases heart disease risk.

<u>Omega-3 Fats</u>. Some types of fish contain unique polyunsaturated fats called Omega-3 fatty acids. These fatty acids seem to make blood platelets less likely to clot, thus decreasing risk of artery blockage and heart attack. Fish with high amounts of Omega-3 include salmon, albacore tuna, mackerel, herring and rainbow trout.

A summary of fat:

When assessing the fat content of food, it is important to look at:
1. The number of <u>grams</u> of fat
2. The <u>percent of calories</u> from fat
3. The <u>type</u> of fat - minimize or avoid saturated fats

One Last Word on Fat: Unsaturated fats do not raise blood cholesterol levels. But too much fat - saturated <u>or</u> unsaturated - may make you fat, and excess body fat is a risk factor for many chronic diseases.

> *On the restaurant menu pages, the asterisk (*) next to the grams of fat indicates that the fat is primarily unsaturated (the "good" type). Look for it!*

Some delicious "Very Low" fat examples:

Notice that many contain primarily unsaturated fat (designated with the *).

Chommanade (Belmont Shores)
PLA KOONG
Shrimps lightly grilled to perfection, sauteed in lime juice & mixed with chili sauce, mint leaves & lemongrass.
✓✓ FAT: Very Low* (2 g)

Jimmy's Fish & Grill (Long Beach)
CIOPINNO *(14 oz. serving)*
✓✓ FAT: Very Low (9 g)

Cutters (Santa Monica)
MUSHROOM GARDEN BURGER
Cutter's no-meat juicy garden burger patty made with whole grains, nuts, fresh mushrooms, cheese & spices. Served with sauteed mushrooms and fresh herbal spread.
✓✓ FAT: Very Low* (9 g)

Shioji (Long Beach Sheraton)
SUSHI DINNER
✓✓ FAT: Very Low* (7 g)

Papa Jon's (West Los Angeles & Long Beach)
SHEPHERD'S PIE
A healthy pie with carrots, spinach, mushrooms, onions, peppers and mashed potatoes.
✓✓ FAT: Very Low* (4 g)

La Salsa (19 locations in Los Angeles County)
FISH TACO (SONORA STYLE)
✓✓ FAT: Very Low* (8 g)

Il Forno (Santa Monica)
SCAMPI MEDITERRANEA
Scampi baked with a touch of brandy, fresh grapefruit juice, green peppercorn & Dijon mustard.
✓✓ FAT: Very Low* (2 g)

Sizzler (throughout Southern California)
LEMON-HERB CHICKEN PLATTER
Two tender breasts of chicken marinated in lemon and herbs.
✓✓ FAT: Very Low (3 g)

JACK IN THE BOX®
CHICKEN TERIYAKI BOWL
Strips of teriyaki-marinated chicken breast, broccoli florets, carrots and teriyaki sauce, all served on a bed of steamed white rice.
✓✓ FAT: Very Low (1½ g)

Eating "Very Low" Fat Becomes Fantastically Delicious When You Have So Many Choices at Los Angeles Restaurants

---

Now - how well are YOU doing?

Now that Los Angeles restaurants are watching how much fat they're adding to your diet, just _how well are you watching?_ Here are some easy ways to add too much fat to your diet - quickly!

High-fat culprits:

	Calories	Fat (g)	Cholest. (mg)	Sodium (mg)
Salad Dressings: (3 Tbs.)				
Blue Cheese	231	24	27	501
Thousand Island	176	17	15	327
French	201	19	6	642
Italian	206	21	0	348
Oil & Vinegar	215	24	0	0
Toppings: (2 Tbs.)				
Butter	200	23	61	232
Margarine	202	23	0	264
Sour Cream	67	6	13	15
Cream Cheese	100	10	31	85
Tarter Sauce	150	16	18	196
Mayonnaise	198	22	16	157
Cheese (1 oz. cheddar)	114	9	30	176
Desserts:				
Cheesecake	386	24	82	284
Apple Pie	323	14	28	207
Chocolate Cake	407	17	5	300
Ice Cream (1 cup)	349	24	88	108

Instead try:

- Reduced-fat salad dressings
- Salsa, low-fat cottage cheese, or yogurt as salad dressing or topping for potatoes
- Only very small amounts of regular or high-fat salad dressings
- Frozen yogurt, sorbet, sherbet or fruit for dessert

CHAPTER 5

Cholesterol - A Hot Topic

Cholesterol continues to be a hot topic enmeshed in controversy. Medical research is progressing on this subject, and we hope to clear up some misconceptions concerning cholesterol.

Where does cholesterol come from?

Most of the cholesterol in your blood is manufactured by your liver. The body produces about 1,000 milligrams (mg.) of cholesterol each day. In addition, the average American consumes 400 to 600 mg. from food each day. The cholesterol we derive from our diets is essentially the same as the cholesterol our bodies manufacture. Our bodies use cholesterol to form hormones and cell membranes.

However, the average high-fat/high-cholesterol diet tends to add too much cholesterol to the bloodstream. The excess cholesterol and other substances accumulate in the walls of the blood vessels. Over time the arteries become narrowed, and eventually the flow of blood is cut off, leading to a heart attack or stroke.

How should blood cholesterol be measured?

To get an accurate and complete cholesterol measure, a tube of blood should be drawn from the arm by a qualified health professional. You should not eat or drink anything (except water) for 12 hours before the blood draw. The laboratory which analyzes the blood sample should follow the reference methods set by the U. S. Centers For Disease Control. The fingertip method found in shopping malls and health fairs may not provide results that are as accurate.

What determines blood cholesterol levels?

1. **Genetics**. Some individuals, no matter how prudent their diet or how regularly they exercise, can't achieve a low cholesterol level without the help of a physician and cholesterol-lowering medications.

2. **Lipoproteins**. Cholesterol is carried through the blood in protein packages called lipoproteins. The amounts and types of lipoproteins are an important indicator of your heart disease risk.

LDLs (low-density lipoproteins) are commonly termed "bad" cholesterol. LDLs increase heart disease risk because they keep cholesterol in blood circulation and carry it to the arteries to be deposited. <u>Excess body fat and a diet high in saturated fat tend to increase LDL levels.</u>

HDLs (high-density lipoproteins) are the "good" cholesterol and protect against heart disease. They actually carry cholesterol AWAY from the arteries to the liver to be excreted from the body. Individuals with high HDL levels have a lower risk of heart disease. <u>Regular exercise, maintaining appropriate body weight, and not smoking help to increase HDL levels.</u>

3. **Diet**. Foods high in saturated fat <u>increase</u> cholesterol levels. These include: butter, whole milk products, palm and coconut oils, cheese, beef, pork, and eggs. In addition, many packaged and processed foods are high in saturated fat or (partially) hydrogenated oils, which also have a cholesterol-raising effect.

A diet *low in total fat*, with fat intake primarily from unsaturated fat sources, <u>reduces</u> cholesterol levels. Unsaturated fats include: olive, corn, safflower, sesame, canola, soybean, and sunflower oils. *High fiber foods*, especially oat bran, apples, carrots, oranges, legumes (beans, peas and lentils) <u>decrease</u> cholesterol levels by inhibiting the absorption of cholesterol into the bloodstream. *Fish and fish oils*, which contain omega-3 fatty acids, also <u>decrease</u> cholesterol levels.

4. **Smoking, stress and some medications** also raise cholesterol levels.

Important facts on dietary cholesterol and fat:

<u>Too much of any fat</u> (even unsaturated oils!) can increase body fat, and excess body fat may increase blood cholesterol levels. Oils, margarine, and butter all have approximately the same number of calories and fat grams per ounce, and so all have the same potential to make you fat. Therefore it's important to limit your total intake of all types of fat.

Even though oils, margarine, and butter have about the same calorie and fat counts, there is a big difference in the chemical make-up of these fats. Butter contains saturated fat, and <u>saturated fats increase blood cholesterol</u> levels. Saturated fats stimulate the production of LDLs ("bad cholesterol"), resulting in increased blood cholesterol levels. Therefore if you avoid only dietary cholesterol in the food you eat, without reducing the amount of saturated fat, you may not decrease your blood cholesterol level at all.

Avoid <u>hydrogenated fats</u> too, because they are also saturated. Margarine, although cholesterol-free, is partially hydrogenated and contains <u>trans-fatty acids</u>, which have been shown to have a cholesterol-raising effect.

Vegetable oils, on the other hand, are predominately <u>unsaturated fats</u>. Liquid oils (such as olive, corn, canola, etc.) in small amounts may help to decrease cholesterol levels. Remember though, that all oils are 100% fat, so use only small amounts.

The <u>amount of cholesterol</u> found in foods is not as important as the <u>amount of saturated fat</u>. But you should minimize intake of very concentrated sources of cholesterol such as egg yolks and liver. Shellfish is very low in saturated fat, but moderately high in cholesterol. Most medical experts seem to agree that shellfish, in small quantities, is a healthy choice.

Cholesterol is found only in animal products. Don't be misled, though. Products which don't contain animal fats may still be loaded with fat. Food packages stating "No Cholesterol" should alert you to look at the nutrition information on the label to determine the amount of total and saturated fat.

How the check mark guidelines for cholesterol were chosen:

The Surgeon General's Office and the American Heart Association recommend that cholesterol consumption be limited to 300 mg. per day. If the day's total were evenly divided in thirds, this would suggest a limit of 100 mg. per meal, which corresponds to our "Very Low" category. If you eat at the "Low" level of 200 mg. per meal for every meal in the day, you would exceed the recommended amount. But since a restaurant meal usually contains a larger portion of meat or other cholesterol-containing foods than side dishes or other meals of the day, we assumed that this cholesterol intake can easily be compensated for by choosing foods with little or no cholesterol for the remaining selections.

If you are watching your blood cholesterol level, select items which are:

1. "Very Low" fat or "Low" fat
2. Primarily unsaturated (designated with the * in this book)
3. "Very Low" or "Low" cholesterol

Examples from Los Angeles restaurants:

Kate Mantilini (Beverly Hills)
LIFE RICE
White rice tossed with chopped steamed broccoli, peas and carrots.
Topped with scrambled egg whites and fresh lime salsa.
✓✓　FAT: Very Low* (10 g)　　✓✓　CHOLESTEROL: Very Low (18 mg)

Bistro 45 (Pasadena)
SEARED SEA SCALLOPS WITH FRUITED TOMATO SAUCE
✓✓　FAT: Very Low* (2 g)　　✓✓　CHOLESTEROL: Very Low (47 mg)

Bombay Cafe (West Los Angeles)
GOBI SABZI
Cauliflower sauteed with green chilies, ginger, coriander, tumeric & cumin seeds.
✓　FAT: Low* (13 g)　　✓✓　CHOLESTEROL: None (0 mg)

Ruby's Diner
VEGGIE RUBYBURGER
(Glendale, Marina Del Rey, Palos Verdes, Seal Beach & Woodland Hills)
Made with a tasty vegetable, rice, oats and wheat patty. Ruby sauce not included in analysis.
✓✓　FAT: Very Low* (8 g)　　✓✓　CHOLESTEROL: Very Low (8 mg)

Michael's (Santa Monica)
MAINE LOBSTER SALAD
with Roma tomatoes, avocado and sweet grilled onions on San Fernando Valley
baby greens with extra virgin olive oil and balsamic vinegar.
✓　FAT: Low* (16 g)　　✓✓　CHOLESTEROL: Very Low (81 mg)

Ca'Brea (Hollywood)
LINGUINETTE ALLE VONGOLE ALL'AGLIO DI FRANTOIO
Linguine pasta with fresh clams in a garlic and white wine sauce.
✓ FAT: Low* (17 g)   ✓✓ CHOLESTEROL: Very Low (48 mg)

El Cholo (Mid-City & La Habra)
CRABMEAT ENCHILADA
with salsa verde with beans and rice (included in analysis).
✓ FAT: Low* (14 g)   ✓✓ CHOLESTEROL: Very Low (99 mg)

Pine Avenue Fish House (Long Beach)
FRESH GRILLED NEW ZEALAND YELLOWTAIL WITH THAI-CHILI SAUCE
✓ FAT: Low* (13 g)   ✓✓ CHOLESTEROL: Very Low (83 mg)

Il Forno Cafe & Pizzeria (Santa Monica)
SPA PIZZA ALLA IL FORNO
Fresh dough baked to crispy perfection and topped with lo-fat cheeses, fresh tomatoes and other assorted fresh vegetables. Seasoned with garlic and herbs.
✓ FAT: Low* (16 g)   ✓✓ CHOLESTEROL: Very Low (32 mg)

Maple Drive (Beverly Hills)
GAZPACHO
✓ FAT: Low* (11 g)   ✓✓ CHOLESTEROL: None (0 mg)

Cafe La Bohème (West Hollywood)
MUSHROOM AND VEGETABLE SPAGHETTINI
soy flavor and olive oil.
✓ FAT: Low* (17 g)   ✓✓ CHOLESTEROL: Very Low (5 mg)

Chin Chin (West Hollywood, Studio City, Brentwood, Marina Del Rey & Encino)
LITE FRAGRANT VEGETABLES WITH KUNG PAO SAUCE
Black bean, sweet & sour orange, curry and garlic sauce also recommended.
✓✓ FAT: Very Low* (2 g)   ✓✓ CHOLESTEROL: None (0 mg)

DC3 (Santa Monica)
SPICY GRILLED TUNA WITH GINGER PINEAPPLE SAUCE
✓ FAT: Low* (16 g)   ✓✓ CHOLESTEROL: Very Low (89 mg)

                    * Primarily unsaturated fat

CHAPTER 6

Sodium - To Salt or Not to Salt?

That is the question. Sodium is an essential nutrient. It helps to maintain blood volume, regulate the balance of water in the cells, and transmit nerve impulses. The kidneys control sodium balance by increasing or decreasing sodium in the urine.

In general, Americans consume more sodium than the body needs. Many foods contain sodium naturally, and it is commonly added to foods during preparation or processing. Sodium is also found in drinking water, prescription drugs and over-the-counter medications.

One teaspoon of salt contains about 2,000 milligrams of sodium, approximately 2/3 of the American Heart Association's recommended daily amount. Other condiments contain significant amounts of sodium, such as seasoning salts (1620 - 1850 mg. per teaspoon), monosodium glutamate - MSG (492 mg. per teaspoon), soy sauce (343 mg. per teaspoon), and meat tenderizer (1750 mg. per teaspoon). Packaged and processed foods also tend to be very high in sodium.

In the United States, about one in four adults has elevated blood pressure. Sodium intake is only one of the factors known to affect high blood pressure, and not everyone is equally susceptible. The sensitivity to sodium seems to be very individualized. At present, there is not a good method to predict who is salt-sensitive or who will develop high blood pressure. Low-sodium diets may help some people avoid high blood pressure. Low-sodium diets may help some people with high blood pressure to control their blood pressure. And in some individuals, a low-sodium diet will not affect blood pressure at all.

Since most Americans consume more sodium than needed, consider reducing your sodium intake. Use less table salt, read labels carefully, and eat sparingly those foods which have large amounts of sodium. Remember that a substantial amount of the sodium you eat may be "hidden" - either occurring naturally in foods or as part of a preservative or flavoring agent that has been added.

To avoid too much sodium:

- Learn to enjoy the flavors of unsalted foods.
- Cook without salt or with only small amounts of added salt.
- Try flavoring foods with herbs, spices, and lemon juice.
- Add little or no salt to food at the table.
- Limit your intake of salty foods such as potato chips, pretzels, salted nuts and popcorn, condiments (soy sauce, steak sauce, garlic salt), pickled foods, cured meats, cheeses, and canned foods.
- Read food labels carefully to determine the amounts of sodium.
- Use lower sodium products, when available, to replace those with higher sodium content.

To avoid too much sodium when dining out:

1. Order entrees with "Low" or "Very Low" sodium levels.
2. Request no added salt whenever possible.

The analyses shown in this book used the sodium content that occurs naturally in food, or salt that is included in a prepared sauce or recipe where the sodium cannot be reduced for an individual portion. However, many chefs cook with salt "to taste" that is not included in the recipes they provided for analysis, so it's very important that you make it very clear that you do not want any extra salt.

> *The ** designation after the sodium values is designed to remind you to specify "no added salt" if it's important to you.*

How the check mark guidelines for sodium were set:

Of the 3000 mg. of sodium recommended per day, we considered a value of 1000 mg. per meal (1/3 of 3000) to be a reasonable level. We assumed 600 mg. could reasonably come from the main entree as a "Low" value, and the remainder from side dishes. A "Very Low" level was chosen as ½ of the "Low" value, or 300 mg.

Examples from Los Angeles restaurants:

La Frite Cafe (Sherman Oaks & Woodland Hills)
GOAT CHEESE & RATATOUILLE CASSEROLE
✓✓ SODIUM: Very Low (89 mg) **

il Moro (West Los Angeles)
CAPPELLINI ALLA CHECCA
Angel hair pasta with fresh diced roma tomatoes, basil, garlic, and extra virgin olive oil.
✓✓ SODIUM: Very Low (84 mg) **

Gaucho Grill (Beverly Ctr, Brentwood, Glendale, Hollywood, Pasadena, Santa Monica, & San Fernando Valley)
BROCHETTE MIXTO
Two skewers (one chicken, one beef) with onions, tomatoes, peppers & mushrooms. All chicken available.
✓✓ SODIUM: Very Low (160 mg) **

Chasen's (West Hollywood)
ANGEL HAIR WITH FRESH TOMATO AND BASIL
✓✓ SODIUM: Very Low (141 mg) **

Four Seasons Hotel Gardens Restaurant (Beverly Hills)
GRILLED VEAL CHOP - SPECIAL REQUEST
with Portobello mushroom steak and orzo pasta. Request light oil (½ oz).
✓✓ SODIUM: Very Low (128 mg) **

CHAPTER 7

Protein, Carbs, & Diabetic Exchanges

Protein: the building blocks

Protein is very important for a healthy body. Protein provides materials for growth, helps to maintain and repair tissues, manufactures the lipoproteins to carry fat, and assists in the maintenance of proper fluid levels.

It is very easy to get protein in our diet, and most Americans consume 2 - 3 times more protein than necessary. Excess protein does not create muscle, as many hope, but is stored as fat. Excess protein puts a strain on the liver and kidneys. In addition, some protein sources are also high in fat, cholesterol and calories, such as: beef, whole milk products, eggs, poultry with skin, cheese and nuts.

The best sources of protein are low-fat foods, including fish, poultry without skin, skim or low-fat milk products and tofu. Whole grains, vegetables and legumes (dried beans, peas and lentils) also contain some protein.

Unless you are a very strict vegetarian, you probably get adequate protein with a balanced diet. If you are a strict vegetarian, it's important to see a nutritionist to analyze your present diet and make sure you're getting adequate amounts of protein.

Carbohydrates: energy

Total carbohydrates are made up of simple sugars, complex carbohydrates, and fiber.

<u>Simple carbohydrates.</u> Sources of simple carbohydrates include: table sugar, candies and other sweets, sodas and bakery goods. These foods contain little or no vitamins and minerals. They provide empty calories, i.e., calories that supply no nutrients and should therefore be minimized.

Fruits and vegetables also contain sugar naturally, and in addition they provide other nutrients, so they are valuable to a healthy diet. The sugar in these foods is in a form that is absorbed quickly by the body, as opposed to the slower-digesting complex carbohydrates.

<u>Complex carbohydrates.</u> These carbohydrates contain many essential nutrients and are the body's most effective source of energy. They are very low in fat and should be a primary source

of calories over the day. It is recommended that 50% to 65% of total daily calories come from nutrient-dense carbohydrates. Foods high in complex carbohydrates include:

- breads and cereals
- dried beans, peas, and lentils
- potatoes and other starchy vegetables
- pasta
- rice and other grain products

<u>Dietary Fiber.</u> The typical American diet is much too low in fiber. The American Cancer Society recommends 20 - 30 grams of fiber daily. The average American consumes only 7 - 8 grams of fiber daily.

Dietary fiber is a term used to describe parts of plant foods which are generally not digestible by humans. Increasing your intake of foods containing complex carbohydrates can also help add dietary fiber to your diet.

There are two main types of fiber: soluble and insoluble. Soluble fiber may help lower blood cholesterol and help to control blood sugar. Soluble fiber is found in oats, beans, carrots, apples and oranges. Insoluble fiber helps to move food through the body quickly and protect against colorectal cancer. Insoluble fiber is found in wheat bran and whole grains. Because both types of fiber have different functions for improving health, a variety of foods with fiber should be included in your diet.

Although fruits and vegetables are not considered complex carbohydrates, they do have significant amounts of nutrients and fiber. Thus, a diet rich in whole grains, breads, cereals, fruits and vegetables will provide optimal amounts of nutrients, fiber and energy.

Diabetic food exchanges

A well-balanced and carefully controlled diet is essential for those with diabetes. Most use the diabetic food exchange system to plan meals. Foods are grouped into the various exchange lists according to their similarities in calories, carbohydrate, protein and fat content, which influences how they are utilized by the body. Although carbohydrates have the largest influence on blood sugar levels, protein and fat also contribute calories and influence the rates of digestion, so they are important to the overall plan.

Even for those without diabetes, the food exchanges which are listed can give useful information about portion size and the balance you are getting between protein and the simple and complex carbohydrates. One meat exchange is equivalent to approximately 7 grams of protein and 3 grams of fat, one bread (starch) exchange contains approximately 15 grams of carbohydrate and 3 grams of protein. Starchy vegetables (potatoes, corn, beans, etc.) are counted as bread (starch) exchanges rather than vegetable exchanges. Vegetable exchanges have less starch and lots of fiber. A fruit exchange contains approximately 15 grams of more easily digested (simple) carbohydrate.

Some diabetic exchange lists use separate categories for lean, medium-fat, and high-fat meats. The computerized system used for the *Healthy Dining* analysis uses the lean meat category which assumes approximately 7 grams of protein and 3 grams of fat per meat exchange. Any added fat from additional ingredients (e.g., butter or oil used in preparation, sauces, spreads, etc.) is counted as separate fat exchanges. This means that the <u>fat exchanges reflect additional fat</u> added to the meat. In most entrees included in the book, the meat is very lean and the total fat from the meat is lower than the 3 grams of fat per meat exchange normally assumed. In these cases we have designated the meat exchanges as <u>"(extra lean)," which indicates that the meat exchange contains less fat</u> than the assumed standard of 3 grams of fat per meat exchange.

In many entrees shown in this book, extra fat (often unsaturated) is added, but with the very lean meat, the total grams of fat still comes out very low. So you don't necessarily need to shy away from a selection that shows Fat exchanges. Looking at the grams of fat probably will give you better information about your overall fat intake.

The food exchanges used by some <u>weight loss programs</u> use an exchange system which is similar to the diabetic food exchange system. Ask your dietitian how to interpret these numbers to meet your particular dietary needs.

CHAPTER 8

Additional Tips for Healthy Dining

Here are some additional dining tips, adapted from "Eating Better When Eating Out," from the USDA Human Nutrition Information Service:

Appetizers: Enjoy raw vegetables dipped in salsa or low-calorie dressing, fruit or steamed seafood. Watch out for rich sauces, dips and batter-fried foods.

Soups: Choose broth or tomato-based soups rather than creamed soups. Lentil, bean and split pea soups are high in fiber. Most soups tend to be high in sodium.

Breads: Bread supplies complex carbohydrates, vitamins, and minerals. Whole grain breads provide fiber. Watch out for breads with added fat or sugar such as croissants, biscuits, cornbread, muffins (e.g., bran, corn, blueberry) and sweet rolls. Use toppings (butter, cream cheese and margarine) very sparingly.

Vegetables and Salads: Plain vegetables are high in fiber and nutrients and very low in calories, fat and sodium. However, butter, margarine and sauces can increase calories, fat, cholesterol and sodium considerably. Look for vegetables seasoned with lemon, herbs or spices rather than fat and salt. Remember - salad dressings and toppings can add a lot of calories, fat and sodium.

Watch out for prepared salads that contain mayonnaise, salad dressing or oil, such as macaroni salad, potato salad, creamy coleslaw, tuna and chicken salad, and marinated vegetables. Some pasta salads are made with large amounts of oily dressing.

Main Entrees: Ask how meals are prepared and what ingredients are used. Is the fish or chicken broiled with butter or other fat? Is it served with a sauce? How large is the portion? Are vegetables fresh or canned, buttered or creamed?

Fish or poultry that is broiled, grilled, baked, steamed or poached is a good choice. However, entrees are often basted with large amounts of fat. Ask to have your entree prepared without added fat, and that chicken be prepared without skin (or remove the skin before eating). Request that lemon juice, wine or only a small amount of fat be used and that no salt be added.

Watch out for menu selections termed "Light fare" or "light." "Light" may or may not mean lower in fat and calories. We have found restaurants in which "On the Light Side" means anything from smaller portions to lower prices!

Choose dishes flavored with herbs and spices rather than rich sauces, gravies, or dressings. If that's not an option, ask for gravies, sour cream, sauces, and other toppings to be served on the side and use sparingly. Limit your use of soy sauce, steak sauce, catsup, mustard, pickles and other condiments to help control sodium.

Portions are often very large. Ask for a take-home bag and eat the remaining portion the next day. Or share an entree with a friend and get an extra appetizer.

Many stir-fried entrees are prepared with very little oil, while some are prepared with too much. Request that yours to be prepared with very little.

Pizza can be a low-fat, nutritious choice if you order yours with half the cheese and only vegetable toppings.

Sandwiches can be an excellent choice if you choose lean deli meats such as turkey or ham (but watch portion size!) instead of higher fat cold cuts, such as bologna or salami. Choose whole grain breads and go easy on or avoid oil, butter and mayonnaise.

Desserts: Fruits are great! Sherbet, sorbet and frozen yogurt are much lower in fat than ice cream. If temptation gets to you - share the dessert with a dinner partner.

Words that signal *high fat* include:

buttered or buttery	creamed or creamy	rich
scalloped	fried	breaded
fritters	tempura	croquettes
crispy	with gravy	in cheese sauce
Hollandaise	au gratin	à la king
Béarnaise	Alfredo	Newburg

Words that signal *high sodium* include:

smoked	barbecued	pickled
broth	soy sauce	teriyaki
creole sauce	marinated	cocktail sauce
tomato base	Parmesan	mustard sauce

Appendix:
Analysis Methods and Accuracy

How was the nutrition analysis done?

We used recipes supplied by the restaurant and performed a computerized nutritional analysis with the Nutritionist IV Computer program developed by N-Squared Computing in Oregon. Research shows the Nutritionist IV Program to be one of the most current and reliable nutrition analysis programs available. It uses the U.S. Department of Agriculture (USDA) data base. We regularly update our program with new data values published by the USDA. If values for recipe ingredients were not available from the USDA data base, we contacted the manufacturer for nutritional information. If the manufacturer did not have nutritional information, we closely matched ingredients to another product with nutritional information.

The data were rounded to the nearest whole number, except for diabetic exchanges, which were rounded to the nearest ¼ exchange unit. We should point out that the numbers coming from the USDA data base and the computer analysis imply a high degree of accuracy. In reality, the USDA found that nutritional values of foods can vary between similar food samples by as much as 20%, and the numbers coming from their measurements represent their average data.

Notes about accuracy

The most accurate method to obtain nutritional information is a chemical analysis performed in a professional laboratory. That is, in fact, how the USDA obtained their information for their data base. It is very expensive (over $1,000 per item) and time-consuming, and therefore unrealistic for this project. Every effort was made to ensure accurate information from the computerized analysis and the USDA data base.

Two main obstacles were encountered with the computerized analysis. First, how much marinade do meats actually absorb, and second, how much oil is absorbed in flash-frying (a method commonly used in Chinese foods)? After numerous conversations with experts throughout the U.S., we found that there has been very little research in these areas. As recommended by nutritionists at the USDA and the Human Nutrition Information Service, we assumed that ¼ to ½ oz. of marinade per 8 oz. of meat was absorbed, depending on the amount of marinading time, and that very little oil (1 teaspoon/6 oz. meat) was absorbed with flash-frying.

Part II
Healthy Dining Menus

Arranged alphabetically
Also see index at the end of this section,
arranged by location, type of cuisine, and alphabetically

Summary of check mark system:

ENTREE GUIDELINES

Calories ✓✓ Very Low = 0 to 350 calories/entree
✓ Low = 350 to 600 calories/entree

Fat ✓✓ Very Low = 0 to 10 grams (g)/entree
✓ Low = 10 to 20 grams (g)/entree

Cholesterol ✓✓ Very Low = 0 to 100 milligrams (mg)/entree
✓ Low = 100 to 200 milligrams (mg)/entree

Sodium ✓✓ Very Low = 0 to 300 milligrams (mg)/entree
✓ Low = 300 to 600 milligrams (mg)/entree

SIDE DISH GUIDELINES†
† Side Dish Guidelines are 1/3 of entree guidelines

Footnotes
* Primarily unsaturated fat
** If you request no added salt

Other Symbols:
$ - Inexpensive, average entree under $10
$$ - Moderate price, average entree $10 - $20
$$$ - Expensive, average entree over $20

Special Request - modification of the usual restaurant recipe or
preparation method. You must ask for the "Special Request" to
make it correspond to the published nutrition information.

Voted #1 Mexican Restaurant for two years in a row by the Readers of LA Opinion Newspaper. Acapulco Restaurant offers a festive atmosphere to enjoy deliciously prepared Mexican dishes. Acapulco's executive chef has worked with time old recipes to refine their food for the more health conscious guest. Be sure to stop in one of 46 locations and enjoy a delicious, health-consciously prepared meal at Acapulco Mexican Restaurant. $

Acapulco locations: Atwater, Azusa, Burbank, Cerritos, Del Amo, Downey, Glendale, Hollywood, La Cienega, Los Angeles (Sunset Blvd.), Monrovia, Montclair, Northridge, Pasadena, Playa Del Rey, Ports O'Call, Puente Hills, Santa Fe Springs, Santa Monica, Sun Valley, Westwood, & Woodland Hills. For additional locations in Orange County, San Diego & Santa Barbara areas, please call 1-800-735-3501.

TORTILLA SOUP

Tender chicken & fresh vegetables in a rich broth, topped with tortilla strips & avocado.

✓✓ CALORIES: Very Low (313)   ✓✓ CHOLESTEROL: Very Low (50 mg)
✓ FAT: Low (14 g)   ✓ SODIUM: Low (502 mg) **
Diabetic Exchanges: 2½ Meat, 1 Bread, ½ Veg, 2 Fat

VEGGIE FAJITAS

Two flour tortillas with a variety of seasonal fresh garden vegetables, served with rice, beans, fruit relish & salsa quemada. Guacamole not included in analysis. Rice & beans shown below.

✓ CALORIES: Low (531)   ✓✓ CHOLESTEROL: None (0 mg)
✓ FAT: Low (20 g)   SODIUM: High (2712 mg) **
Diabetic Exchanges: 2¾ Bread, 4¾ Veg, ¼ Fruit, 3¾ Fat

GARDEN TOSTADA - REQUEST WITHOUT DRESSING

Lettuce, vegetables, black beans, tomatoes & relish. Analysis does not include tostada shell or dressing.

✓ CALORIES: Low (600)   ✓✓ CHOLESTEROL: None (0 mg)
✓ FAT: Low* (18 g)   SODIUM: High (2347 mg) **
Diabetic Exchanges: 1¼ Meat, 4¼ Bread, 2¼ Veg, ¼ Fruit, 3 Fat

CHICKEN TACO AL CARBON - REQUEST BLACK BEANS RATHER THAN REFRIED

Analysis is for 4 corn tortillas (2 flour tortillas similar). Served with beans (request black beans instead of refried) and rice (see analysis below).

✓ CALORIES: Low (468)   ✓ CHOLESTEROL: Low (120 mg)
✓✓ FAT: Very Low (8 g)   SODIUM: High (1455 mg) **
Diabetic Exchanges: 6¼ Meat (extra lean), 3¼ Bread, ¼ Veg, ½ Fat

GRILLED CHICKEN BREAST - REQUEST VEGETABLES STEAMED

Marinated in salsa, grilled & served with vegetables (request steamed instead of sauteed) & rice (see below).

✓ CALORIES: Low (552)   ✓ CHOLESTEROL: Low (168 mg)
✓ FAT: Low (20 g)   SODIUM: High (1451 mg) **
Diabetic Exchanges: 8¾ Meat (extra lean), ¼ Bread, 2¼ Veg, ¼ Fruit, 2¾ Fat

RICE WITH RELLENO SAUCE

146 calories, 1 g fat*, <1 mg cholesterol, 506 mg sodium**; Diabetic Exchanges: 2 Bread, ¼ Veg

BLACK BEANS

230 calories, 7 g fat*, 0 cholesterol, 373 mg sodium**; Diabetic Exchanges: 2 Bread, 1¼ Fat

   ✓ Low ✓✓ Very Low
†Side dish guidelines are 1/3 of entree guidelines

BeauRivage

(310) 456-5733

26025 W. Pacific Coast Highway, Malibu   (2 miles north of Pepperdine at Corral Canyon)

Established in 1982, BeauRivage is the premier Mediterranean restaurant to offer innovative as well as authentic and creative specialties from the countries bordering this captivating sea. Our award-winning chef, Paolo Giovanni will delight in preparing the freshest food with delicate sauces or simply treated, grilled, or steamed with locally grown fresh herbs. Located on the shore of the Pacific, BeauRivage offers a breathtaking view from every one of its seven dining areas, including the spectacular patio or the romantic atmosphere with candlelight and fireplace featuring soft piano or guitar dinner music. $$$

MINESTRA DI VERDURA†

Minestrone soup (bowl)†

✓ CALORIES: Low (164) ✓✓ CHOLESTEROL: None (0 mg)
FAT: Moderate* (5 g) ✓✓ SODIUM: Very Low (43 mg)
Diabetic Exchanges: 2¾ Veg, 1 Bread, ¾ Fat

TAGLIERINI POLLO - SPECIAL REQUEST

Smoked chicken, shallots, tomatoes, mushrooms, white wine and herbes de Provence. Request no butter.

✓ CALORIES: Low (549) ✓ CHOLESTEROL: Low (146 mg)
✓✓ FAT: Very Low (7 g) SODIUM: High (1700 mg) **
Diabetic Exchanges: 3 Meat (extra lean), 3½ Bread, 1½ Veg

CAPPELLACCI NAPOLETANA

A folded sheet of pasta, filled with spinach and ricotta cheese and served with fresh tomatoes, basil and parmesan.

✓ CALORIES: Low (600) ✓ CHOLESTEROL: Low (135 mg)
✓ FAT: Low (20 g) ✓ SODIUM: Low (393 mg) **
Diabetic Exchanges: 2 Meat, 3½ Bread, 1½ Veg, 2¼ Fat

MEDITERRANEAN SEA BASS

✓ CALORIES: Low (365) ✓ CHOLESTEROL: Low (117 mg)
✓ FAT: Low* (16 g) ✓✓ SODIUM: Very Low (194 mg) **
Diabetic Exchanges: 7 Meat (extra lean), 2 Fat

BAKED CHICKEN - SPECIAL REQUEST

Served with vegetables & roasted potatoes. Request steamed vegetables & skinless chicken. Potatoes not included in analysis (see below).

✓ CALORIES: Low (587) CHOLESTEROL: Moderate (219 mg)
✓ FAT: Low (15 g) ✓✓ SODIUM: Very Low (256 mg) **
Diabetic Exchanges: 11¼ Meat (extra lean), 2¼ Veg, 1 Fat

ROASTED POTATOES†

CALORIES: Moderate (430) ✓✓ CHOLESTEROL: None (0 mg)
✓ FAT: Low* (7 g) ✓✓ SODIUM: Very Low (27 mg) **
Diabetic Exchanges: 5 Bread, 1½ Fat

---

* Primarily unsaturated fat
** If you request no added salt

Inside this beautiful art deco building you'll find dishes that are every bit as artistic as the paintings around the room. Bistro 45 has received much acclaim from the media, including The Los Angeles Times, L.A. Weekly, Zagat and Gourmet Magazine who called it "Wonderful", "Remarkably Refreshing", "Sensational" and "Exceptional". $$

Bistro 45

45 S. Mentor Ave., Pasadena, CA 91106
(818) 795-2478

GRILLED SEASONAL VEGETABLES - ENTREE PORTION
Brushed with a garlic-herb vinaigrette. Saffron rice included in analysis.

✓✓ CALORIES: Very Low (330)   ✓✓ CHOLESTEROL: None (0 mg)
✓✓ FAT: Very Low* (6 g)   ✓✓ SODIUM: Very Low (24 mg) **
Diabetic Exchanges: 4¼ Veg, 2 Bread, 1 Fat

SEARED AHI WITH PICKLED VEGETABLES AND POMEGRANATE DRESSING
- ENTREE PORTION *Served with rice or potatoes (not included in analysis).*

✓ CALORIES: Low (435)   ✓✓ CHOLESTEROL: Very Low (76 mg)
✓✓ FAT: Very Low* (5 g)   ✓✓ SODIUM: Very Low (136 mg) **
Diabetic Exchanges: 5½ Meat (extra lean), 3½ Veg, 2¼ Fruit, ½ Fat

SEARED SEA SCALLOPS WITH FRUITED TOMATO SAUCE
Served with potatoes or rice (not included in analysis).

✓✓ CALORIES: Very Low (228)   ✓✓ CHOLESTEROL: Very Low (47 mg)
✓✓ FAT: Very Low* (2 g)   SODIUM: Moderate (657 mg) **
Diabetic Exchanges: 3¼ Meat (extra lean), 1 Veg, 1 Fruit

BOUILLABAISSE (1 SERVING)
Fresh seasonal fish and shellfish served in a garlic-saffron broth with fresh herbs, tomato, croutons and aioli. Croutons not included in analysis.

✓✓ CALORIES: Very Low (294)   ✓ CHOLESTEROL: Low (157 mg)
✓✓ FAT: Very Low* (8 g)   ✓ SODIUM: Low (315 mg) **
Diabetic Exchanges: 6¾ Meat (extra lean)

ROASTED CHICKEN WITH GARLIC AND NATURAL JUICES - REQUEST SKINLESS
Served with steamed vegetables (included in analysis) and mashed potatoes (not included in analysis).

✓ CALORIES: Low (569)   ✓ CHOLESTEROL: Low (192 mg)
FAT: Moderate (23 g)   ✓✓ SODIUM: Very Low (238 mg) **
Diabetic Exchanges: 10 Meat (extra lean), 2¼ Veg, 2¾ Fat

✓ Low ✓✓ Very Low

   †Side dish guidelines are 1/3 of entree guidelines

Unique among Los Angeles' Indian restaurants, Bombay Cafe offers a mix of savory "street" foods, tandoor-cooked fish, chicken, lamb, breads, and light traditional Indian home cooking. See for yourself why "Gourmet" magazine raved "I've never tasted better spicing". Sample one of our 15 house-made chutneys and see why Ruth Reichl put them in her list of LA restaurant's top 40 dishes. Try our California Tandoori Salad and see why Zagat Survey consistently rates us LA's best Indian restaurant. Open Tues.- Fri. 11:30 am to 10:00 pm; Sat. & Sun. 4:00 pm to 10:00 pm. $$

Bombay Cafe
12113 Santa Monica Blvd. #205
Los Angeles, CA 90025   (310) 820-2070

CALIFORNIA TANDOORI SALAD
Warm tandoori chicken, mushrooms, paneer, romaine, scallions and cilantro. Request lemon-cilantro dressing on the side and use sparingly (59 calories, 6 g fat, 234 mg sodium per Tbs.)

✓✓ CALORIES: Very Low (296)   ✓ CHOLESTEROL: Low (102 mg)
✓✓ FAT: Very Low (9 g)   ✓✓ SODIUM: Very Low (193 mg) **
Diabetic Exchanges: 5 Meat (extra lean), 2 Veg, ¾ Fat

MIRCH MASALA TIKKA (CHICKEN TIKKA KABAB)
with mint yogurt chutney (included in analysis).

✓ CALORIES: Low (409)   ✓ CHOLESTEROL: Low (195 mg)
✓✓ FAT: Very Low (9 g)   ✓ SODIUM: Low (454 mg) **
Diabetic Exchanges: 10 Meat (extra lean), ¼ Veg

UTTAPAM
A semolina griddle cake topped with tomato, onion, green chili and cilantro. Served with coconut chutney & garnishes (included in analysis).
✓✓ CALORIES: Very Low (280)   ✓✓ CHOLESTEROL: Very Low (10 mg)
✓✓ FAT: Very Low (7 g)   SODIUM: Moderate (753 mg) **
Diabetic Exchanges: 2¼ Bread, 1 Veg, ¼ Milk, 1¼ Fat

JALPARI TIKKA (FISH KABAB)
✓ CALORIES: Low (379)   ✓ CHOLESTEROL: Low (109 mg)
✓✓ FAT: Very Low* (8 g)   ✓✓ SODIUM: Very Low (254 mg) **
Diabetic Exchanges: 7¾ Meat (extra lean), ¼ Veg

GOBI SABZI
Cauliflower sauteed with green chilies, ginger, coriander, tumeric & cumin seeds.
✓✓ CALORIES: Very Low (189)   ✓✓ CHOLESTEROL: None (0 mg)
✓ FAT: Low* (13 g)   ✓ SODIUM: Low (560 mg) **
Diabetic Exchanges: 3 Veg, 2½ Fat

* Primarily unsaturated fat
** If you request no added salt

Mary Sue Milliken and Susan Feniger, the celebrated chefs/owners of Border Grill, have developed a menu which pays homage to the bold flavors from the border, coastal Mexico and beyond. With a colorful, festive ambience and a surprisingly light cuisine that is more authentic than the fat-laden food served in the majority of Mexican restaurants, Border Grill is undoubtedly an original, and one of the city's 40 best restaurants according to the LA Times. $$

Border Grill   1445 Fourth St, Santa Monica, CA 90401 (310) 451-1655

CHICKEN GRIDDLED TACOS
Our homemade corn tortillas with chicken, avocado, and salsa. Analysis is for 3 tacos.
- ✓ CALORIES: Low (382)
- ✓✓ CHOLESTEROL: Very Low (40 mg)
- ✓ FAT: Low (18 g)
- ✓ SODIUM: Low (416 mg) **

Diabetic Exchanges: 1½ Meat, 2½ Bread, ½ Veg, 2½ Fat

GRIDDLED FISH TACOS
Our homemade corn tortillas with sea bass, avocado, & cucumber relish. Analysis is for 2 tacos.
- ✓✓ CALORIES: Very Low (211)
- ✓✓ CHOLESTEROL: Very Low (30 mg)
- ✓✓ FAT: Very Low* (4 g)
- ✓✓ SODIUM: Very Low (167 mg) **

Diabetic Exchanges: 2 Meat (extra lean), 1½ Bread, ½ Fat

BORDER VEGETARIAN - REQUEST LIGHT OIL
Plateful of assorted steamed, grilled and roasted vegetables with rice and beans (included in analysis). Request light oil (1 Tbs.)
- ✓ CALORIES: Low (578)
- ✓✓ CHOLESTEROL: Very Low (3 mg)
- ✓ FAT: Low* (20 g)
- SODIUM: Moderate (612 mg) **

Diabetic Exchanges: 3½ Bread, 4 Veg, 4 Fat

CHICKEN AL CARBON - REQUEST WITHOUT SKIN
Marinated with citrus and morita chile, and topped with orange salsa. Served with black beans and rice (see analysis below).
- ✓ CALORIES: Low (487)
- ✓ CHOLESTEROL: Low (192 mg)
- ✓ FAT: Low (19 g)
- ✓ SODIUM: Low (565 mg) **

Diabetic Exchanges: 10 Meat (extra lean), 2¼ Fat

PESCADO VERACRUZANA
Pan seared & baked fish with tomatoes, jalapenos, olives & oregano. Served with rice (see below).
- ✓✓ CALORIES: Very Low (316)
- ✓✓ CHOLESTEROL: Very Low (62 mg)
- ✓ FAT: Low* (19 g)
- ✓✓ SODIUM: Very Low (186 mg) **

Diabetic Exchanges: 4¾ Meat (extra lean), ¼ Veg, 3 Fat

WHITE OR RED RICE† *(3 oz.)*
- ✓✓ CALORIES: Very Low (96)
- ✓✓ CHOLESTEROL: Very Low (6 mg)
- ✓✓ FAT: Very Low* (2 g)
- SODIUM: Moderate (359 mg)

Diabetic Exchanges: 1 Bread, ½ Fat

REFRIED BLACK BEANS† *(3 oz.)*
- ✓ CALORIES: Low (129)
- ✓✓ CHOLESTEROL: None (0 mg)
- ✓ FAT: Low* (6 g)
- SODIUM: Moderate (314 mg)

Diabetic Exchanges: ¾ Bread, ¼ Veg, 1 Fat

✓ Low ✓✓ Very Low

   †Side dish guidelines are 1/3 of entree guidelines

Stop! Look for the flavor! Where is it hiding? Bring it out through roasting, sautéing, stir frying, grilling, sweating and poaching. Stay away from frying! Anything more than a sear is not really necessary, nor will it add to the life of the food. Incorporate as much live food in your diet as possible. Always working within the natural state of anything allows its to keep its attributes. Healthy dining is the only way we can rebuild ourselves and allow for tremendous growth, and it is much simpler today than ever before. A little education is all that is needed for great rewards. Love and patience! Are they not the making for a great strawberry whole wheat soufflé!? $$

- Ernest Lepore

Bravo Cucina

1319 3rd Street, Promenade
Santa Monica, CA 90401   (310) 394-0374

SEARED AHI TUNA WITH SHALLOT INFUSION

Analysis also includes low-fat mashed potatoes and fresh vegetables.

✓ CALORIES: Low (541)   CHOLESTEROL: Moderate (249 mg)
✓✓ FAT: Very Low (10 g)   ✓ SODIUM: Low (350 mg)
Diabetic Exchanges: 8 Meat (extra lean), 1½ Bread, 2¼ Veg, 1¼ Fat

PRIMAVERA PASTA - SPECIAL REQUEST

Assorted vegetables served over fresh carrot fettucine. <u>*Request reduced oil*</u> *(1 Tbs).*

✓ CALORIES: Low (513)   ✓✓ CHOLESTEROL: Very Low (43 mg)
✓ FAT: Low* (18 g)   ✓✓ SODIUM: Very Low (207 mg) **
Diabetic Exchanges: 3 Bread, ¼ Meat, 3 Veg, 2¾ Fat

CAPPELLINI ALLA RUSTICA - SPECIAL REQUEST

Angel hair pasta with roasted eggplant, zucchini, tomatoes, capers, calamata olives and pinenuts in BRAVO's classic tomato sauce. <u>*Request reduced oil*</u> *(1 Tbs).*

✓ CALORIES: Low (599)   ✓✓ CHOLESTEROL: None (0 mg)
✓ FAT: Low* (20 g)   ✓ SODIUM: Low (560 mg) **
Diabetic Exchanges: 4¾ Bread, 2¾ Veg, 3¾ Fat

CHICKEN "SAUSAGE" PASTA - SPECIAL REQUEST

No sausage used, but so rich and delicious --- you'll never miss it! <u>*Request reduced cream*</u>.

CALORIES: Moderate (667)   ✓ CHOLESTEROL: Low (126 mg)
✓ FAT: Low (20 g)   ✓✓ SODIUM: Very Low (198 mg) **
Diabetic Exchanges: 5 Meat, 4¼ Bread, ¼ Milk, 2½ Fat

---

* Primarily unsaturated fat
** If you request no added salt

Bristol's Café

Located inside Bristol Farms Manhattan Beach, Bristol's Café offers breakfast, lunch and dinner menus. We feature a variety of farm fresh breakfasts, a selection of classic sandwiches, crisp salads, hand tossed pizzas and homemade soups for lunch, and an array of wonderful dinners and fresh baked desserts. Bristol's Café also offers beer and wine tastings, special winery dinners, patio dining and free cooking classes. Hours are 8 am to 9 pm daily. $

Bristol Farms locations:

1570 Rosecrans Ave, Manhattan Beach, CA 90266 (310) 643-5229
837 Silver Spur Rd, Rolling Hills Estates, CA 90274 (310) 541-9157
606 Fair Oaks Avenue, Pasadena, CA 91031 (818) 441-5450

The menu items shown below are available at the Manhattan Beach location only.

VEGGIE BURGER - WITHOUT CHEESE

Garden veggie patty, lettuce, tomato, and lo-cal mayo on an onion roll. (Swiss cheese not included in analysis). Served with Garden Vegetable Pasta (see analysis below).
- ✓ CALORIES: Low (533)
- ✓ FAT: Low* (15 g)
- ✓✓ CHOLESTEROL: Very Low (7 mg)
- SODIUM: Moderate (884 mg) **

Diabetic Exchanges: ½ Meat, 5 Bread, ¼ Veg, 2½ Fat

GRILLED VEGGIE MOZZARELLA SANDWICH

Fresh mozzarella, grilled eggplant, zucchini, summer squash, onions, mushrooms, roasted red bell pepper, tomatoes, and fresh herbs on a baguette. Served with Garden Vegetable Pasta (see analysis below).
- ✓ CALORIES: Low (433)
- ✓ FAT: Low (14 g)
- ✓✓ CHOLESTEROL: Very Low (22 mg)
- SODIUM: Moderate (714 mg) **

Diabetic Exchanges: ½ Meat, 3½ Bread, 1 Veg, 2 Fat

CAPELLINI NOODLES WITH TOMATO CONCASSE

Fresh tomatoes, basil and garlic sauteed in olive oil, tossed with capellini noodles and topped with ricotta-salada cheese. Analysis includes steamed vegetables.
- ✓ CALORIES: Low (486)
- ✓ FAT: Low* (20 g)
- ✓✓ CHOLESTEROL: Very Low (10 mg)
- ✓ SODIUM: Low (357 mg) **

Diabetic Exchanges: ¾ Meat, 3¼ Bread, 1¾ Veg, 3¼ Fat

MEDITERRANEAN MEDLEY - REQUEST NO BUTTER

Bay scallops, baby clams & large prawns, sauteed with garlic, peppers, capers & tomatoes in a white wine sauce; served over linguini. <u>Request no butter.</u>
- ✓ CALORIES: Low (600)
- ✓ FAT: Low* (15 g)
- ✓ CHOLESTEROL: Low (158 mg)
- SODIUM: High (1079 mg) **

Diabetic Exchanges: 4 Meat (extra lean), 3 Bread, 1½ Veg, 2¼ Fat

CATCH OF THE DAY

Specially picked from our seafood department and cooked to perfection. Analysis is for swordfish; other fish similar. Served with steamed vegetables (included in analysis).
- ✓ CALORIES: Low (356)
- ✓ FAT: Low* (20 g)
- ✓✓ CHOLESTEROL: Very Low (66 mg)
- ✓✓ SODIUM: Very Low (183 mg) **

Diabetic Exchanges: 4½ Meat (extra lean), ¾ Veg, 2¾ Fat

GARDEN VEGETABLE PASTA† *(3 oz. portion)*
- ✓ CALORIES: Low (133)
- ✓ FAT: Low* (5 g)
- ✓✓ CHOLESTEROL: Very Low (19 mg)
- SODIUM: Moderate (357 mg) **

Diabetic Exchanges: 1 Bread, ¼ Veg, 1 Fat

✓ Low ✓✓ Very Low

†Side dish guidelines are 1/3 of entree guidelines

Ca'Brea serves the finest in Northern Italian cuisine in a comfortable setting of casual country elegance. Local and national publications continue to pick Ca'Brea as one of Los Angeles' best restaurants. Daily specials augment the regular menu, allowing for plenty of variety for even the most frequent patrons. Private rooms available for parties up to 60. Excellent food quality and reasonable prices along with attentive service keep Ca'Brea full and reservations advisable. $$

Ca'Brea
(213) 938-2863

346 South La Brea Ave., Los Angeles, CA 90036

INSALATA TIEPIDA DI FRUTTI DI MARE CON ORTAGGI, OLIO E LIMONE
Fresh seafood salad with marinated vegetables in a lemon and garlic dressing.

✓✓ CALORIES: Very Low (285) ✓ CHOLESTEROL: Low (142 mg)
✓ FAT: Low* (17 g) ✓✓ SODIUM: Very Low (280 mg) **
Diabetic Exchanges: 3 Meat (extra lean), 1½ Veg, 3¼ Fat

LINGUINETTE ALLE VONGOLE ALL'AGLIO DI FRANTOIO
Linguine pasta with fresh clams in a garlic and white wine sauce. (Large serving)

CALORIES: Moderate (688) ✓✓ CHOLESTEROL: Very Low (48 mg)
✓ FAT: Low* (17 g) ✓✓ SODIUM: Very Low (91 mg) **
Diabetic Exchanges: 2½ Meat, 5½ Bread, ¼ Fruit, 2¾ Fat

PENNETTE RUSTICHE AL POMODORO ED ERBETTE AROMATICHE
Short tube pasta with aromatic herbs in a garlic tomato sauce (spicy).

✓ CALORIES: Low (478) ✓✓ CHOLESTEROL: None (0 mg)
✓✓ FAT: Very Low* (5 g) ✓✓ SODIUM: Very Low (198 mg) **
Diabetic Exchanges: 5½ Bread, 1½ Veg, ½ Fat

PESCE DEL GIORNO
Fish of the day. Analysis for red snapper (other fish similar).
Served with steamed spinach and roasted potatoes (included in analysis).

✓ CALORIES: Low (456) ✓✓ CHOLESTEROL: Very Low (84 mg)
✓ FAT: Low* (16 g) SODIUM: Moderate (677 mg) **
Diabetic Exchanges: 6¾ Meat (extra lean), 1¼ Bread, 1¼ Veg, 2½ Fat

* Primarily unsaturated fat
** If you request no added salt

Dining at Cafe La Bohème gives you the opportunity to enjoy tastes from around the world. The eclectic menu includes dishes from Japan, Italy, France and Asia. Preparation and presentation of the innovative dishes are superb. The elaborate and elegant setting at Cafe La Bohème makes your dining experience unique and memorable. $$

Cafe La Bohème   8400 Santa Monica Blvd., West Hollywood, CA 90069   (213) 848-2360

MUSHROOM AND VEGETABLE SPAGHETTINI
soy flavor and olive oil.

✓ CALORIES: Low (476)   ✓✓ CHOLESTEROL: Very Low (5 mg)
✓ FAT: Low* (17 g)   SODIUM: High (1035 mg) **
Diabetic Exchanges: 4 Bread, ½ Veg, 3 Fat

TOMATO AND BASIL SPAGHETTINI - SPECIAL REQUEST
with Italian tomato sauce. <u>*Request light oil*</u> *(½ oz).*

✓ CALORIES: Low (554)   ✓✓ CHOLESTEROL: None (0 mg)
✓ FAT: Low* (20 g)   ✓✓ SODIUM: Very Low (242 mg) **
Diabetic Exchanges: 4 Bread, 2¾ Veg, 3¾ Fat

VEGETARIAN PIZZA (½ PIZZA)
Vine ripened organic tomato, endive, roasted eggplant, raddicchio & lettuce. Analysis for ½ pizza.

✓ CALORIES: Low (389)   ✓✓ CHOLESTEROL: Very Low (11 mg)
✓ FAT: Low (18 g)   ✓ SODIUM: Low (515 mg) **
Diabetic Exchanges: ¼ Meat, 2½ Bread, ½ Veg, 3 Fat

GRILLED CHICKEN WITH CILANTRO JALAPENO SAUCE
- REQUEST CHICKEN WITHOUT SKIN
Analysis does not include potatoes (see below) or tortilla salad.

✓ CALORIES: Low (591)   CHOLESTEROL: Moderate (289 mg)
✓ FAT: Low (14 g)   ✓ SODIUM: Low (477 mg) **
Diabetic Exchanges: 15 Meat (extra lean), ¼ Veg, ¼ Fat

GRILLED SWORDFISH WITH ONION PEPPERCORN SAUCE
- REQUEST SAUCE ON SIDE
Served with sauteed spinach (included) and mashed potatoes (see below). <u>*Request sauce on the side*</u> *and use sparingly (not included in analysis).*

✓ CALORIES: Low (370)   ✓✓ CHOLESTEROL: Very Low (66 mg)
✓ FAT: Low* (20 g)   ✓✓ SODIUM: Very Low (297 mg) **
Diabetic Exchanges: 4½ Meat, ½ Veg, 2¾ Fat

MASHED POTATOES†

✓ CALORIES: Low (138)   ✓✓ CHOLESTEROL: Very Low (24 mg)
✓ FAT: Low (7 g)   ✓ SODIUM: Low (141 mg)
Diabetic Exchanges: 1 Bread, 1½ Fat

✓ Low ✓✓ Very Low

   †Side dish guidelines are 1/3 of entree guidelines

Cafe Nordstrom

Cafe Nordstrom offers a wide selection of breakfast items, hot and cold sandwiches, specialty salads and freshly baked pastries to hungry shoppers. Especially popular with our lunch crowd is our Blue Plate Souper which features a bowl of soup, green salad and a half sandwich. At Cafe Nordstrom we take pride in the freshness and quality of our food. $

Glendale: 200 W. Broadway, Glendale, CA 91204   (818) 502-9922 x 1610
Topanga: 6602 Topanga Canyon Rd., Canoga Park, CA 91303   (818) 884-7900 x 1610
Santa Anita: 400 S. Baldwin, Ste. 200, Arcadia, CA 91007   (818) 821-6363 x 1610
Southbay Galleria: 1835 Hawthorne Blvd, Redondo Beach, CA 90278   (310) 542-9440 x 1610
Westside: 10830 W. Pico Blvd., Los Angeles 90064   (310) 470-6155 x 1610

BREAST OF TURKEY SANDWICH - SPECIAL REQUEST
Order whole wheat bread and <u>mustard instead of mayonnaise</u>.
✓✓ CALORIES: Very Low (333)   ✓✓ CHOLESTEROL: Very Low (79 mg)
✓✓ FAT: Very Low (6 g)   SODIUM: Moderate (620 mg) **
Diabetic Exchanges: 3¾ Meat (extra lean), 1½ Bread, ¼ Veg, ½ Fat

BREAST OF CHICKEN SANDWICH - SPECIAL REQUEST
<u>Request mustard rather than mayonnaise and no cheese</u>.
✓ CALORIES: Low (395)   ✓✓ CHOLESTEROL: Very Low (96 mg)
✓✓ FAT: Very Low (10 g)   SODIUM: Moderate (618 mg) **
Diabetic Exchanges: 4 Meat (extra lean), 2 Bread, ¼ Veg, 1½ Fat

VEGETARIAN CHILI WITH BEANS - SPECIAL REQUEST
<u>Request cheese on the side</u> and use sparingly (not included in analysis).
✓✓ CALORIES: Very Low (194)   ✓✓ CHOLESTEROL: None (0 mg)
✓✓ FAT: Very Low (2 g)   ✓ SODIUM: Low (493 mg) **
Diabetic Exchanges: 2¼ Bread, ½ Fat

MEDITERRANEAN VEGETARIAN ON FOCCACIA
Cucumber, sun dried tomatoes, avocado, mozzarella, lettuce and herbs on foccacia bread. You may request less cheese and/or avocado to reduce fat.
✓ CALORIES: Low (583)   ✓✓ CHOLESTEROL: Very Low (25 mg)
FAT: Moderate* (28 g)   SODIUM: Moderate (840 mg) **
Diabetic Exchanges: 1 Meat, 3 Bread, 1 Veg, 4 Fat

* Primarily unsaturated fat
** If you request no added salt

Welcome to Carrows, "Home of America's Favorite Food." With comfortable surroundings, friendly service and an extensive menu featuring a wide range of breakfast, lunch and dinner choices, Carrows is the perfect setting for traditional family dining. You'll love the homestyle freshness and abundant portions of our meals, and of course you'll want to save room for one of our irresistible desserts.

*For our senior guests, we offer a new menu with reduced prices. Our bakeries (in select locations), offer baked goods like fresh muffins, cookies, cornbread and our **no sugar added** Lite Apple Pie. Visit Carrows 7 days a week, from 6:00 am to 12:00 midnight (hours vary by location). $*

Carrows

Locations in Alhambra, Cerritos, Chatsworth, Commerce, Downey, Gardena, Highland Park, Inglewood, Long Beach, Montebello, Northridge, Norwalk, Panorama City, Playa Del Rey, Rosemead, San Pedro, Santa Fe Springs, Santa Monica, South Pasadena, Tarzana, Torrance, West Covina & Whittier.

CHICKEN DELUXE SANDWICH
Lightly seasoned skinless chicken breast, topped with tomato, red onion, sprouts and Grey Poupon Dijon mustard sauce. We recommend salad with low-cal dressing and fresh fruit instead of fries as the side dishes (not included in analysis).
✓ CALORIES: Low (456)   ✓ CHOLESTEROL: Low (128 mg)
✓ FAT: Low (18 g)   ✓ SODIUM: Low (557 mg) **
Diabetic Exchanges: 6¼ Meat (extra lean), 1¼ Bread, ¼ Veg, 2½ Fat

EGGSTRÓDNAIRE GARDEN OMELETTE - SPECIAL REQUEST
Spinach, tomatoes, onions, Jack and Cheddar cheese. <u>Request ½ portion cheese and sauce on the side</u>. Analysis for omelette only, without sauce.
✓✓ CALORIES: Very Low (258)   ✓ CHOLESTEROL: Low (143 mg)
✓ FAT: Low (17 g)   ✓ SODIUM: Low (589 mg) **
Diabetic Exchanges: 2¾ Meat, ¾ Veg, 2 Fat

FRESH VEGETABLE PLATTER
A medley of seasonal fresh vegetables, served with seasoned new potatoes (included in analysis) and bread (not included). We recommend <u>low-cal dressing instead of Hollandaise or melted butter</u> (not included in analysis).
✓✓ CALORIES: Very Low (323)   ✓✓ CHOLESTEROL: Very Low (16 mg)
✓✓ FAT: Very Low (7 g)   ✓✓ SODIUM: Very Low (152 mg) **
Diabetic Exchanges: 4½ Veg, 2¼ Bread, 1 Fat

OLD-FASHIONED SPAGHETTI WITH MARINARA
Tender spaghetti topped with marinara sauce.
✓ CALORIES: Low (538)   ✓✓ CHOLESTEROL: Very Low (5 mg)
✓✓ FAT: Very Low* (10 g)   SODIUM: High (1043 mg) **
Diabetic Exchanges: ¼ Meat, 4¾ Bread, 4½ Veg

BROILED SEAFOOD PLATTER - SPECIAL REQUEST
A tempting selection of Alaskan halibut, skewered shrimp and sea scallops broiled to perfection. <u>Request no butter</u>. Served with rice pilaf and fresh vegetables (included in analysis).
✓ CALORIES: Low (569)   CHOLESTEROL: Moderate (293 mg)
✓ FAT: Low* (13 g)   SODIUM: High (1118 mg) **
Diabetic Exchanges: 8¾ Meat (extra lean), 1¾ Bread, 1 Veg, 1½ Fat

✓ Low ✓✓ Very Low
†Side dish guidelines are 1/3 of entree guidelines

Everybody knows Chasen's. Created in 1936 by vaudevillian performer Dave Chasen, it is more than a restaurant. It is a legend - a Hollywood institution known for its warm and elegant ambiance, known also for the Hollywood stars, writers, sports personalities, big business CEO's and politicians who are its "regulars." Whether you're a movie star, a sports celebrity, or an individual who simply appreciates the finest in cuisine and hospitality, any occasion is cause for celebration...at Chasen's. $$$

Chasen's

9039 Beverly Boulevard, West Hollywood, CA 90048   (310) 271-2168

ANGEL HAIR WITH FRESH TOMATO AND BASIL

✓ CALORIES: Low (521)   ✓✓ CHOLESTEROL: Very Low (31 mg)
✓ FAT: Low (20 g)   ✓✓ SODIUM: Very Low (141 mg) **
Diabetic Exchanges: 4 Bread, 1½ Veg, 3½ Fat

BREAST OF CHICKEN PEPPERONATA

Served with rice and vegetables (included in analysis).

✓ CALORIES: Low (594)   ✓ CHOLESTEROL: Low (192 mg)
✓ FAT: Low (17 g)   ✓ SODIUM: Low (350 mg) **
Diabetic Exchanges: 10 Meat (extra lean), 1½ Bread, 1¼ Veg, 1¾ Fat

CHICKEN CURRY - SPECIAL REQUEST

Request light sauce (½ portion). Served with rice pilaf and assorted garnishes (not included in analysis).

✓ CALORIES: Low (572)   ✓ CHOLESTEROL: Low (189 mg)
✓ FAT: Low (20 g)   ✓ SODIUM: Low (356 mg) **
Diabetic Exchanges: 8¾ Meat (extra lean), ¼ Bread, ¼ Veg, 1 Fruit, 2½ Fat

SEAFOOD BROCHETTE (DINNER MENU ONLY)

Served with rice pilaf and vegetables (included in analysis). Butter served on the side is not included.

✓ CALORIES: Low (557)   ✓ CHOLESTEROL: Low (128 mg)
✓ FAT: Low* (20 g)   ✓ SODIUM: Low (469 mg) **
Diabetic Exchanges: 4½ Meat (extra lean), 2½ Bread, 1¼ Veg, 3½ Fat

* Primarily unsaturated fat
** If you request no added salt

Chin Chin

West Hollywood: 8618 Sunset Blvd. (310) 652-1818
Studio City: 12215 Ventura Blvd. (818) 985-9090
Brentwood: 11740 San Vicente Blvd. (310) 826-2525
Marina Del Rey: 13455 Maxella Ave. (310) 823-9999
Encino: 16101 Ventura Boulevard (818) 783-1717

"Chin Chin" not only means "to your health" but it is also known as a popular hotspot for Chinese food. It has been dubbed "fun food" by Merrill Shindler of the Daily News. Chin Chin offers generous portions served in a contemporary setting with a bustling atmosphere. Chin Chin is committed to preparing light and healthy food, and now offers its new **Chin Chin Lite Menu** *which features Chinese dishes prepared with little or no oil.* $$

Below are a few of our many items containing little or no oil from our **Lite Menu***.*

LITE FRAGRANT VEGETABLES WITH KUNG PAO SAUCE
Black bean, sweet & sour orange, curry and garlic sauce also recommended.

✓ CALORIES: Low (373) ✓✓ CHOLESTEROL: None (0 mg)
✓✓ FAT: Very Low* (2 g) SODIUM: High (2388 mg)
Diabetic Exch: 3 Veg, 3¼ Bread

LITE GARLIC CHICKEN

✓ CALORIES: Low (570) ✓ CHOLESTEROL: Low (144 mg)
✓✓ FAT: Very Low (7 g) SODIUM: High (1023 mg)
Diabetic Exchanges: 7½ Meat (extra lean), 1 Bread, 4½ Veg

LITE SWEET & SOUR ORANGE CHICKEN

✓ CALORIES: Low (570) ✓ CHOLESTEROL: Low (144 mg)
✓✓ FAT: Very Low (6 g) SODIUM: High (1666 mg)
Diabetic Exchanges: 7½ Meat (extra lean), 4 Bread, 1½ Veg

LITE SHRIMP WITH BLACK BEANS

✓ CALORIES: Low (364) CHOLESTEROL: Moderate (283 mg)
✓✓ FAT: Very Low* (3 g) SODIUM: High (2351 mg)
Diabetic Exchanges: 4 Meat (extra lean), 1¼ Bread, 2½ Veg, ¼ Fat

VEGETABLE "UNFRIED" FRIED RICE - SPECIAL REQUEST
Request no egg.

✓ CALORIES: Low (465) ✓✓ CHOLESTEROL: Very Low (5 mg)
✓✓ FAT: Very Low* (1 g) SODIUM: High (1900 mg)
Diabetic Exchanges: 5¾ Bread, ¾ Veg

✓ Low ✓✓ Very Low

  †Side dish guidelines are 1/3 of entree guidelines

Chommanade

Welcome to Chommanade, where you will experience sensational Thai cuisine at very reasonable prices. With a unique and creative flair, Chommanade offers authentic Thai dishes in an elegant, yet casual atmosphere. All items prepared without MSG. Come and enjoy healthful and wonderful Thai dining every day from 5:00 - 9:30 pm. $

Chommanade 5009 E. 2nd St., Belmont Shore, CA 90803   (310) 433-1037

#7 PLA KOONG

Shrimps lightly grilled to perfection, sauteed in lime juice and mixed with chili sauce, mint leaves and lemongrass.

✓✓ CALORIES: Very Low (293)   CHOLESTEROL: Moderate (236 mg)
✓✓ FAT: Very Low* (2 g)   SODIUM: High (1953 mg)
Diabetic Exchanges: 3½ Meat (extra lean), 2 Bread, 1 Veg, ¼ Fruit

#12 TOM YUM KAI (SOUP)

Chicken in delicious hot and sour broth with mushrooms.

✓✓ CALORIES: Very Low (252)   ✓✓ CHOLESTEROL: Very Low (73 mg)
✓✓ FAT: Very Low (6 g)   SODIUM: High (1903 mg)
Diabetic Exchanges: 3 Meat, ½ Bread, ½ Veg, ¼ Fruit

#14 TOM YUM KOONG (SOUP)

Shrimps in delicious hot and sour broth with mushrooms.

✓✓ CALORIES: Very Low (215)   ✓ CHOLESTEROL: Low (180 mg)
✓✓ FAT: Very Low* (4 g)   SODIUM: High (2040 mg)
Diabetic Exchanges: 2½ Meat (extra lean), ½ Bread, ½ Veg, ¼ Fruit

#32 GINGER CHICKEN

Stir-fried with fresh ginger, mushrooms and green onions.

✓ CALORIES: Low (402)   ✓✓ CHOLESTEROL: Very Low (84 mg)
✓ FAT: Low (18 g)   SODIUM: High (3042 mg)
Diabetic Exchanges: 3 Meat, 1½ Bread, 1½ Veg, 2¾ Fat

#37 VEGETARIAN DELIGHT

Mixture of fresh crisp vegetables cooked in light sesame oil with a touch of garlic.

✓✓ CALORIES: Very Low (288)   ✓✓ CHOLESTEROL: Very Low (9 mg)
✓ FAT: Low* (14 g)   SODIUM: High (2256 mg)
Diabetic Exchanges: ¼ Meat, 1½ Bread, 2½ Veg, 2¾ Fat

#38 SPICY TOFU - REQUEST STEAMED

Tofu curd topped with spicy mint chili sauce. Request tofu steamed rather than fried.

✓ CALORIES: Low (375)   ✓✓ CHOLESTEROL: Very Low (9 mg)
✓ FAT: Low* (20 g)   SODIUM: High (1287 mg)
Diabetic Exchanges: 1¾ Meat, 1¼ Bread, 1½ Veg, 6½ Fat

---

* Primarily unsaturated fat
** If you request no added salt

"You are what you eat" has never been truer. We're changing the way we eat -- and CLEARWATER CAFE has responded by using the best fish and seafood from around the world. Indoor-outdoor dining and a charming rustic atmosphere sets the scene for sunny weekend breakfasts, lunches after shopping in Old Town Pasadena, and romantic dinners.

$$

Clearwater Cafe

168 West Colorado Blvd.
Pasadena, CA 91105
(818) 356-0959

PENNE WITH SAUTEED FRESH VEGETABLES

✓ CALORIES: Low (600)   ✓✓ CHOLESTEROL: None (0 mg)
✓ FAT: Low* (16 g)   ✓✓ SODIUM: Very Low (80 mg) **
Diabetic Exchanges: 5½ Bread, 2 Veg, 2¾ Fat

MIXED GRILL OF VEGETABLES WITH CREAMY POLENTA

✓✓ CALORIES: Very Low (300)   ✓✓ CHOLESTEROL: None (0 mg)
✓✓ FAT: Very Low* (8 g)   ✓ SODIUM: Low (390 mg) **
Diabetic Exchanges: 2¼ Bread, 1½ Veg, ¾ Fruit, ½ Fat

GRILLED HAWAIIAN MAHI-MAHI

with achiote marinade and black bean chili. Served with Jasmine rice (included in analysis).

✓ CALORIES: Low (479)   ✓ CHOLESTEROL: Low (124 mg)
✓✓ FAT: Very Low* (6 g)   ✓ SODIUM: Low (539 mg) **
Diabetic Exchanges: 5 Meat (extra lean), 3½ Bread, ½ Veg, ¼ Fat

GRILLED MEXICAN YELLOWTAIL

with teriyaki glaze and grilled eggplant. Served with Jasmine rice (included in analysis).

✓ CALORIES: Low (596)   ✓✓ CHOLESTEROL: Very Low (72 mg)
✓ FAT: Low* (12 g)   SODIUM: High (1225 mg) **
Diabetic Exchanges: 5½ Meat (extra lean), 4 Bread

✓ Low ✓✓ Very Low

†Side dish guidelines are 1/3 of entree guidelines

After four years of continuous operation surviving fires, floods and earthquakes, Coogie's continues to be Malibu's foremost family restaurant. Located in the Malibu Colony Plaza, it offers a casual, relaxed atmosphere. From fresh fish to unique salads, their creative menu satisfies everyone's needs. Open 7 days a week for breakfast, lunch and dinner. $

Coogie's Beach Cafe

23755 West Malibu Road
Malibu, CA 90265   (310) 317-1444

COOGIE'S BAJA DELIGHT

A House Favorite! Two large fresh grilled fish tacos with smoked chili sauce, guacamole, salsa & cabbage in soft wheat tortillas.

✓ CALORIES: Low (485)   ✓✓ CHOLESTEROL: Very Low (83 mg)
✓ FAT: Low* (15 g)   ✓ SODIUM: Low (590 mg) **
Diabetic Exchanges: 4¼ Meat (extra lean), 2½ Bread, 1 Veg, 2½ Fat

STEAMED ORIENTAL VEGETABLES

A fresh assortment of garden vegetables steamed in a ginger soy broth and served over a wild rice blend.

✓ CALORIES: Low (460)   ✓✓ CHOLESTEROL: None (0 mg)
✓✓ FAT: Very Low* (2 g)   SODIUM: High (1287 mg) **
Diabetic Exchanges: 1 Veg, 3 Bread

CHARBROILED GARLIC TURKEY SALAD

Charbroiled tenderloin of turkey in a garlic marinade, sliced over a bed of wild greens, with parmesan dressing, roasted peppers, tomatoes, mandarin oranges & new potatoes.

✓ CALORIES: Low (506)   ✓ CHOLESTEROL: Low (138 mg)
✓ FAT: Low (20 g)   ✓ SODIUM: Low (599 mg) **
Diabetic Exchanges: 7½ Meat (extra lean), ¾ Bread, ¾ Veg, ¼ Fruit, 3½ Fat

PAPAYA MANGO SALMON

Fresh baked North Atlantic Salmon on a lemon-lime sauce and topped with fresh papaya mango salsa.

✓ CALORIES: Low (400)   ✓ CHOLESTEROL: Low (119 mg)
✓ FAT: Low* (18 g)   ✓✓ SODIUM: Very Low (177 mg) **
Diabetic Exchanges: 6 Meat, ¾ Veg, ½ Fruit, ¾ Fat

FARFALLONI PASTA

Bow tie pasta with chicken breast, sundried tomatoes, broccoli, and red chili flakes in a light garlic chicken broth. Topped with parmesan cheese.

✓ CALORIES: Low (584)   ✓ CHOLESTEROL: Low (153 mg)
✓ FAT: Low (20 g)   ✓✓ SODIUM: Very Low (144 mg) **
Diabetic Exchanges: 5 Meat (extra lean), 3 Bread, ¼ Veg, 2¾ Fat

* Primarily unsaturated fat
** If you request no added salt

An exiting bistro with a fresh approach to fresh fish and seafood, salads, homemade pastas, chicken and beef - a menu that has something for everyone! At Cutters you can count on high quality food at reasonable prices and great service from our courteous staff. $

Santa Monica's go anytime order anything bistro!

Cutters   2425 Colorado Avenue, Santa Monica, CA 90404   (310) 453-3588

SESAME CHICKEN SALAD
Crisp romaine tossed with chicken, won ton strips, sliced celery, red bell peppers, almonds and scallions in a tangy sweet-and-sour sauce.
- ✓ CALORIES: Low (480)
- ✓ FAT: Low (11 g)
- ✓ CHOLESTEROL: Low (101 mg)
- SODIUM: High (1491 mg) **

Diabetic Exchanges: 4½ Meat, 3 Bread, ¾ Veg, ¾ Fat

MUSHROOM GARDEN BURGER
Cutters' no-meat juicy garden burger patty made with whole grains, nuts, fresh mushrooms, cheese & spices. Served with sauteed mushrooms and fresh herbal spread. Request low-fat slaw (included in analysis) instead of fries.
- ✓ CALORIES: Low (476)
- ✓✓ FAT: Very Low* (9 g)
- ✓✓ CHOLESTEROL: Very Low (8 mg)
- SODIUM: High (1502 mg) **

Diabetic Exchanges: ½ Meat, 4¾ Bread, 1½ Veg, 1½ Fat

MESQUITE-GRILLED THAI CHICKEN SANDWICH
Mesquite-grilled skinless breast of chicken marinated in olive oil, Thai chili-garlic paste and lemon juice. Served with Thai basil, crisp iceberg, sliced fresh tomato and onion on a Kaiser roll. Request low-fat slaw (included in analysis) instead of fries.
- ✓ CALORIES: Low (544)
- ✓✓ FAT: Very Low (10 g)
- ✓ CHOLESTEROL: Low (120 mg)
- SODIUM: High (1649 mg) **

Diabetic Exchanges: 6¼ Meat (extra lean), 1 Veg, 2¾ Bread, 1 Fat

SPAGHETTINI WITH HERB PESTO AND TOMATO-BASIL SALSA
Tender spaghettini tossed with vegetable broth and crowned with chunky tomato basil salsa, fresh herb pesto and grated Parmesan.
- ✓ CALORIES: Low (395)
- ✓✓ FAT: Very Low* (9 g)
- ✓✓ CHOLESTEROL: Very Low (2 mg)
- SODIUM: High (1184 mg) **

Diabetic Exchanges: 4 Bread, ¾ Veg, 1½ Fat

MESQUITE-GRILLED APRICOT CILANTRO CHICKEN
Skinless breast of chicken mesquite-grilled and topped with a fresh fruit salsa of apricots, plum tomatoes, fresh ginger & cilantro. Served with vegetable medley (included in analysis).
- ✓ CALORIES: Low (495)
- ✓ FAT: Low (12 g)
- ✓ CHOLESTEROL: Low (144 mg)
- SODIUM: High (1429 mg)

Diabetic Exchanges: 7½ Meat (extra lean), ¾ Bread, 1½ Veg, ½ Fruit, 1 Fat

FRESH FISH SELECTION WITH HEART-HEALTHY PREPARATION
also available daily.

✓ Low ✓✓ Very Low

†Side dish guidelines are 1/3 of entree guidelines

Dante's Italian Cuisine

Dante's award-winning Italian cuisine is hailed as one of the South Bay's best eating experiences. Salvatore Costa, the owner and chef, is very meticulous about the quality and freshness in every dish he prepares. No wonder he was given a 3-star rating. He was born in Palermo, Sicily, but many dishes have a northern touch since he lived many years in Milan. The restaurant has a wonderful Old World ambiance with a contemporary look. The staff is friendly and jovial and help to make the atmosphere at Dante's warm and inviting. Prices are extremely reasonable. All major cards accepted. Reservations suggested. Full bar. $$

Dante's 1611 S. Catalina Ave, Redondo Beach, CA 90277 (310) 792-1972

CONTADINA SALAD
Whole corn, tomatoes, romaine, mushrooms and grilled breast of chicken.
Dressing served on the side (not included in analysis - use sparingly).
✓✓ CALORIES: Very Low (333)   ✓ CHOLESTEROL: Low (144 mg)
✓✓ FAT: Very Low (7 g)   ✓✓ SODIUM: Very Low (141 mg) **
Diabetic Exchanges: 7½ Meat (extra lean), ¼ Bread, 1 Veg

PASTA POMODORO FRESCO - SPECIAL REQUEST
Fresh tomatoes with fresh garlic and sweet basil. Request reduced oil (1 Tbs).
✓ CALORIES: Low (402)   ✓✓ CHOLESTEROL: None (0 mg)
✓ FAT: Low* (16 g)   ✓✓ SODIUM: Very Low (24 mg) **
Diabetic Exchanges: 3 Bread, 2 Veg, 3 Fat

PASTA COZZE
Fresh mussels in red sauce.
✓ CALORIES: Low (499)   ✓✓ CHOLESTEROL: Very Low (48 mg)
✓ FAT: Low* (14 g)   SODIUM: Moderate (828 mg) **
Diabetic Exchanges: 1½ Meat, 3½ Bread, 1½ Veg, 2 Fat

PASTA VEGETARIANA - SPECIAL REQUEST
A variety of sauteed vegetables with fresh tomatoes. Request reduced oil (1 Tbs).
✓ CALORIES: Low (463)   ✓✓ CHOLESTEROL: None (0 mg)
✓ FAT: Low* (18 g)   ✓✓ SODIUM: Very Low (233 mg) **
Diabetic Exchanges: 3 Bread, 3½ Veg, 3½ Fat

SCAMPI DEL CAPITANO - SPECIAL REQUEST
Made with fresh tomatoes, brandy, garlic and touch of Grey Poupon. Request reduced oil (1 Tbs).
✓ CALORIES: Low (378)   CHOLESTEROL: Moderate (277 mg)
✓ FAT: Low* (18 g)   SODIUM: Moderate (627 mg) **
Diabetic Exchanges: 4 Meat (extra lean), ¾ Veg, 3 Fat

---

* Primarily unsaturated fat
** If you request no added salt

Da Pasquale is a small family Italian bistro with great food you'll remember. Da Pasquale is located in Beverly Hills and operated by Anna and Pasquale Morra, the former "original pizza chef" at Angeli Caffe's. Pastas, risotto, fish specials and very thin-crusted pizza are prepared daily. The smells alone will knock you off your feet and have you coming back for more. Lunch served Monday to Friday; dinner Monday to Saturday. Catering and takeout available. $$

Da Pasquale

9749 Little Santa Monica Boulevard, Beverly Hills, CA 90210   (310) 859-3884

LINGUINE ALLE VONGOLE - SPECIAL REQUEST

Linguine with clams, olive oil, hot pepper, parsley and white wine. <u>Request light oil</u> (1 Tbs).

✓ CALORIES: Low (563)   ✓✓ CHOLESTEROL: Very Low (38 mg)
✓ FAT: Low* (20 g)   ✓✓ SODIUM: Very Low (71 mg) **
Diabetic Exchanges: 2 Meat, 4 Bread, ¼ Veg, 3½ Fat

LINGUINE CON ARAGOSTA - SPECIAL REQUEST

Baby lobster tail, garlic, parsley and tomatoes. <u>Request light oil</u> (1 Tbs).

✓ CALORIES: Low (594)   ✓✓ CHOLESTEROL: Very Low (81 mg)
✓ FAT: Low* (20 g)   ✓ SODIUM: Low (448 mg) **
Diabetic Exchanges: 3¼ Meat (extra lean), 4 Bread, 1 Veg, 3½ Fat

SPAGHETTI AL CARCIOFI - SPECIAL REQUEST

Artichokes, garlic, olive oil, parsley, black olives and capers. <u>Request light oil</u> (1 Tbs).

✓ CALORIES: Low (549)   ✓✓ CHOLESTEROL: None (0 mg)
FAT: Moderate* (23 g)   SODIUM: High (1136 mg) **
Diabetic Exchanges: 4 Bread, 3 Veg, 5 Fat

LINGUINE AL GAMBERI - SPECIAL REQUEST

Shrimp sauteed in olive oil, garlic, hot peppers and tomatoes. <u>Request light oil</u> (1 Tbs).

✓ CALORIES: Low (566)   ✓ CHOLESTEROL: Low (163 mg)
✓ FAT: Low* (20 g)   ✓✓ SODIUM: Very Low (204 mg) **
Diabetic Exchanges: 2 Meat, 4 Bread, 1 Veg, 3½ Fat

RAVIOLI AL POMODORO - SPECIAL REQUEST
<u>Request light oil</u> (½ Tbs).

✓ CALORIES: Low (449)   ✓✓ CHOLESTEROL: Very Low (89 mg)
✓ FAT: Low (18 g)   ✓✓ SODIUM: Very Low (216 mg) **
Diabetic Exchanges: 1½ Meat, 3 Bread, 1½ Veg, 1¾ Fat

✓ Low ✓✓ Very Low
†Side dish guidelines are 1/3 of entree guidelines

Located at the historical Santa Monica Airport, the DC3 Restaurant and Catering offers an incredible dining experience with award-winning Euro-Pacific cuisine and ocean-view seating. Home for aviation legends, culinary Epicureans, and all others who enjoy great food, great pours, and the thrill of flight. At DC3, let your tastes soar! $$

DC3   (310) 399-2323
2800 Donald Douglas Loop North
Santa Monica, CA 90405

SEABASS
Served over wild mushroom ragout with yellow pepper sauce. Served with herb mashed potatoes (included in analysis).

✓ CALORIES: Low (463)   ✓ CHOLESTEROL: Low (102 mg)
✓ FAT: Low (16 g)   ✓✓ SODIUM: Very Low (229 mg) **
Diabetic Exchanges: 5 Meat (extra lean), 1¾ Bread, 1½ Veg, 2¼ Fat

GRILLED BREAST OF TURKEY
with red wine mushroom sauce, roasted potatoes & sauteed carrots (included in analysis).
Request roasted new potatoes instead of mashed.

✓ CALORIES: Low (573)   ✓ CHOLESTEROL: Low (165 mg)
✓ FAT: Low (16 g)   ✓✓ SODIUM: Very Low (134 mg) **
Diabetic Exchanges: 8½ Meat (extra lean), 2½ Bread, 1¼ Veg, 1¾ Fat

SPICY GRILLED TUNA WITH GINGER PINEAPPLE SAUCE

✓ CALORIES: Low (486)   ✓✓ CHOLESTEROL: Very Low (89 mg)
✓ FAT: Low* (16 g)   SODIUM: Moderate (821 mg) **
Diabetic Exchanges: 6¼ Meat (extra lean), ½ Bread, 1½ Veg, 1 Fruit, 2¾ Fat

CHARRED SWORDFISH
with sauteed asparagus and red new potatoes (included in analysis).
Request sauce on the side and use sparingly (see note below).

✓ CALORIES: Low (418)   ✓✓ CHOLESTEROL: Very Low (88 mg)
✓ FAT: Low (12 g)   ✓✓ SODIUM: Very Low (226 mg)
Diabetic Exchanges: 5 Meat, 2 Bread, ½ Veg, ¾ Fat

CHICKEN WITH ROASTED GARLIC SAUCE
Served with mashed potatoes and grilled vegetables (included in analysis).

✓ CALORIES: Low (554)   ✓ CHOLESTEROL: Low (165 mg)
✓ FAT: Low (20 g)   ✓✓ SODIUM: Very Low (198 mg) **
Diabetic Exchanges: 7½ Meat (extra lean), 1½ Bread, ½ Veg, 2½ Fat

SAUCES (CITRUS, LEMON BUTTER, AND TOMATO LEMON BASIL)
contain approx. 80 CALORIES, 9 g FAT, 20 mg CHOLESTEROL, 140 mg SODIUM per Tablespoon.

* Primarily unsaturated fat
** If you request no added salt

In the comfortable, sleek and cosmopolitan atmosphere, Drago remarkably preserves the unique influences of Italy. If your desires are adventurous, the Sicilian specialties are sure to please. Enjoy exquisite Italian food with flavors pure and delightful. $$

Drago   2628 Wilshire Boulevard, Santa Monica, CA 90403   (310) 828-1585

CARPACCIO DI PESCE SPADA, INSALATA DI CETRIOLI - SPECIAL REQUEST
Smoked swordfish carpaccio and cucumber salad. <u>Request light oil</u> (1 tsp).

✓✓ CALORIES: Very Low (143)   ✓✓ CHOLESTEROL: Very Low (33 mg)
✓✓ FAT: Very Low* (7 g)   SODIUM: Moderate (666 mg) **
    Diabetic Exchanges: 2½ Meat (extra lean), ¼ Veg, ¾ Fat

INSALATA DI FAGIOLI E TONNO - SPECIAL REQUEST
Tuna and white bean salad. <u>Request light oil</u> (1 Tbs).

✓✓ CALORIES: Very Low (267)   ✓✓ CHOLESTEROL: Very Low (12 mg)
 ✓ FAT: Low* (17 g)   ✓✓ SODIUM: Very Low (178 mg) **
    Diabetic Exchanges: 1¼ Meat (extra lean), ¾ Bread, ½ Veg, 3¼ Fat

PASTA PRIMAVERA
 ✓ CALORIES: Low (539)   ✓✓ CHOLESTEROL: None (0 mg)
✓✓ FAT: Very Low* (9 g)   ✓ SODIUM: Low (539 mg) **
    Diabetic Exchanges: 6 Bread, ¾ Veg, 1½ Fat

GALLETTO CON PEPERONATA
Cornish game hen with bell peppers.

 ✓ CALORIES: Low (563)   ✓ CHOLESTEROL: Low (193 mg)
 ✓ FAT: Low (19 g)   ✓ SODIUM: Low (422 mg) **
    Diabetic Exchanges: 10 Meat (extra lean), 3½ Veg, 2 Fat

✓ Low ✓✓ Very Low
†Side dish guidelines are 1/3 of entree guidelines

Earth, Wind & Flour

Encino: 17644 Ventura Boulevard (near White Oak Ave.) (818) 986-0772
Santa Monica: 2222 Wilshire Boulevard (corner of 23rd) (310) 829-7829
Westwood: 1776 Westwood Boulevard (corner of Santa Monica) (310) 470-2499

PIZZA ALTOBELLO - REQUEST EASY CHEESE (½ PIZZA)

Extra thin crusted. Mushrooms, eggplant, basil, cilantro with mozzarella, white cheddar and parmesan. Request easy cheese (½ portion of cheese). Analysis is for ½ pizza.

✓ CALORIES: Low (584) ✓✓ CHOLESTEROL: Very Low (44 mg)
✓ FAT: Low (20 g) SODIUM: High (1443 mg) **
Diabetic Exchanges: 1½ Meat, 4¼ Bread, ¾ Veg, 2½ Fat

PASTA PRIMAVERA - REQUEST STEAMED

A medley of fresh broccoli, mushrooms, carrots, and snow peas - request steamed. Topped with diced red peppers and served with choice of pasta. Analysis is for regular sized serving.

✓ CALORIES: Low (398) ✓✓ CHOLESTEROL: Very Low (76 mg)
✓✓ FAT: Very Low* (3 g) ✓✓ SODIUM: Very Low (182 mg) **
Diabetic Exchanges: 4¼ Bread, 2¼ Veg

PASTA MARINARA

Tomatoes, garlic and Italian spices, masterfully combined to create this robust Italian classic. Analysis is for regular sized serving.

✓✓ CALORIES: Very Low (312) ✓✓ CHOLESTEROL: None (0 mg)
✓✓ FAT: Very Low* (3 g) ✓ SODIUM: Low (503 mg) **
Diabetic Exchanges: 4 Bread, 1 Veg

PASTA POMODORO - REQUEST LIGHT OIL

The classic dish made better - tomatoes, garlic, basil and extra virgin olive oil with just of touch of our marinara sauce. Request light oil (½ oz). Analysis is for a regular serving.

✓ CALORIES: Low (454) ✓✓ CHOLESTEROL: None (0 mg)
✓ FAT: Low* (17 g) ✓ SODIUM: Low (345 mg) **
Diabetic Exchanges: 4 Bread, 2 Veg, 2¾ Fat

CHINESE CHICKEN SALAD (DINNER SIZE) - REQUEST DRESSING ON THE SIDE

A California favorite. Fresh lettuce, sliced water chestnuts, mandarin oranges, chicken, rice noodles, cashews, and our homemade pineapple sesame dressing. Request dressing on the side and use sparingly (not included in analysis).

✓ CALORIES: Low (528) ✓✓ CHOLESTEROL: Very Low (48 mg)
✓ FAT: Low (20 g) SODIUM: Moderate (655 mg) **
Diabetic Exchanges: 2½ Meat (extra lean), 2¼ Bread, ¼ Veg, ¼ Fruit, 3¾ Fat

---

* Primarily unsaturated fat
** If you request no added salt

Since 1946 we have been dedicated to the food service industry, with an emphasis on fine meats. This enables us to excel in our selection of quality meat, fish and produce. We offer VARIETY, QUALITY and VALUE, served in a casual, tiffany lamp filled Victorian atmosphere. Within our menu are 2 menus, a "Big Eaters Menu" and a "Little Eaters Menu." Both offer full meals, a variety of healthy side dishes, Edward's quality and value. But we give you, THE CUSTOMER, the choice of how much you want to eat and spend. We are committed to meeting your changing and more healthy eating habits. $

Fine Steaks • Broiled Fresh Fish
Super Lean Ground Beef

Edward's Steak House 9600 Flair Dr., El Monte, CA 91731 (818) 442-2400

LILLY LANGTREE (LITTLE EATERS MENU)
Lean pink slices of USDA choice roasted beef au jus.

✓✓ CALORIES: Very Low (183)   ✓✓ CHOLESTEROL: Very Low (77 mg)
✓✓ FAT: Very Low (8 g)   ✓✓ SODIUM: Very Low (186 mg) **
Diabetic Exchanges: 3½ Meat

JUDGE ROY BEAN (LITTLE EATERS MENU)
Lean slices of USDA choice roasted beef "on the well side" with fresh mushroom sauce.

✓✓ CALORIES: Very Low (256)   ✓✓ CHOLESTEROL: Very Low (68 mg)
✓ FAT: Low (12 g)   SODIUM: High (3606 mg) **
Diabetic Exchanges: 3¼ Meat, ½ Bread, ¼ Veg, ¾ Fat

BROCHETTE OF CHICKEN BREAST (BIG EATERS MENU) - SPECIAL REQUEST
Savory chunks of boneless and skinless chicken breast laced with onions, bell peppers and mushrooms. Served with gringo salsa. <u>Request light margarine</u> (½ oz).

✓ CALORIES: Low (496)   ✓ CHOLESTEROL: Low (180 mg)
✓ FAT: Low (19 g)   ✓ SODIUM: Low (536 mg) **
Diabetic Exchanges: 9¼ Meat (extra lean), 1½ Veg, 2¼ Fat

BROILED FRESH FISH (BIG EATERS MENU - 7 OZ. PORTION)
Analysis is for halibut; similar analysis for orange roughy and red snapper.

✓✓ CALORIES: Very Low (220)   ✓✓ CHOLESTEROL: Very Low (63 mg)
✓✓ FAT: Very Low* (5 g)   ✓✓ SODIUM: Very Low (216 mg) **
Diabetic Exchanges: 5¾ Meat (extra lean)

TENDER CHUNKS OF WHITE CHICKEN BREAST SALAD - SPECIAL REQUEST
with lettuce, roasted almond slivers and sesame seeds. <u>Request light almonds</u> (½ oz).

✓ CALORIES: Low (471)   ✓✓ CHOLESTEROL: Very Low (96 mg)
✓ FAT: Low (17 g)   SODIUM: High (1572 mg) **
Diabetic Exchanges: 5 Meat (extra lean), 1¼ Bread, ¼ Veg, 2¼ Fat

RECOMMENDED ACCOMPANIMENTS:
Salad with house dressing or herb dressing, plain baked potato, fresh fruit, rice, sliced tomatoes, fresh vegetables, seasoned spinach, gringo salsa, apple butter.

✓ Low ✓✓ Very Low

     †Side dish guidelines are 1/3 of entree guidelines

"A legend in its own time" according to Southern California Restaurant Writers. 65 years of superb cuisine at moderate prices. "The Mexican against which all others must be judged." - Zagat Survey. $

El Cholo Mexican Restaurant

1121 S. Western Avenue, Los Angeles, CA 90006   (213) 734-2773
840 E. Whittier Boulevard, La Habra, CA 90631   (714) 525-1320

FRESH FISH SOFT TACOS

Fresh fish seared in Mexican spices and served with black beans (included in analysis).

✓ CALORIES: Low (378)   ✓✓ CHOLESTEROL: Very Low (97 mg)
✓✓ FAT: Very Low* (8 g)   ✓✓ SODIUM: Very Low (201 mg) **
Diabetic Exchanges: 3 Meat (extra lean), 2½ Bread, ½ Veg, 1 Fat

CHICKEN SOFT TACOS

Skinless barbecued chicken breast with a medley of fresh vegetables and served with black beans (included in analysis).

✓ CALORIES: Low (575)   ✓ CHOLESTEROL: Low (120 mg)
✓✓ FAT: Very Low (9 g)   SODIUM: Moderate (735 mg) **
Diabetic Exchanges: 6¼ Meat (extra lean), 3½ Bread, ¾ Veg, ½ Fat

VEGETARIAN ENCHILADA

A combination of fresh vegetables with corn and tomato salsa. Analysis also includes black beans and rice.

✓ CALORIES: Low (588)   ✓✓ CHOLESTEROL: Very Low (52 mg)
✓ FAT: Low (20 g)   SODIUM: Moderate (709 mg) **
Diabetic Exchanges: 2¼ Meat, 4 Bread, 1¾ Veg, 2½ Fat

CRABMEAT ENCHILADA

with salsa verde, beans and rice (included in analysis). Analysis does not include sour cream or avocado - omit or use sparingly.

✓ CALORIES: Low (462)   ✓✓ CHOLESTEROL: Very Low (99 mg)
✓ FAT: Low* (14 g)   SODIUM: High (1047 mg) **
Diabetic Exchanges: 2½ Meat (extra lean), 3 Bread, ½ Veg, 2 Fat

CHICKEN TOSTADITA

Analysis does not include tortilla shell.

✓ CALORIES: Low (404)   ✓ CHOLESTEROL: Low (104 mg)
✓ FAT: Low (15 g)   ✓✓ SODIUM: Very Low (246 mg) **
Diabetic Exchanges: 5¼ Meat (extra lean), ¾ Bread, 1¾ Veg, 2 Fat

---

* Primarily unsaturated fat
** If you request no added salt

This restored 1902 Venice firehouse, open since 1986, offers breakfast, lunch, dinner and a full bar. The atmosphere is casual and neighborly, featuring body builders specials and other healthy dishes. Restaurant open daily from 7 am weekdays & 8 am weekends 'till 11 pm. Bar open 'till 1 am. $

The Firehouse   (310) 396-6810
213 Rose Avenue, Venice, CA   90291

Pasta with Eggplant and Tomato
✓ CALORIES: Low (465)   ✓✓ CHOLESTEROL: None (0 mg)
✓✓ FAT: Very Low* (6 g)   ✓✓ SODIUM: Very Low (41 mg) **
Diabetic Exchanges: 4¾ Bread, 2½ Veg, 1 Fat

Fish Tacos
Mahi Mahi tacos with beans, salsa and guacamole.
✓ CALORIES: Low (488)   ✓✓ CHOLESTEROL: Very Low (94 mg)
✓ FAT: Low* (12 g)   SODIUM: High (1197 mg) **
Diabetic Exchanges: 3 Meat (extra lean), 2½ Bread, 4 Veg, 1 Fat

Body Builders Lunch
Pasta and chicken breast with side of marinara.
CALORIES: Moderate (758)   ✓ CHOLESTEROL: Low (144 mg)
✓✓ FAT: Very Low (7 g)   ✓ SODIUM: Low (535 mg) **
Diabetic Exchanges: 7½ Meat (extra lean), 5¾ Bread, 2 Veg

Stir Fried Vegetables with Steamed Rice
✓✓ CALORIES: Very Low (339) ✓✓ CHOLESTEROL: None (0 mg)
✓✓ FAT: Very Low* (6 g)   SODIUM: Moderate (619 mg) **
Diabetic Exchanges: ¼ Meat, 3 Bread, 3½ Veg, 1 Fat

Halibut Veracruz
Served with rice and steamed vegetables (included in analysis).
✓ CALORIES: Low (587)   ✓✓ CHOLESTEROL: Very Low (66 mg)
✓ FAT: Low* (11 g)   SODIUM: High (1238 mg) **
Diabetic Exchanges: 5¾ Meat (extra lean), 3 Bread, 3¾ Veg, 1 Fat

Tandoori Chicken
Marinated in yogurt and Indian spices. Served with raita and mango chutney (included) and pita bread. Pita bread not included in analysis.
✓ CALORIES: Low (508)   ✓ CHOLESTEROL: Low (198 mg)
✓✓ FAT: Very Low (9 g)   ✓✓ SODIUM: Very Low (233 mg) **
Diabetic Exchanges: 10 Meat (extra lean), ½ Milk, 1¼ Fruit, ¼ Fat

✓ Low ✓✓ Very Low

   †Side dish guidelines are 1/3 of entree guidelines

FOUR SEASONS HOTEL
Los Angeles at Beverly Hills
A FOUR SEASONS · REGENT HOTEL

Elegant, yet comfortable, Gardens Restaurant at the Four Seasons Hotel at Beverly Hills offers a seasonal menu featuring contemporary California cuisine. Gardens Restaurant has been awarded Four Stars, the highest rating, by the California Restaurant Writers Association for both the restaurant and the wine list. Gardens Restaurant serves the Four Seasons Alternative Cuisine. These selections are nutritionally balanced, lower in calories, cholesterol, sodium and fat for the health-conscious gourmet. The following are examples of Alternative Cuisine items offered. The menu changes seasonally. $$$

Gardens Restaurant - Four Seasons Hotel at Beverly Hills

300 South Doheny Drive, Los Angeles, CA 90048 (310) 273-2222

ORECCHIETTE PASTA
with fresh pizzaiolo sauce and buffalo mozzarella.
✓✓ CALORIES: Very Low (300) ✓✓ CHOLESTEROL: Very Low (37 mg)
✓ FAT: Low (18 g) ✓✓ SODIUM: Very Low (70 mg) **
Diabetic Exchanges: ¼ Meat, 1¼ Bread, ¾ Veg, 3¼ Fat

SPINACH AND WILD MUSHROOM CANNELONI
with charred tomato sauce.
✓✓ CALORIES: Very Low (285) ✓✓ CHOLESTEROL: Very Low (57 mg)
✓✓ FAT: Very Low (9 g) ✓✓ SODIUM: Very Low (84 mg) **
Diabetic Exchanges: ¾ Meat, 3¾ Bread, ¾ Veg, 3 Fat

GRILLED SWORDFISH
with pepe pasta-vegetable and roasted pepper infusion.
✓✓ CALORIES: Very Low (345) ✓✓ CHOLESTEROL: Very Low (77 mg)
✓ FAT: Low* (15 g) ✓✓ SODIUM: Very Low (179 mg) **
Diabetic Exchanges: 5¼ Meat (extra lean), ¼ Bread, ½ Veg, 1½ Fat

SEARED DOUBLE BREAST OF CHICKEN - SPECIAL REQUEST
with garden vegetables and braised garlic mashed potatoes. Request skinless chicken.
✓ CALORIES: Low (584) ✓ CHOLESTEROL: Low (168 mg)
✓ FAT: Low (20 g) ✓✓ SODIUM: Very Low (181 mg) **
Diabetic Exchanges: 8¾ Meat (extra lean), 1½ Bread, 1 Veg, 2¾ Fat

GRILLED VEAL CHOP - SPECIAL REQUEST
with Portobello mushroom steak and orzo pasta. Request light oil (½ oz).
✓ CALORIES: Low (448) ✓ CHOLESTEROL: Low (147 mg)
FAT: Moderate (22 g) ✓✓ SODIUM: Very Low (128 mg) **
Diabetic Exchanges: 5¼ Meat, ¾ Bread, ½ Veg, 2¾ Fat

* Primarily unsaturated fat
** If you request no added salt

The Fourth Street Grille is a casual dining room located at the corner of 4th Street and the 10 Freeway in the Guest Quarters Suite Hotel in Santa Monica. The restaurant specializes in grilled beef, fish, poultry and veal and serves breakfast, lunch, and dinner every day of the year, and offers specialty brunches on holidays. Complimentary parking and complimentary selections for kids from the children's menu when adult guests purchase an entree. $$

Fourth Street Grille - Guest Quarters Suite Hotel

1707 Fourth Street, Santa Monica, CA 90401   (310) 395-3332

ANGEL HAIR PASTA NESTED WITH SCALLOPS AND SAFFRON BROTH

✓ CALORIES: Low (541)   ✓✓ CHOLESTEROL: Very Low (38 mg)
✓ FAT: Low* (16 g)   ✓✓ SODIUM: Very Low (189 mg) **
Diabetic Exchanges: 2½ Meat (extra lean), 4 Bread, ¼ Veg, 2¾ Fat

SWORDFISH WITH CUCUMBER SALSA

Served with rice, potato or pasta (not included in analysis).

✓✓ CALORIES: Very Low (307)   ✓✓ CHOLESTEROL: Very Low (66 mg)
✓ FAT: Low* (16 g)   ✓✓ SODIUM: Very Low (156 mg) **
Diabetic Exchanges: 4½ Meat (extra lean), ¼ Fruit, 1¾ Fat

CHICKEN SCALLOPINI

✓ CALORIES: Low (458)   ✓ CHOLESTEROL: Low (168 mg)
✓ FAT: Low (17 g)   ✓✓ SODIUM: Very Low (197 mg) **
Diabetic Exchanges: 8¾ Meat (extra lean), 1¼ Veg, 1¾ Fat

VEGETARIAN SANDWICH

Assorted vegetables with cilantro mayonnaise, served on roll.
Request fresh fruit as the accompaniment (included in analysis).

✓ CALORIES: Low (455)   ✓✓ CHOLESTEROL: Very Low (2 mg)
✓✓ FAT: Very Low* (10 g)   SODIUM: Moderate (736 mg) **
Diabetic Exchanges: 4 Bread, ½ Veg, 1 Fruit, 1½ Fat

HALIBUT WITH STEAMED ASPARAGUS AND PAPAYA SALSA

Served with rice, potato, or pasta (not included in analysis).

✓ CALORIES: Low (421)   ✓✓ CHOLESTEROL: Very Low (64 mg)
✓ FAT: Low* (19 g)   ✓✓ SODIUM: Very Low (123 mg) **
Diabetic Exchanges: 4½ Meat (extra lean), ½ Veg, 1 Fruit, 2¾ Fat

✓ Low ✓✓ Very Low
†Side dish guidelines are 1/3 of entree guidelines

Gaucho Grill restaurants combine good food, a relaxed atmosphere, and reasonable prices. The wide variety of delicious and healthy foods is guaranteed to please. Gaucho Grill offers the best in quality and value. Come enjoy a wonderful lunch or dinner at Gaucho Grill. $

Gaucho Grill

Beverly Ctr. - 121 N. La Cienega, Beverly Hills   (310) 657-9104
Brentwood - 11754 San Vicente Boulevard   (310) 447-7898
Glendale City Ctr. - 101 N. Brand Blvd. Su. 220   (818) 247-9534
Hollywood - 7980 Sunset Boulevard   (213) 656-4152
Pasadena - 121 W. Colorado   (818) 683-3580
Santa Monica - 1253 Third St. Promenade   (310) 394-4966
Studio City - 12050 Venture Blvd. Su. A202   (818) 508-1030
Woodland Hills - 6435 Canoga Avenue   (818) 992-6416

We recommend ordering rice (see analysis below) rather than fries with your meal.

POLLO DESHUESDAO - REQUEST SKINLESS
Marinated grilled boneless breast of chicken.

✓✓ CALORIES: Very Low (329)   ✓ CHOLESTEROL: Low (168 mg)
✓✓ FAT: Very Low (7 g)   ✓✓ SODIUM: Very Low (145 mg) **
Diabetic Exchanges: 8¾ Meat (extra lean)

GRILLED SALMON - REQUEST NO OIL

✓ CALORIES: Low (413)   ✓ CHOLESTEROL: Low (160 mg)
✓ FAT: Low* (18 g)   ✓✓ SODIUM: Very Low (128 mg) **
Diabetic Exchanges: 8 Meat

GAUCHO CHICKEN SALAD - REQUEST LIGHT (½ PORTION) DRESSING
Grilled boneless chicken chopped on a bed of fresh spinach, romaine, and iceberg lettuce, with tomatoes, green and red peppers, red onions topped with feta cheese and picante sauce.

✓ CALORIES: Low (407)   ✓ CHOLESTEROL: Low (103 mg)
✓ FAT: Low (20 g)   SODIUM: Moderate (841 mg) **
Diabetic Exchanges: 5 Meat (extra lean), 1¾ Veg, 3 Fat

VEGETABLE BROCHETTE - REQUEST GRILLED
Two skewers with grilled peppers, onions, zucchini, mushrooms, eggplant, and tomatoes, served with salsa (included in analysis) and rice (see analysis below).

✓✓ CALORIES: Very Low (219)   ✓✓ CHOLESTEROL: Very Low (2 mg)
✓ FAT: Low* (14 g)   ✓ SODIUM: Low (459 mg) **
Diabetic Exchanges: ¼ Bread, 2½ Veg, 2¾ Fat

BROCHETTE MIXTO
Two skewers (one chicken, one beef) with onions, tomatoes, peppers & mushrooms. All chicken available.

✓ CALORIES: Low (431)   ✓ CHOLESTEROL: Low (184 mg)
✓ FAT: Low (13 g)   ✓✓ SODIUM: Very Low (160 mg) **
Diabetic Exchanges: 9½ Meat (extra lean), 1 Veg

RICE† *(9½ oz.)*

CALORIES: Moderate (401)   ✓✓ CHOLESTEROL: Very Low (<1 mg)
✓ FAT: Low* (5 g)   SODIUM: Information not available
Diabetic Exchanges: 5 Bread, ¼ Veg, 1 Fat

* Primarily unsaturated fat
** If you request no added salt

Inspired by the flavors and colors of the Mediterranean, designer Barbara Lazaroff has incorporated soft lighting, curves, textured glass and custom-glazed tile to give the illusion of a three-dimensional watercolor. Outdoor dining and an open kitchen are featured. Granita's cuisine spotlights the efforts of Wolfgang Puck and chef Kevin Ripley with seasonal selections of fresh fish and seafood. Open for lunch Wed. - Fri. 11:30 am to 2:00 pm, brunch Sat. & Sun. 11:00 am to 2:30 pm. Dinner from 6:00 pm weeknights and 5:30 pm weekends. Reservations recommended. $$$

Granita

23725 W. Malibu Road (Malibu Colony Plaza), Malibu, CA 90265   (310) 456-0488

CHATHAM CLAMS ON LINGUINE WITH CAPERS AND ROASTED PEPPERS - SPECIAL REQUEST

Request parmesan cheese served on the side (use sparingly - not included in analysis).

✓ CALORIES: Low (600)　　　✓ CHOLESTEROL: Low (113 mg)
✓ FAT: Low* (16 g)　　　✓ SODIUM: Low (481 mg) **
Diabetic Exchanges: 1½ Meat (extra lean), 3¾ Bread, 1½ Veg, 3½ Fat

ALASKAN SALMON ON SPICY GREENS - SPECIAL REQUEST

*with roma tomato, pinenuts and white truffle oil vinaigrette.
Request light portion of vinaigrette (1 oz).*

✓ CALORIES: Low (369)　　　✓✓ CHOLESTEROL: Very Low (83 mg)
✓ FAT: Low* (18 g)　　　✓✓ SODIUM: Very Low (103 mg) **
Diabetic Exchanges: 6½ Meat, ¼ Veg, 1 Fat

GRILLED SWORDFISH WITH CHINO CHERRY TOMATO AND FAVA SALSA - SPECIAL REQUEST *Request light oil (1 tsp).*

✓ CALORIES: Low (390)　　　✓✓ CHOLESTEROL: Very Low (67 mg)
✓ FAT: Low* (20 g)　　　✓✓ SODIUM: Very Low (202 mg) **
Diabetic Exchanges: 4¼ Meat (extra lean), ½ Bread, ¾ Veg, 2¾ Fat

GRILLED SALMON WITH ROASTED EGGPLANT BROTH - SPECIAL REQUEST *Request no added butter.*

✓ CALORIES: Low (462)　　　✓✓ CHOLESTEROL: Very Low (85 mg)
✓ FAT: Low (20 g)　　　✓ SODIUM: Low (544 mg) **
Diabetic Exchanges: 5¾ Meat, ¼ Bread, 2½ Veg, 1½ Fat

　　　✓ Low ✓✓ Very Low
†Side dish guidelines are 1/3 of entree guidelines

"Truly amazing," "Incredible" and "Addictive" - Gratis opened its doors to such rave reviews in April 1994, and has since enjoyed unparalleled success. It offers guilt-free cuisine with fat-free foods that are as good as, or better than, their fat-laden counterparts. Choose from a variety of muffins, salads, soups, chili, pizzas, pastas and salad dressings and feast your eyes on fabulous desserts. Fat-free food can and does taste great - at Gratis. Open seven days a week from 11 am - 10 pm, Fridays & Saturdays until 10:30 pm. $

Gratis   11658 San Vicente Boulevard, Los Angeles, CA 90049   (310) 571-2345

SOUTHWEST SALAD
with vegetarian chili, black beans & cilantro lime dressing. (20 oz.)
✓ CALORIES: Low (436)　　✓✓ CHOLESTEROL: Very Low (6 mg)
✓✓ FAT: Very Low* (1 g)　　　SODIUM: Moderate (917 mg)

CHOPPED VEGETABLE SALAD
(10 oz. portion) with balsamic vinaigrette.
✓✓ CALORIES: Very Low (148)　　✓✓ CHOLESTEROL: Very Low (11 mg)
✓✓ FAT: Very Low* (<1 g)　　　SODIUM: Moderate (780 mg)

GRILLED JAPANESE EGGPLANT AND SHITTAKE MUSHROOM PIZZA
Analysis is for a whole 10" pizza (6 slices).
✓ CALORIES: Low (491)　　✓✓ CHOLESTEROL: Very Low (8 mg)
✓✓ FAT: Very Low* (2 g)　　　SODIUM: Moderate (921 mg)

SPINACH & MUSHROOM LASAGNA *(15 oz.)*
✓✓ CALORIES: Very Low (281)　　✓✓ CHOLESTEROL: Very Low (18 mg)
✓✓ FAT: Very Low* (1 g)　　　SODIUM: High (2135 mg)

TRIPLE LAYER CHOCOLATE CAKE† *(6 oz.)*
　CALORIES: Moderate (206)　　✓✓ CHOLESTEROL: Very Low (1 mg)
✓✓ FAT: Very Low* (1 g)　　　SODIUM: High (730 mg)

VANILLA BEAN CHEESECAKE† *(7½ oz.)*
　CALORIES: Moderate (299)　　✓✓ CHOLESTEROL: Very Low (18 mg)
✓✓ FAT: Very Low* (<1 g)　　　SODIUM: High (837 mg)

Nutrition information was supplied by Gratis Restaurant.

* Primarily unsaturated fat
** If you request no added salt

Green Street

Modern decor, fresh flowers, an airy heated patio for year-round dining - and, of course the food. The menu offers over 150 items, many of which will delight the healthy diner. Green Street is also known for their versatile approach - they will prepare any item exactly to your specification, such as omelettes cooked with only egg whites, salads tossed with dressing supplied by the guest, sandwiches with high calorie items deleted or substituted. Green Street Restaurant, with their fresh approach to the American Classics, has become Pasadena's favorite cafe. $

Green Street   146 S. Shoppers Lane, Pasadena, CA 91101 (818) 577-7170

JERK CHICKEN AND VEGETABLES - SPECIAL REQUEST
Chicken breast with sauteed vegetables topped with Jamaican sauce. <u>Request very light oil</u> (½ oz).

✓ CALORIES: Low (486)   ✓ CHOLESTEROL: Low (144 mg)
✓ FAT: Low (20 g)   SODIUM: Moderate (840 mg)
Diabetic Exchanges: 7½ Meat (extra lean), ¼ Bread, 3 Veg, 2¾ Fat

SNAPPER PICADO - SPECIAL REQUEST
Red snapper with brown rice and salsa. <u>Request very light oil</u> (½ oz) <u>and no butter.</u>

✓ CALORIES: Low (492)   ✓✓ CHOLESTEROL: Very Low (42 mg)
✓ FAT: Low* (19 g)   SODIUM: High (1082 mg)
Diabetic Exchanges: 3¼ Meat, 3 Bread, 2¾ Fat

PASTA AND PEPPERS - SPECIAL REQUEST
Penne pasta with red bell peppers, garlic, tomatoes and onions. <u>Request very light oil</u> (½ oz).

✓ CALORIES: Low (505)   ✓✓ CHOLESTEROL: Very Low (14 mg)
✓ FAT: Low (19 g)   ✓✓ SODIUM: Very Low (184 mg) **
Diabetic Exchanges: 3¼ Bread, ½ Meat, 2¾ Veg, 3 Fat

VEGETABLE BURRITO - SPECIAL REQUEST
with fresh vegetables, beans, rice, salsa and cheese. <u>Request light (1 oz) cheese.</u>

✓ CALORIES: Low (520)   ✓✓ CHOLESTEROL: Very Low (30 mg)
✓ FAT: Low (18 g)   SODIUM: High (1155 mg)
Diabetic Exchanges: 1¼ Meat, 4 Bread, 2 Veg, 2¼ Fat

CHICKEN AND VEGETABLES - SPECIAL REQUEST
Chicken breast with sauteed vegetables. <u>Request very light oil</u> (½ oz).

✓ CALORIES: Low (466)   ✓ CHOLESTEROL: Low (144 mg)
✓ FAT: Low (20 g)   ✓✓ SODIUM: Very Low (163 mg) **
Diabetic Exchanges: 7½ Meat (extra lean), 3 Veg, 2¾ Fat

    ✓ Low ✓✓ Very Low
†Side dish guidelines are 1/3 of entree guidelines

Hugo's, the famous hot spot in West Hollywood, is in its 15th year as a restaurant. Known primarily as the breakfast hangout for the Hollywood crowd, Hugo's continues to be innovative and progressive for breakfast, lunch and dinner. From the spacious dining room, you can watch the breads, pastas, and pastries being made in the open kitchen. The new coffee/juice/wine bar has a myriad of choices to accompany the large, fun, healthy menu. $

PUMPKIN PANCAKES (3 PANCAKES)

Golden pancakes made with spiced pumpkin puree.
✓✓ CALORIES: Very Low (193)　✓✓ CHOLESTEROL: Very Low (3 mg)
✓✓ FAT: Very Low* (1 g)　✓ SODIUM: Low (500 mg)
Diabetic Exchanges: 2 Bread, ½ Fruit, ¼ Fat

WILD MUSHROOM SCRAMBLE - REQUEST EGG WHITES

Wild mushrooms, onions, carrots, goat cheese, sage and marjoram. Request preparation with egg whites and turmeric-rice as the accompaniment (included in analysis).
✓ CALORIES: Low (399)　✓✓ CHOLESTEROL: Very Low (33 mg)
✓ FAT: Low (17 g)　SODIUM: Moderate (609 mg) **
Diabetic Exchanges: 2¾ Meat (extra lean), 1½ Bread, 1¼ Veg, 2¾ Fat

PASTA POMODORO PRIMAVERA

Diced tomatoes, garlic and basil lightly sauteed in extra-virgin olive oil.
✓ CALORIES: Low (502)　✓✓ CHOLESTEROL: Very Low (83 mg)
✓ FAT: Low* (17 g)　✓✓ SODIUM: Very Low (55 mg) **
Diabetic Exchanges: 3½ Bread, 2¼ Veg, 2¾ Fat

CHICKEN EGGPLANT SANDWICH WITH FRUIT SALAD

Grilled chicken, eggplant, sun dried tomato, and greens. Request balsamic vinaigrette dressing on the side and use sparingly (not included in analysis). Analysis includes fruit salad as the accompaniment.
✓ CALORIES: Low (534)　✓✓ CHOLESTEROL: Very Low (96 mg)
✓✓ FAT: Very Low (9 g)　SODIUM: Moderate (760 mg) **
Diabetic Exchanges: 5 Meat (extra lean), 3¾ Bread, 1 Fruit, ½ Fat

MUNG BEANS AND RICE

Tender mung beans, basmati rice, tiny chunks of vegetables, onion, garlic, ginger and an exotic blend of Indian spices.
✓✓ CALORIES: Very Low (249)　✓✓ CHOLESTEROL: None (0 mg)
✓✓ FAT: Very Low* (2 g)　SODIUM: Moderate (741 mg) **
Diabetic Exchanges: ¼ Meat, 2¾ Bread, ¾ Veg, ¼ Fat

ESAU STEW

A thick red lentil stew with beets, five onions, carrots, vegetable juice and potato.
✓✓ CALORIES: Very Low (247)　✓✓ CHOLESTEROL: None (0 mg)
✓✓ FAT: Very Low* (1 g)　SODIUM: Moderate (610 mg) **
Diabetic Exchanges: 2½ Bread, ¾ Veg

* Primarily unsaturated fat
** If you request no added salt

i. CUGINI

Where the warmth of the Mediterranean meets the Pacific Ocean, i Cugini is Santa Monica's liveliest and most beautiful Italian restaurant. Be part of the excitement indoors or relax on the Mediterranean-style patio. Dinner at i Cugini, a landmark Italian restaurant at the corner of Broadway and Ocean Avenue. $$

i Cugini Trattoria   1501 Ocean Avenue, Santa Monica, CA 90401 (310) 451-4595

PRIMAVERA PIZZA (½ PIZZA)
with fresh vegetables, oven-dried tomato sauce, spinach & Parmesan.
Analysis is for ½ of whole pizza.

✓ CALORIES: Low (511)   ✓✓ CHOLESTEROL: Very Low (2 mg)
✓ FAT: Low* (15 g)   SODIUM: High (1170 mg)
Diabetic Exchanges: ¼ Meat, 4¼ Bread, 1 Veg, 2½ Fat

SPAGHETTI CON FRUTTI DI MARE (¾ SERVING)
Thin pasta with shrimp, mussels, clams, scallops, squid and spicy tomato sauce.
Analysis is for ¾ of "piccolo" (individual) serving.

✓ CALORIES: Low (466)   ✓ CHOLESTEROL: Low (103 mg)
✓✓ FAT: Very Low (3 g)   SODIUM: Moderate (815 mg)
Diabetic Exchanges: 2¾ Meat (extra lean), 4¼ Bread, 1½ Veg

PESCE AL FERRI ALLA MODA DELL'ADRIATICO
Chilean sea bass baked Adriatic style with potatoes, rosemary & olives.

✓ CALORIES: Low (417)   ✓✓ CHOLESTEROL: Very Low (70 mg)
✓ FAT: Low* (19 g)   ✓ SODIUM: Low (427 mg)
Diabetic Exchanges: 4½ Meat (extra lean), 1½ Bread, ¾ Veg, 3 Fat

RIGATONI CON MELANZANE (¾ SERVING)
Hollow tube pasta, eggplant, tomato, hot pepper, garlic and olive oil.
Analysis is for ¾ serving.

✓ CALORIES: Low (457)   ✓✓ CHOLESTEROL: None (0 mg)
✓ FAT: Low* (12 g)   ✓ SODIUM: Low (422 mg)
Diabetic Exchanges: 4¼ Bread, 2 Veg, 2 Fat

✓ Low ✓✓ Very Low
†Side dish guidelines are 1/3 of entree guidelines

Il Cielo brings northern Italian country cooking to Beverly Hills, and is perfect for that romantic occasion or business lunch or dinner. Enjoy dining in our gardens or by our fireplace underneath the fresco and be transported to an Italian villa. Strolling guitarist on weekends. Our specialties include oven-baked whole striped bass, incredible pastas and homemade desserts. $$

Il Cielo
(310) 276-9990
9018 Burton Way, Beverly Hills, CA 90210

RISOTTO DEL CIELO
Risotto with fresh vegetables.
✓ CALORIES: Low (499)   ✓✓ CHOLESTEROL: None (0 mg)
✓ FAT: Low* (15 g)   ✓ SODIUM: Low (504 mg) **
Diabetic Exchanges: 4¾ Bread, 1 Veg, 2¾ Fat

BRANZINO AL FORNO CON SALSA VERDE
Italian sea bass grilled and baked with fresh herbs.
✓ CALORIES: Low (417)   ✓ CHOLESTEROL: Low (118 mg)
✓ FAT: Low* (19 g)   ✓✓ SODIUM: Very Low (197 mg) **
Diabetic Exchanges: 5¾ Meat (extra lean), ¼ Veg, 2¾ Fat

SOGLIOLA AL FORNO
Imported Dover sole baked with white wine. Served with fresh vegetables (included in analysis).
✓ CALORIES: Low (454)   ✓ CHOLESTEROL: Low (106 mg)
✓ FAT: Low* (20 g)   ✓✓ SODIUM: Very Low (201 mg) **
Diabetic Exchanges: 5½ Meat (extra lean), ¾ Veg, 3½ Fat

TAGLIOLINI DELLA NONNA ANTONELLA (2/3 SERVING)
Chicken breast and broccoli with white wine and onions over pasta. Analysis is for 2/3 of a full serving.
✓ CALORIES: Low (540)   ✓✓ CHOLESTEROL: Very Low (58 mg)
✓ FAT: Low (16 g)   ✓✓ SODIUM: Very Low (231 mg) **
Diabetic Exchanges: 2½ Meat (extra lean), 3¾ Bread, ¾ Veg, 2½ Fat

PETTO DI POLLO AL CIELO - SPECIAL REQUEST
Chicken breast grilled with lemon. Request light oil (½ Tbs).
✓ CALORIES: Low (551)   CHOLESTEROL: Moderate (241 mg)
✓ FAT: Low (17 g)   ✓✓ SODIUM: Very Low (213 mg) **
Diabetic Exchanges: 12½ Meat (extra lean), ¼ Fruit, 1¼ Fat

PENNETTE CON MALANZANE (2/3 SERVING)
Fillet of eggplant, anchovies, garlic and fresh tomatoes with pasta. Analysis is for 2/3 of a full serving.
✓ CALORIES: Low (528)   ✓✓ CHOLESTEROL: Very Low (4 mg)
✓ FAT: Low* (20 g)   ✓✓ SODIUM: Very Low (210 mg) **
Diabetic Exchanges: 4 Bread, ½ Veg, 3½ Fat

* Primarily unsaturated fat
** If you request no added salt

Enter Il Fornaio Cucina Italiana and feel as if you've been transported to Italy! Authentic Italian cuisine is served in a traditional trattoria-style setting. Munch on a basket of freshly baked breads and rolls while selecting from an extensive menu. Choose from a variety of homemade pastas, grilled meats and fowl from the rotisserie, garden fresh salads and pizzas from the wood-burning oven. Be sure to save room for classic Italian desserts and espresso drinks. All major credit cards accepted. $$

Il Fornaio Cucina Italiana

24 W. Union Street, Pasadena, CA 91103   (818) 683-9797
301 N. Beverly Drive, Beverly Hills, CA 90210   (310) 550-8330

PIZZA VEGETARIANA (½ PIZZA)

Tomato sauce, tomatoes, red onions, sweet peppers, artichokes, and zucchini (no cheese).
Analysis is for ½ pizza.

✓✓ CALORIES: Very Low (300)   ✓✓ CHOLESTEROL: None (0 mg)
✓✓ FAT: Very Low* (9 g)   ✓ SODIUM: Low (549 mg) **
Diabetic Exchanges: 2¼ Bread, ¾ Veg, 1¾ Fat

PIZZA ADRIATICA (½ PIZZA) - SPECIAL REQUEST

Fresh tomato sauce, marinated shrimp, grilled zucchini, feta cheese & basil. <u>Request light cheese</u> (1 oz).

✓✓ CALORIES: Very Low (301)   ✓✓ CHOLESTEROL: Very Low (68 mg)
✓✓ FAT: Very Low (6 g)   SODIUM: Moderate (924 mg) **
Diabetic Exchanges: 1 Meat, 2½ Bread, ½ Veg, ¾ Fat

PENNE AI VEGETALI

Whole wheat pasta tubes, fresh vegetables and herbs (no butter or salt).

✓ CALORIES: Low (600)   ✓✓ CHOLESTEROL: None (0 mg)
✓ FAT: Low* (16 g)   ✓✓ SODIUM: Very Low (56 mg) **
Diabetic Exchanges: 5¾ Bread, 2 Veg, 2¾ Fat

CONCHIGLIE CON MELANZANE AL FORNO - SPECIAL REQUEST

Pasta shells, eggplant, tomato, smoked mozzarella; baked
in a wood-burning oven. <u>Request light cheese</u> (1 oz).

✓✓ CALORIES: Very Low (342)   ✓✓ CHOLESTEROL: Very Low (33 mg)
✓✓ FAT: Very Low (10 g)   ✓ SODIUM: Low (427 mg) **
Diabetic Exchanges: 1 Meat, 2½ Bread, ½ Veg, 1 Fat

PIATTO DI VERDURE - SPECIAL REQUEST

A selection of seasonal vegetables and garlic roasted in the oakwood-burning oven.
<u>Request light oil</u> (½ oz). Served with polenta (not included in analysis).

✓ CALORIES: Low (420)   ✓✓ CHOLESTEROL: None (0 mg)
✓ FAT: Low* (14 g)   ✓✓ SODIUM: Very Low (37 mg) **
Diabetic Exchanges: 2½ Bread, 3¾ Veg, 2¾ Fat

POLLO ALL'AGLIO E ROSMARINO

Grilled pounded chicken breast with puree of roasted garlic and rosemary,
served on a bed of steamed spinach (no butter or salt).

✓ CALORIES: Low (600)   CHOLESTEROL: Moderate (265 mg)
✓ FAT: Low (12 g)   ✓✓ SODIUM: Very Low (287 mg) **
Diabetic Exchanges: 13½ Meat, 4 Veg

✓ Low ✓✓ Very Low
†Side dish guidelines are 1/3 of entree guidelines

Il Forno is a Northern Italian restaurant with the flavor of California and a warm, welcoming atmosphere where each diner is treated with friendly hospitality. Superior and innovative food includes creations by Chef Domenico Salvatore, a highly respected culinary artist. The "Spa Cuisine" caters to many southern Californians' interest in lighter, healthier eating. $$

Il Forno Caffe & Pizzeria

2901 Ocean Park Blvd, Santa Monica, CA 90405   (310) 450-1241

FETTUCCINE ALLA SPORTIVA

Fresh homemade fettuccine, yogurt, ricotta cheese, herbs and chicken consomme.
✓ CALORIES: Low (595)　　✓ CHOLESTEROL: Low (145 mg)
✓ FAT: Low (14 g)　　✓✓ SODIUM: Very Low (293 mg) **
Diabetic Exchanges: 2½ Meat, 4 Bread, ¾ Milk, 2 Fat

SEDANINI TRE COLORI

Three color short tube pasta with chopped fresh tomato, eggplant, green peas, fresh roasted garlic, basil & black pepper prepared with a touch of no-cholesterol oil.
✓ CALORIES: Low (451)　　✓✓ CHOLESTEROL: Very Low (100 mg)
✓✓ FAT: Very Low* (5 g)　　✓✓ SODIUM: Very Low (118 mg) **
Diabetic Exchanges: ½ Meat, 4 Bread, 3¼ Veg, 1½ Fat

SPAGHETTINI ESPRESSI

Thin spaghetti, fresh tomato sauce, basil & garlic.
✓ CALORIES: Low (389)　　✓✓ CHOLESTEROL: Very Low (100 mg)
✓✓ FAT: Very Low* (4 g)　　✓✓ SODIUM: Very Low (50 mg) **
Diabetic Exchanges: ½ Meat, 4 Bread, ¾ Veg, 1¼ Fat

SCAMPI MEDITERRANEA

Scampi baked in the oven with a touch of brandy, fresh grapefruit juice, green peppercorn & Dijon mustard.
✓✓ CALORIES: Very Low (158)　　CHOLESTEROL: Moderate (218 mg)
✓✓ FAT: Very Low* (2 g)　　✓ SODIUM: Low (361 mg) **
Diabetic Exchanges: 2½ Meat, 1 Veg, ¼ Fruit

SPA PIZZA ALLA IL FORNO

Fresh dough baked to crispy perfection and topped with lo-fat cheeses, fresh tomatoes and other assorted fresh vegetables. Seasoned with garlic and herbs.
✓ CALORIES: Low (581)　　✓✓ CHOLESTEROL: Very Low (32 mg)
✓ FAT: Low* (16 g)　　SODIUM: Moderate (733 mg) **
Diabetic Exchanges: 2 Meat, 4½ Bread, 1½ Veg, 1¾ Fat

* Primarily unsaturated fat
** If you request no added salt

Il Moro is the largest addition to the growing family of restaurants created by Jean Louis De Mori and Antonio Tommasi, which already include Locanda Veneta and Ca'Brea. Our emphasis at Il Moro, as at our other restaurants, is on serving you fresh, wholesome and healthy Italian food. We use only high quality products such as extra virgin olive oil and daily selected produce when preparing our dishes. Our goal is to present a whole new menu of delicious foods at affordable prices. $

Il Moro

(310) 575-3530
11400 W. Olympic Blvd., Los Angeles, CA 90064

CAPPELLINI ALLA CHECCA
Angel hair pasta with fresh diced roma tomatoes, basil, garlic, and extra virgin olive oil.
- ✓ CALORIES: Low (516)
- ✓✓ CHOLESTEROL: Very Low (62 mg)
- ✓ FAT: Low* (18 g)
- ✓✓ SODIUM: Very Low (84 mg) **

Diabetic Exchanges: 2½ Bread, 5 Veg, 2¾ Fat

CUFFIE DEL PAPA
Homemade Pope hat shaped pasta with tomato sauce, porcini mushroom, black olives and capers.
- ✓ CALORIES: Low (402)
- ✓✓ CHOLESTEROL: Very Low (62 mg)
- ✓ FAT: Low* (17 g)
- ✓ SODIUM: Low (459 mg) **

Diabetic Exchanges: 2½ Bread, ¼ Veg, 3 Fat

PENNE ALL'ARRABIATA
Homemade short tube pasta with a spicy garlic tomato sauce.
- ✓ CALORIES: Low (393)
- ✓✓ CHOLESTEROL: Very Low (62 mg)
- ✓ FAT: Low* (16 g)
- ✓ SODIUM: Low (370 mg) **

Diabetic Exchanges: 2¾ Bread, ¼ Veg, 2¾ Fat

LINGUINE ALLO SCOGLIO
Linguine pasta with prawns, clams and calamari in a white wine and garlic broth, light and spicy.
- ✓ CALORIES: Low (567)
- CHOLESTEROL: Moderate (204 mg)
- ✓ FAT: Low* (13 g)
- ✓ SODIUM: Low (580 mg) **

Diabetic Exchanges: 1½ Meat, 3½ Bread, 1¾ Fat

PIZZA FUNGHI E POLLO
Tomato, smoked mozzarella, roasted chicken and a medley of mushrooms with herbs
- ✓ CALORIES: Low (433)
- ✓✓ CHOLESTEROL: Very Low (49 mg)
- ✓ FAT: Low (11 g)
- SODIUM: High (1577 mg) **

Diabetic Exchanges: 1½ Meat, 4½ Bread, ¼ Veg, ½ Fat

✓ Low ✓✓ Very Low

   †Side dish guidelines are 1/3 of entree guidelines

il Pastaio

One of Beverly Hills' favorite and most talented chefs, Celestino Drago, has created **il Pastaio** *("the macaroni maker") with his brother Giacomino as the chef. Pasta, risotto and carpaccio become elegant dishes with the beautiful yet simple way each plate is presented. There's pasta in many forms - fresh or dried; black, white, green and yellow; in shapes of hearts, half and full moons, ears, tubes, butterflies and stars. Service is warm, intelligent, and gracious with the ambiance of a neighborhood cafe in Rome. $*

il Pastaio

400 N. Canon Drive, Beverly Hills, CA 90210   (310) 205-5444
141 South Lake Avenue, Pasadena, CA 91101   (818) 795-4006

SMOKED SWORDFISH CARPACCIO - SPECIAL REQUEST
with fennel and oranges. Request light oil (1 tsp).
✓✓ CALORIES: Very Low (172)   ✓✓ CHOLESTEROL: Very Low (33 mg)
✓✓ FAT: Very Low* (8 g)   SODIUM: Moderate (667 mg) **
Diabetic Exchanges: 2 Meat, ½ Fruit, 1 Fat

GRILLED VEGETABLES
Belgian endive, shitake mushrooms, zucchini, eggplant, bell peppers, radicchio, tomato and asparagus with olive oil and balsamic vinegar.
✓✓ CALORIES: Very Low (159)   ✓✓ CHOLESTEROL: None (0 mg)
✓✓ FAT: Very Low* (7 g)   ✓✓ SODIUM: Very Low (26 mg) **
Diabetic Exchanges: ¾ Bread, 1¼ Veg, 1¼ Fat

RISOTTO VERDE, SPINACI E PISELLI
Puree of spinach and peas.
✓✓ CALORIES: Very Low (313)   ✓✓ CHOLESTEROL: Very Low (5 mg)
✓✓ FAT: Very Low* (4 g)   ✓ SODIUM: Low (482 mg) **
Diabetic Exchanges: ¼ Meat, 3¼ Bread, ¼ Veg

PAGLIA E FIENO CON PESTO ALLA TRAPANESE
Green and white tagliolini with Sicilian style pesto.
✓ CALORIES: Low (437)   ✓✓ CHOLESTEROL: Very Low (67 mg)
✓ FAT: Low* (19 g)   ✓ SODIUM: Low (406 mg) **
Diabetic Exchanges: ¼ Meat, 2½ Bread, 1½ Veg, 3 Fat

CAPELLINI AL POMODORE E BASILICO
✓ CALORIES: Low (450)   ✓✓ CHOLESTEROL: None (0 mg)
✓ FAT: Low* (15 g)   ✓✓ SODIUM: Very Low (12 mg) **
Diabetic Exchanges: 4 Bread, ½ Veg, 2¾ Fat

---

* Primarily unsaturated fat
** If you request no added salt

A lovely country gourmet restaurant specializing in natural foods, with creekside dining. Under the sycamores, beside a babbling brook, you'll listen to the mellow sounds of classical music. Called L.A.'s most romantic restaurant, nestled in the heart of Topanga Canyon. A must visit for lovers and out-of-town guests. $$

Inn of the Seventh Ray
128 Old Topanga Canyon Road
Topanga, CA 90290   (310) 455-1311

UDON NOODLE SALAD, SZECHUAN STYLE
Udon noodles with bell peppers, snap peas and roasted peanuts. Request peanut dressing on the side and use sparingly (57 calories, 5 g fat, 75 mg sodium per Tbs.)

✓✓ CALORIES: Very Low (329)   ✓✓ CHOLESTEROL: None (0 mg)
✓ FAT: Low* (19 g)   ✓✓ SODIUM: Very Low (61 mg) **
Diabetic Exchanges: ¾ Meat, 1½ Bread, ½ Veg, 3¾ Fat

TOFU SANTA FE
Marinated tofu charbroiled and topped with bean pate, soy cheese and cactus salsa.

✓✓ CALORIES: Very Low (212)   ✓✓ CHOLESTEROL: Very Low (12 mg)
✓ FAT: Low (14 g)   ✓ SODIUM: Low (598 mg) **
Diabetic Exchanges: 2¼ Meat, 1 Fat

SEITAN BURGER
High protein wheat gluten burger on whole wheat bun with sprouts, tomatoes and mushrooms.

✓ CALORIES: Low (579)   ✓✓ CHOLESTEROL: None (0 mg)
✓ FAT: Low* (12 g)   SODIUM: Moderate (656 mg) **
Diabetic Exchanges: 2¾ Bread, ¼ Veg, 1 Fat

SHITAKE MUSHROOM STIRFRY
Served over whole wheat noodles (included in analysis).

✓ CALORIES: Low (499)   ✓✓ CHOLESTEROL: None (0 mg)
✓ FAT: Low* (20 g)   SODIUM: Moderate (827 mg) **
Diabetic Exchanges: 4 Bread, 2 Veg, 3¾ Fat

WATERCRESS, DAIKON, PEPPERS AND ARAME SALAD
Request dressing on the side. Analysis includes 4 Tbs. dressing.

✓✓ CALORIES: Very Low (266)   ✓✓ CHOLESTEROL: None (0 mg)
✓ FAT: Low* (13 g)   SODIUM: Moderate (834 mg) **
Diabetic Exchanges: ½ Meat, 5¾ Veg, 2¼ Fat

✓ Low ✓✓ Very Low

   †Side dish guidelines are 1/3 of entree guidelines

Italy's Little Kitchen has won numerous awards and garnered critical acclaim for its outstanding food preparation. In addition to great flavor, the health of their patrons is always foremost on their minds. They make their own breads and pizza dough fresh daily without any shortening or oil, so they have no fat or cholesterol. The majority of the sauces are free of butter or fat, and when they saute, they use extra virgin olive oil. The seafood is fresh. The menu emphasizes chicken, fish, pastas, grains and steamed vegetables. You may request very little or no cheese, or substitute goat cheese which is lower in calories, cholesterol and fat. If you have specific dietary preferences, please let them know. They welcome special requests. For a healthy low-fat or non-fat meal, Italy's Little Kitchen is your ideal restaurant! $

Italy's Little Kitchen

West Los Angeles: 11651 Santa Monica Blvd. (310) 996-1172
Westchester/Playa del Rey: 8516 Lincoln Blvd. (310) 645-1220 and 642-9775
Manhattan Beach: 921 Sepulveda Blvd. (310) 374-9210 and 374-9905

IAPALUCCI PIZZA "THE HOUSE FAVORITE" (2 SLICES)

Grilled eggplant, artichoke hearts, broccoli rapini, mozzarella and parmesan. Analysis is for 2 slices of a large pizza.

✓ CALORIES: Low (357)   ✓✓ CHOLESTEROL: Very Low (27 mg)
✓✓ FAT: Very Low (10 g)   SODIUM: Moderate (686 mg) **
Diabetic Exchanges: ¾ Meat, 3 Bread, ½ Veg, 1 Fat

FETTUCCINI PRIMAVERA WITH SAUTEED VEGETABLES

✓ CALORIES: Low (411)   ✓✓ CHOLESTEROL: None (0 mg)
✓ FAT: Low* (12 g)   ✓ SODIUM: Low (450 mg) **
Diabetic Exchanges: 3 Bread, 2 Veg, 2 Fat

BROCCOLI RAPINI MOSTACCIOLI

Wild Italian broccoli and sun dried tomatoes.

✓ CALORIES: Low (479)   ✓✓ CHOLESTEROL: Very Low (2 mg)
✓ FAT: Low* (11 g)   ✓✓ SODIUM: Very Low (82 mg) **
Diabetic Exchanges: 3¾ Bread, ¼ Veg, 1¾ Fat

SALMORIGLIO

Grilled fish with lemon herbs. Analysis includes steamed vegetables.

✓ CALORIES: Low (370)   ✓✓ CHOLESTEROL: Very Low (63 mg)
✓ FAT: Low* (18 g)   ✓✓ SODIUM: Very Low (139 mg) **
Diabetic Exchanges: 5¾ Meat, ¾ Veg, 2½ Fat

PENNE WITH MARINARA

✓ CALORIES: Low (447)   ✓✓ CHOLESTEROL: None (0 mg)
✓✓ FAT: Very Low* (4 g)   ✓ SODIUM: Low (585 mg) **
Diabetic Exchanges: 5¼ Bread, 1¼ Veg, ¼ Fat

* Primarily unsaturated fat
** If you request no added salt

JIMMY'S
RESTAURANT

Since its opening in 1978, Jimmy's has been the Westside gathering place for Los Angeles celebrities, business leaders and social figures. The setting of "belle epoque" luxury is a backdrop for the high-profile clientele who dine at lunch or dinner daily on contemporary California-influenced French cuisine. The bar is lively at night with a pianist at the baby grand playing for dancing or listening. Host and principal Jimmy Murphy is always on-hand with his son, Sean, maitre d' of the restaurant, to personally welcome guests with his warm Irish hospitality. $$$

Jimmy's Restaurant 201 Moreno Dr., Beverly Hills, CA 90212 (310) 552-2394

WARM SALAD WITH CUBES OF SWORDFISH AND GARLIC DRESSING

✓✓ CALORIES: Very Low (222) ✓✓ CHOLESTEROL: Very Low (28 mg)
✓ FAT: Low* (16 g) ✓✓ SODIUM: Very Low (70 mg) **
Diabetic Exchanges: 2 Meat (extra lean), ¼ Veg, 2¾ Fat

WILD RICE SALAD - REQUEST DRESSING ON THE SIDE
Request dressing on the side and use sparingly (not included in analysis).

✓ CALORIES: Low (431) ✓✓ CHOLESTEROL: None (0 mg)
✓✓ FAT: Very Low* (3 g) ✓✓ SODIUM: Very Low (50 mg) **
Diabetic Exchanges: ½ Meat, 5½ Bread, 1¾ Veg

PAUPIETTE OF SEA BASS WITH NOPALES LEAVES

✓✓ CALORIES: Very Low (320) ✓ CHOLESTEROL: Low (165 mg)
✓ FAT: Low* (19 g) ✓✓ SODIUM: Very Low (112 mg) **
Diabetic Exchanges: 3¾ Meat (extra lean), 1 Veg, 3 Fat

SLICED BREAST OF CHICKEN WITH PROVENCALE HERBS & LINGUINE PRIMAVERA
- SPECIAL REQUEST *Request light oil (1 Tbs.)*

✓ CALORIES: Low (499) ✓ CHOLESTEROL: Low (120 mg)
✓ FAT: Low (19 g) ✓✓ SODIUM: Very Low (123 mg) **
Diabetic Exchanges: 6¼ Meat, 1½ Bread, ¾ Veg, 2¾ Fat

HAWAIIAN AHI TUNA GRILLED, WITH TROPICAL FRUIT SALSA

✓ CALORIES: Low (554) ✓✓ CHOLESTEROL: Very Low (98 mg)
✓ FAT: Low* (18 g) ✓✓ SODIUM: Very Low (121 mg) **
Diabetic Exchanges: 7¼ Meat, 2½ Fruit, 2¾ Fat

DESSERT: ### BAKED BANANAS WITH ORANGE SAUCE†

CALORIES: Moderate (321) ✓✓ CHOLESTEROL: Very Low (10 mg)
✓ FAT: Low* (5 g) ✓✓ SODIUM: Very Low (42 mg)
Diabetic Exchanges: 3¾ Fruit, ¾ Fat

✓ Low ✓✓ Very Low

  †Side dish guidelines are 1/3 of entree guidelines

Seafood at its finest! Serving over 20 fresh fish daily, Jimmy's Fish and Grill is an Award-winner with both the Southern California Restaurant Writers and the California Restaurant Writers. Located in the Market Place. Lunch served 11 am to 4 pm; dinner until 10 pm Monday through Thursday, until 11 pm Friday and Saturday, and until 9 pm on Sunday. $$

Jimmy's Fish & Grill

6563 E. Pacific Coast Hwy., Long Beach, CA 90803   (310) 594-9479

CIOPINNO *(14 oz. serving)*

✓✓ CALORIES: Very Low (277)   ✓ CHOLESTEROL: Low (129 mg)
✓✓ FAT: Very Low (9 g)   SODIUM: High (1269 mg) **
Diabetic Exchanges: 4½ Meat (extra lean), 1¼ Veg, ¾ Fat

MESQUITE GRILLED FISH (8 OZ.)
Served with fresh vegetables (included in analysis) and choice of side dishes (see below).
Analysis is for halibut; other fish also recommended.
✓✓ CALORIES: Very Low (324)   ✓✓ CHOLESTEROL: Very Low (83 mg)
✓✓ FAT: Very Low (10 g)   ✓✓ SODIUM: Very Low (202 mg) **
Diabetic Exchanges: 5 Meat (extra lean), 1¾ Veg, ¾ Fat

TERIYAKI CHICKEN BREAST
Served with fresh vegetables (included in analysis) and choice of side dishes (see recommendations below).
✓ CALORIES: Low (447)   ✓ CHOLESTEROL: Low (192 mg)
✓✓ FAT: Very Low (9 g)   SODIUM: High (1409 mg) **
Diabetic Exchanges: 10 Meat (extra lean), 1¾ Veg

LINGUINI AND CLAMS WITH RED SAUCE (¾ SERVING)
Fresh little neck clams simmered in clam nectar and wine. Served over linguini. Request with red sauce. Analysis is for ¾ of a large serving.
✓ CALORIES: Low (575)   ✓✓ CHOLESTEROL: Very Low (65 mg)
✓ FAT: Low* (17 g)   ✓ SODIUM: Low (429 mg) **
Diabetic Exchanges: 3 Meat (extra lean), 4 Bread, 1 Veg, 2½ Fat

PASTA SEAL BEACH (¾ SERVING)
Fresh salmon chunks sauteed with olives, capers and cilantro in a tomato sauce. Served over linguini. Analysis is for ¾ of a large serving.
✓ CALORIES: Low (571)   ✓✓ CHOLESTEROL: Very Low (70 mg)
✓ FAT: Low* (18 g)   ✓ SODIUM: Low (340 mg) **
Diabetic Exchanges: 3 Meat, 4¼ Bread, 1 Veg, 1½ Fat

RECOMMENDED SIDE DISHES:
Manhattan Chowder, Salad (nonfat dressing available), Fruit, Tomato Slices, Steamed Rice, Red Potatoes, Baked Potato.

* Primarily unsaturated fat
** If you request no added salt

Healthy Dining in Los Angeles **81**

Enjoy exotic Cal/Asian cuisine at its very best. Our chefs mix philosophies and cuisines to bring you flavors that are out of this world. Imagine the aromatic style of grilling and barbecuing married with delicate spices from the Far East, like ginger, cumin and nutmeg! All this in a sophisticated but relaxed setting. Menu changes quarterly. The following are examples of menu items offered. $$

JW's Restaurant & Lounge - JW Marriott Hotel at Century City

2151 Avenue of the Stars, Los Angeles, CA 90067   (310) 556-8225

BARBEQUED AHI TUNA SALAD
with sweet and sour dressing.
✓ CALORIES: Low (354)   ✓✓ CHOLESTEROL: Very Low (64 mg)
✓✓ FAT: Very Low* (9 g)   ✓✓ SODIUM: Very Low (281 mg) **
Diabetic Exchanges: 4½ Meat (extra lean), 1¼ Bread, 1¼ Veg, 1½ Fat

FLAME GRILLED VEGETABLE SALAD
with roasted rouge royal vinaigrette.
✓✓ CALORIES: Very Low (129)   ✓✓ CHOLESTEROL: None (0 mg)
✓✓ FAT: Very Low* (6 g)   ✓✓ SODIUM: Very Low (111 mg) **
Diabetic Exchanges: ¼ Bread, 1¾ Veg, 1 Fat

FLAME BROILED BLUENOSE SEA BASS WITH GRILLED MUSHROOM SALSA
Served with curried basmati rice and steamed vegetables (included in analysis).
✓ CALORIES: Low (386)   ✓✓ CHOLESTEROL: Very Low (70 mg)
✓ FAT: Low* (12 g)   ✓✓ SODIUM: Very Low (275 mg) **
Diabetic Exchanges: 4¼ Meat (extra lean), 1¼ Bread, 2¼ Veg, 1¾ Fat

SEARED PACIFIC TUNA WITH LIME PEPPER CRUST & ORANGE MINT SALSA
Served with Japanese rice and steamed vegetables (included in analysis).
✓ CALORIES: Low (391)   ✓✓ CHOLESTEROL: Very Low (76 mg)
✓✓ FAT: Very Low* (8 g)   ✓✓ SODIUM: Very Low (226 mg) **
Diabetic Exchanges: 5½ Meat (extra lean), 1 Bread, ¼ Fruit, 1½ Veg, 1 Fat

ORIENTAL MARINATED SWORDFISH WITH ASIAN PEAR SALSA
Served with Japanese rice and steamed vegetables (included in analysis).
✓ CALORIES: Low (381)   ✓✓ CHOLESTEROL: Very Low (66 mg)
✓ FAT: Low* (12 g)   ✓✓ SODIUM: Very Low (297 mg) **
Diabetic Exchanges: 4½ Meat (extra lean), 1 Bread, ¼ Fruit, 1½ Veg, 1 Fat

SAMBAL TERIYAKI CHICKEN BREAST WITH PINEAPPLE PLUM & CHINESE PARSLEY
Served with steamed vegetables (included in analysis).
✓ CALORIES: Low (416)   ✓ CHOLESTEROL: Low (144 mg)
✓ FAT: Low (14 g)   ✓ SODIUM: Low (498 mg) **
Diabetic Exchanges: 7½ Meat (extra lean), ¼ Fruit, 1¾ Veg, 1½ Fat

✓ Low   ✓✓ Very Low

    †Side dish guidelines are 1/3 of entree guidelines

KATE MANTILINI

Kate Mantilini   9101 Wilshire Blvd., Beverly Hills, CA 90210   (310) 278-3699

All items shown below are from our Healthy Alternatives Menu

PENNE WITH BROCCOLI AND SUN-DRIED TOMATOES

with garlic and hot chile peppers. Order with a little parmesan and no oil.

✓ CALORIES: Low (523)   ✓✓ CHOLESTEROL: Very Low (72 mg)

✓✓ FAT: Very Low* (9 g)   ✓ SODIUM: Low (480 mg) **

Diabetic Exchanges: 1 Meat, 2¾ Bread, 1¼ Veg, ¾ Fat

LIFE RICE

White rice tossed with chopped steamed broccoli, peas and carrots.
Topped with scrambled egg whites and fresh lime salsa.

✓ CALORIES: Low (447)   ✓✓ CHOLESTEROL: Very Low (18 mg)

✓✓ FAT: Very Low* (10 g)   SODIUM: Moderate (974 mg) **

Diabetic Exchanges: 1½ Meat (extra lean), 3¾ Bread, 1½ Veg, 1¾ Fat

GRILLED CHICKEN PAILLARD

Served with tomatillo sauce (included in analysis).

✓ CALORIES: Low (558)   CHOLESTEROL: Moderate (241 mg)

✓ FAT: Low (20 g)   ✓✓ SODIUM: Very Low (238 mg) **

Diabetic Exchanges: 12½ Meat (extra lean), ¼ Veg, 1¾ Fat

SEARED SEA SCALLOPS WITH FRESH CITRUS FRUITS

Drizzled lightly with hot chili oil and a mixed tangle of wild greens. Served with rice (see analysis below).

✓✓ CALORIES: Very Low (288)   ✓✓ CHOLESTEROL: Very Low (38 mg)

✓ FAT: Low* (17 g)   ✓✓ SODIUM: Very Low (247 mg) **

Diabetic Exchanges: 2½ Meat (extra lean), ½ Fruit, ¼ Veg, 3¼ Fat

FRESH GROUND TURKEY BURGER

All white meat on sunflower cracked wheat toast from La Brea Bakery. Topped with lively lime salsa and fresh fruit. Served with rice (see analysis below).

✓ CALORIES: Low (583)   ✓✓ CHOLESTEROL: Very Low (72 mg)

FAT: Moderate (23 g)   ✓✓ SODIUM: Very Low (174 mg)**

Diabetic Exchanges: 3 Meat, 3 Bread, ½ Fruit, 1½ Fat

RICE *(1 cup)* 241 calories, 6 g fat*, 14 mg cholesterol, 455 mg sodium; Diabetic Exch: 2¾ Bread, 1 Fat

* Primarily unsaturated fat
** If you request no added salt

KELLY'S

est. 1958

A dining tradition in Long Beach for over 35 years. Long known for its prime rib, steaks, fresh fish, seafood and daily specials, Kelly's has added a low fat, low cholesterol menu to complement the traditional menu. Three Star Award from California Restaurant Writers. Cocktails, wines by glass, and their famous Irish coffee. Open daily at 4 pm. Reservations suggested. $$

Kelly's   5716 E. 2nd Street, Naples Island, Long Beach, CA 90803   (310) 433-4983

Entrees served with salad with non-fat dressing and your choice of baked potato with fat-free toppings, fat-free wild rice pilaf, or fresh vegetables prepared in Butter Buds.

PASTA MARINARA WITH CHICKEN
Angel hair or fettuccine tossed with fresh garlic and tomatoes, topped with skinless, broiled chicken (no oil or cheese).
- ✓ CALORIES: Low (578)
- ✓ CHOLESTEROL: Low (168 mg)
- ✓✓ FAT: Very Low (9 g)
-   SODIUM: Moderate (831 mg) **

Diabetic Exchanges: 8¾ Meat (extra lean), 2½ Bread, 2¼ Veg

PASTA TOMATILLO WITH CHICKEN
Angel hair or fettuccine tossed with fresh garlic, veal stock, tomatillo salsa, fresh vegetable and topped with skinless broiled chicken (no oil or cheese).
- ✓ CALORIES: Low (597)
- ✓ CHOLESTEROL: Low (168 mg)
- ✓✓ FAT: Very Low (9 g)
-   SODIUM: Moderate (629 mg) **

Diabetic Exchanges: 8¾ Meat (extra lean), 3¼ Bread, ¾ Veg

CHICKEN DIANE
Boneless, skinless breast served in a sauce prepared with Dijon mustard, shallots and demi-glace.
- ✓ CALORIES: Low (420)
- ✓ CHOLESTEROL: Low (192 mg)
- ✓✓ FAT: Very Low (9 g)
- ✓ SODIUM: Low (557 mg) **

Diabetic Exchanges: 10 Meat (extra lean)

BROILED FRESH FISH OF THE DAY
Daily selection served with Butter Buds, lemon juice, white wine, shallots and fresh herbs (no oil or cream). Analysis is for halibut; other fish similar.
- ✓✓ CALORIES: Very Low (340)
- ✓✓ CHOLESTEROL: Very Low (91 mg)
- ✓✓ FAT: Very Low* (7 g)
- ✓✓ SODIUM: Very Low (225 mg) **

Diabetic Exchanges: 6½ Meat (extra lean)

VEGETARIAN PLATE
A medley of fresh vegetables chosen by the chef, with Butter Buds on the side.
- ✓✓ CALORIES: Very Low (272)
- ✓✓ CHOLESTEROL: None (0 mg)
- ✓✓ FAT: Very Low* (2 g)
-   SODIUM: High (1337 mg) **

Diabetic Exchanges: 2¾ Bread, 2 Veg

VEAL PICCATA
Thinly sliced veal with shallots, capers, lemon juice, white wine, Butter Buds, fresh herbs and veal stock (no oil).
- ✓✓ CALORIES: Very Low (293)
- ✓ CHOLESTEROL: Low (133 mg)
- ✓ FAT: Low (11 g)
- ✓ SODIUM: Low (456 mg) **

Diabetic Exchanges: 5¼ Meat, ½ Fat

✓ Low ✓✓ Very Low
†Side dish guidelines are 1/3 of entree guidelines

KOO KOO ROO California Kitchen features Original Skinless Flame-Broiled Chicken, Fresh Oven-Roasted Turkey, Rotisserie Chicken, salads, and gourmet side dishes. Food is made fresh throughout the day and appeals to those who appreciate delicious, high quality, fresh food that can be enjoyed on the premises or as a home meal replacement. Catering available. $

Koo Koo Roo locations

Beverly Hills: 262 S. Beverly Dr. (310) 274-3121
Brentwood: 1150 San Vincente Bl. (310) 207-3232
Encino: 17136 Ventura Blvd. (818) 783-5576
Long Beach: 245 Pine Ave. (310) 590-8002

Los Angeles: 8393 Beverly Blvd. (213) 655-9045
Marina Del Rey: 4352 Glencoe Ave. (310) 305-8100
Santa Monica: 2002 Wilshire Blvd. (310) 453-8767
West LA: 11066 Santa Monica Blvd. (310) 473-5858

ORIGINAL SKINLESS FLAME BROILED CHICKEN - ¼ CHICKEN
Includes breast and wing. Analysis for side dishes below.
- ✓ CALORIES: Low (394)
- ✓ FAT: Low (14 g)
- ✓ CHOLESTEROL: Low (164 mg)
- ✓ SODIUM: Low (580 mg)

Diabetic Exchanges: 8½ Meat (extra lean), ¼ Veg, ¾ Fat

ORIGINAL SKINLESS FLAME BROILED CHICKEN - 2 BREASTS
Analysis for side dishes shown below.
- ✓ CALORIES: Low (503)
- ✓ FAT: Low (14 g)
- CHOLESTEROL: Moderate (231 mg)
- SODIUM: Moderate (628 mg)

Diabetic Exchanges: 12 Meat (extra lean), ¼ Veg, ¾ Fat

ORIGINAL CHICKEN BREAST SANDWICH (WITHOUT SPREAD)
Analysis does not include sandwich spread - request without or use sparingly.
- ✓ CALORIES: Low (534)
- ✓✓ FAT: Very Low (9 g)
- ✓ CHOLESTEROL: Low (116 mg)
- SODIUM: Moderate (939 mg)

Diabetic Exchanges: 6 Meat (extra lean), 3½ Bread, ¼ Veg, ½ Fat

TURKEY BREAST SANDWICH - REQUEST WITHOUT MAYONNAISE
Analysis does not include mayonnaise. Request without or only small amount.
- ✓ CALORIES: Low (521)
- ✓✓ FAT: Very Low (7 g)
- ✓ CHOLESTEROL: Low (118 mg)
- SODIUM: Moderate (907 mg)

Diabetic Exchanges: 6 Meat (extra lean), 3¼ Bread, ¼ Veg, 1 Fat

CRACKED WHEAT RICE† *(3½ oz. individual size)*
119 calories, 2 g fat*, 0 cholesterol, 220 mg sodium; Diabetic Exchanges: 1 Bread, ¾ Veg, ¼ Fat

CORN ON THE COB† *(½ ear)*
58 calories, < 1 g fat*, 0 cholesterol, 3 mg sodium; Diabetic Exchanges: ¾ Bread

STEAMED VEGETABLES† *(3¾ oz. individual size)*
34 calories, <1 g fat*, 0 cholesterol, 32 mg sodium; Diabetic Exchanges: 1¼ Veg

BUTTERNUT SQUASH† *(5½ oz. individual size)*
62 calories, < 1 g fat*, 0 cholesterol, 6 mg sodium; Diabetic Exchanges: 1 Bread

* Primarily unsaturated fat
** If you request no added salt

*For the 20 years since the popular French Bistro **La Frite Cafe** opened its doors, homesick Parisians and Californians have been savoring its culinary delights. In quaint, comfortable surroundings, you can enjoy your choice of French or California cuisine, including fish specials, quiches, crepes, salads, and delicious desserts. This is the place to come to kibbutz over coffee and dessert. $$*

La Frite Cafe

15013 Ventura Blvd., Sherman Oaks, CA 91403 (818) 990-1791
22616 Ventura Blvd., Woodland Hills, CA 91364 (818) 225-1331

GOAT CHEESE AND RATATOUILLE CASSEROLE - SPECIAL REQUEST
Request light cheese (½ oz).

✓✓ CALORIES: Very Low (235) ✓✓ CHOLESTEROL: Very Low (12 mg)
✓ FAT: Low (17 g) ✓✓ SODIUM: Very Low (89 mg) **
Diabetic Exchanges: ½ Meat, 2¾ Veg, 3 Fat

SALADE NICOISE - SPECIAL REQUEST
Request dressing served on the side and use sparingly (not included in analysis).

✓✓ CALORIES: Very Low (339) ✓✓ CHOLESTEROL: Very Low (58 mg)
✓✓ FAT: Very Low* (9 g) SODIUM: High (1032 mg) **
Diabetic Exchanges: 4½ Meat, 1¼ Bread, 2 Veg, 1¼ Fat

VEGETARIAN BOWTIE PASTA - SPECIAL REQUEST
Request light oil (1 Tbs.) and parmesan cheese on the side.

✓ CALORIES: Low (569) ✓✓ CHOLESTEROL: Very Low (92 mg)
✓ FAT: Low* (19 g) ✓✓ SODIUM: Very Low (77 mg) **
Diabetic Exchanges: 5 Bread, 2¼ Veg 3½ Fat

GRILLED TURKEY BURGER ON WHOLE WHEAT BUN
includes lettuce and tomato topping.

✓ CALORIES: Low (512) ✓ CHOLESTEROL: Low (158 mg)
✓ FAT: Low (11 g) SODIUM: Moderate (839 mg) **
Diabetic Exchanges: 6 Meat, 2¾ Bread, ½ Veg, ¾ Fat

✓ Low ✓✓ Very Low

  †Side dish guidelines are 1/3 of entree guidelines

Located at the south end of the Larchmont district, La Luna combines a friendly neighborhood atmosphere with fabulous Northern Italian cuisine. New and traditional dishes are prepared the true Italian way - fresh and light. Chef/proprietor Robertino Giovannelli emphasizes that everything is made at the moment - right before the customers eyes - nothing is prepared in advance. Come experience the wonderful cuisine and comfortable atmosphere of La Luna. $$

La Luna

113 North Larchmont Boulevard
Los Angeles, CA 90004 (213) 962-2130

INSALATA DEL FATTORE

Calamari, string beans and potatoes in Italian vinaigrette.

- ✓ CALORIES: Low (472)
- ✓ FAT: Low* (16 g)
- CHOLESTEROL: Moderate (264 mg)
- ✓✓ SODIUM: Very Low (68 mg) **

Diabetic Exchanges: 2½ Meat (extra lean), 4¼ Bread, 2¾ Fat

SPAGHETTI MISTO FUNGHI (2/3 SERVING)

with mixed wild mushrooms in garlic and white wine sauce. Analysis is for 2/3 of a full serving.

- ✓ CALORIES: Low (538)
- ✓ FAT: Low (16 g)
- ✓✓ CHOLESTEROL: Very Low (15 mg)
- ✓ SODIUM: Low (362 mg) **

Diabetic Exchanges: 1 Meat, 4¼ Bread, 2¼ Fat

TAGLIOLINI CON SCAMPI & CARCIOFI (2/3 SERVING)

Home-made pasta with shrimp, artichoke and fresh tomato. Analysis is for 2/3 of a full serving.

- ✓ CALORIES: Low (442)
- ✓ FAT: Low (13 g)
- ✓ CHOLESTEROL: Low (181 mg)
- ✓ SODIUM: Low (435 mg) **

Diabetic Exchanges: 3½ Meat, 1¾ Bread, 2 Veg, 1¼ Fat

PETTO DI POLLO CON FUNGHI & ASPARAGI - SPECIAL REQUEST

Chicken breast with mushrooms & asparagus sauteed in white wine. Request light oil (1 Tbs).

- ✓ CALORIES: Low (556)
- ✓ FAT: Low (20 g)
- ✓ CHOLESTEROL: Low (168 mg)
- ✓✓ SODIUM: Very Low (191 mg) **

Diabetic Exchanges: 8¾ Meat (extra lean), ½ Veg, 2¾ Fat

BAKED ORANGE ROUGHY

baked with zucchini and fresh tomato.

- ✓✓ CALORIES: Very Low (230)
- ✓✓ FAT: Very Low* (9 g)
- ✓✓ CHOLESTEROL: Very Low (40 mg)
- ✓✓ SODIUM: Very Low (170 mg) **

Diabetic Exchanges: 4 Meat (extra lean), 1 Veg, 1¼ Fat

* Primarily unsaturated fat
** If you request no added salt

Set among the shops and galleries of Main Street in Santa Monica is La Vecchia Cucina, "The Old Kitchen." This restaurant has all the ingredients of a neighborhood trattoria. Charm, intimacy, a casual setting and a great menu make it a fashionable secret for clientele who return time and again. La Vecchia is noted for its homemade breads, pizzas, award-winning traditional Italian dishes and friendly atmosphere. $

La Vecchia Cucina 2654 Main Street, Santa Monica, CA 90405 (310) 399-7979

SAGNE A PEZZI
Homemade square pasta with shiitake mushrooms and basil in a chopped tomato sauce.
✓ CALORIES: Low (422)   ✓✓ CHOLESTEROL: Very Low (62 mg)
✓ FAT: Low* (13 g)   SODIUM: High (1053 mg) **
Diabetic Exchanges: 3¼ Bread, ¼ Veg, 2 Fat

SPAGHETTI AL FILETTO DI POMODORO
Spaghetti in tomato sauce with fresh basil.
✓ CALORIES: Low (391)   ✓✓ CHOLESTEROL: None (0 mg)
✓✓ FAT: Very Low* (5 g)   SODIUM: Moderate (864 mg) **
Diabetic Exchanges: 4¼ Bread, ½ Fat

LINGUINE ZINGARA
Grilled chicken breast, sun dried tomatoes, leeks, zucchini, fresh tomatoes, olive oil and garlic.
✓ CALORIES: Low (541)   ✓✓ CHOLESTEROL: Very Low (72 mg)
✓✓ FAT: Very Low (8 g)   ✓✓ SODIUM: Very Low (91 mg) **
Diabetic Exchanges: 3¾ Meat (extra lean), 4 Bread, ¾ Veg, ½ Fat

PAPPARDELLE ALLA FRA DIAVOLA
Homemade pasta with shrimp and shiitake mushrooms in a spicy tomato sauce.
✓ CALORIES: Low (527)   CHOLESTEROL: Moderate (304 mg)
✓✓ FAT: Very Low* (4 g)   SODIUM: High (1314 mg) **
Diabetic Exchanges: 3¼ Meat (extra lean), 4 Bread, ¼ Veg

PESCE BIANCO ALLA LIVORNESE
Sauteed white fish in marinara sauce. Includes steamed vegetables.
✓✓ CALORIES: Very Low (292)   ✓✓ CHOLESTEROL: Very Low (64 mg)
✓✓ FAT: Very Low (10 g)   SODIUM: Moderate (668 mg) **
Diabetic Exchanges: 5 Meat (extra lean), ½ Veg, 1¼ Fat

POLLO AL LIMONE
Chicken breast with lemon sauce. Includes steamed vegetables.
✓ CALORIES: Low (424)   ✓ CHOLESTEROL: Low (155 mg)
✓ FAT: Low (17 g)   ✓✓ SODIUM: Very Low (191 mg)
Diabetic Exchanges: 7½ Meat, ½ Veg, ¼ Fruit, 2 Fat

✓ Low ✓✓ Very Low

   †Side dish guidelines are 1/3 of entree guidelines

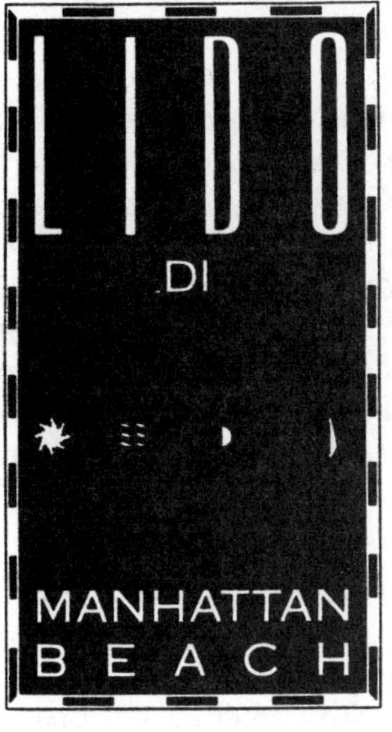

Lido di Manhattan Beach offers contemporary yet elegant surroundings and a combination of food, music and art unrivaled in the South Bay - a combination which caused regular patrons to recently vote Lido to be "Best All-Around Restaurant." The menu features our pasta, made fresh daily, alongside local seafood, beef and poultry. We are located only 3 convenient miles from LAX, and offer lunch and dinner Monday - Friday, dinner only Saturdays and Sundays. $$

Lido di Manhattan Beach

1550 Rosecrans Ave. "G"
Manhattan Beach, CA 90266   (310) 536-0730

PASTA PICANTE

*Italian olives, capers, pine nuts, tomatoes, hot peppers and parsley,
tossed with parmesan cheese and black pepper spaghettini.*

✓ CALORIES: Low (588)   ✓✓ CHOLESTEROL: Very Low (2 mg)
✓ FAT: Low* (14 g)   ✓✓ SODIUM: Very Low (298 mg) **
Diabetic Exchanges: 5½ Bread, 1½ Veg, 2 Fat

HALIBUT CHARDONNAY

*Poached in chardonnay with fresh baby artichoke hearts, mushrooms and capers, and served over black
and white linguine with sesame ginger long beans (all included in analysis).*

✓ CALORIES: Low (593)   ✓✓ CHOLESTEROL: Very Low (63 mg)
✓✓ FAT: Very Low* (10 g)   ✓✓ SODIUM: Very Low (294 mg) **
Diabetic Exchanges: 5¾ Meat (extra lean), 3½ Bread, 1 Veg, ¾ Fat

JUMBO SEA SCALLOPS - SPECIAL REQUEST

*Charbroiled, served on Santa Fe red bell pepper puree with angel hair pasta.
Request light oil (½ Tbs.) with pasta. Polenta not included in analysis.*

✓ CALORIES: Low (568)   ✓ CHOLESTEROL: Low (120 mg)
✓ FAT: Low* (14 g)   ✓ SODIUM: Low (382 mg) **
Diabetic Exchanges: 2½ Meat (extra lean), 3½ Bread, 1¾ Veg, 2 Fat

CHARBROILED CHICKEN, SUNDRIED TOMATOES & SPINACH WITH LINGUINE
- SPECIAL REQUEST

*Charbroiled breast of chicken, sauteed with sundried tomatoes and spinach, tossed
with parmesan cheese and linguine. Request light oil (¾ Tbs).*

✓ CALORIES: Low (449)   ✓ CHOLESTEROL: Low (149 mg)
✓ FAT: Low (19 g)   SODIUM: Moderate (660 mg) **
Diabetic Exchanges: 8 Meat (extra lean), ½ Bread, ½ Veg, 2¼ Fat

* Primarily unsaturated fat
** If you request no added salt

At Louise's, we continually strive, through education and training, to better understand the rich diversity of the Italian cuisine. Our goal is to constantly improve the culinary products for you, our guest. We import some of the finest Italian products available which we use in the preparation of the dishes listed below. We hope you enjoy these special items we are preparing for this Healthy menu. We've done this with all our knowledge and all our hearts. $

Louise's Locations:

Beverly Hills: 342 N. Beverly Hills Dr.
Brentwood: 11645 San Vicente Blvd.
Glendale: 130 N. Maryland Ave.
Huntington Beach: 300 Pacific Coast Hwy. #200
Larchmont: 232 N. Larchmont Blvd.
Los Feliz: 4500 Los Feliz Blvd.

Melrose: 7505 Melrose Ave.
Pasadena: 2 E. Colorado Blvd.
Pico: 10645 Pico Boulevard
Redondo Beach: 1430 Pacific Coast Hwy.
Santa Monica: 1008 Montana Ave.
Santa Monica: 264 26th Street
Studio City: 12050 Ventura Blvd., A-201

ANGEL HAIR WITH PLUM TOMATO CONCASSE AND BASIL - SPECIAL REQUEST
Request light oil (½ oz) and light cheese (½ oz).
- ✓ CALORIES: Low (398)
- ✓ FAT: Low (20 g)
- ✓✓ CHOLESTEROL: Very Low (49 mg)
- ✓✓ SODIUM: Very Low (296 mg) **

Diabetic Exchanges: ¾ Meat, 2 Bread, 2 Veg, 3 Fat

PENNE ALL'ARRABBIATA - SPECIAL REQUEST
with tomato, garlic and red chili pepper. Request light oil (½ oz) and no cheese.
- ✓ CALORIES: Low (452)
- ✓ FAT: Low* (20 g)
- ✓✓ CHOLESTEROL: Very Low (57 mg)
- ✓✓ SODIUM: Very Low (291 mg) **

Diabetic Exchanges: 3 Bread, 1¼ Veg, 4 Fat

TAGLIOLINI ALLE VONGOLE - SPECIAL REQUEST
Thin fettucine with fresh clams and extra virgin olive oil. Request light oil (½ oz).
- ✓ CALORIES: Low (401)
- ✓ FAT: Low* (16 g)
- ✓✓ CHOLESTEROL: Very Low (86 mg)
- ✓✓ SODIUM: Very Low (212 mg) **

Diabetic Exchanges: 2 Meat (extra lean), 2½ Bread, 2¾ Fat

RIGATONI WITH GRILLED VEGETABLES - SPECIAL REQUEST
Tossed in extra virgin olive oil. Request light oil (½ oz).
- ✓ CALORIES: Low (484)
- ✓ FAT: Low* (20 g)
- ✓✓ CHOLESTEROL: Very Low (68 mg)
- ✓✓ SODIUM: Very Low (293 mg) **

Diabetic Exchanges: ¾ Meat, 3 Bread, 2 Veg, 3 Fat

THREE CITRUS GRILLED CHICKEN - SPECIAL REQUEST
Request light oil (¼ oz) and steamed vegetables. Served with pasta (not included in analysis).
- ✓ CALORIES: Low (582)
- ✓ FAT: Low (17 g)
- CHOLESTEROL: Moderate (241 mg)
- ✓✓ SODIUM: Very Low (266 mg) **

Diabetic Exchanges: 12½ Meat (extra lean), 1 Veg, ½ Fruit, 1¼ Fat

✓ Low ✓✓ Very Low

†Side dish guidelines are 1/3 of entree guidelines

RESTAURANT AND JAZZ CLUB

"Riviera Reverie - Hot jazz, cool prices, warm setting - all this and fine French Provencal fare too!", says the LA Times. Lunaria's intimately appealing atmosphere and comfortable setting allow you to savor the best Provencale cuisine in town as you relax to the cool jazz sounds of the evening's entertainment (live nightly). Luncheon Mon - Fri 11:30am - 2:30pm; Dinner Tues-Thurs 5:30pm - 10:30pm; Fri-Sat 5:30pm-12:00. Reservations recommended. $$

Lunaria Restaurant and Jazz Club

10351 Santa Monica Boulevard (at Beverly Glen), Los Angeles, CA 90025 (310) 282-8870

GRILLED CHICKEN BREAST (LUNCH MENU) - REQUEST WITHOUT SKIN

With vegetable couscous and spicy bell pepper coulis.

- ✓ CALORIES: Low (584)
- ✓ FAT: Low (18 g)
- CHOLESTEROL: Moderate (217 mg)
- ✓ SODIUM: Low (518 mg) **

Diabetic Exchanges: 11¼ Meat (extra lean), 1 Bread, 1 Veg, 1½ Fat

GRILLED CHICKEN SALAD (LUNCH MENU ONLY)

Coconut and curry marinated with roasted vegetables and mixed greens.

- ✓ CALORIES: Low (437)
- ✓ FAT: Low (14 g)
- ✓ CHOLESTEROL: Low (147 mg)
- ✓ SODIUM: Low (583 mg) **

Diabetic Exchanges: 7½ Meat (extra lean), ½ Bread, 1¼ Veg, 1¼ Fat

BRAISED CHILEAN SEABASS - SPECIAL REQUEST

Potato fennel puree, cold pressed olive oil, tomato & capers. Request very light oil (¼ portion).

- ✓ CALORIES: Low (507)
- ✓ FAT: Low (20 g)
- ✓ CHOLESTEROL: Low (136 mg)
- ✓ SODIUM: Low (525 mg) **

Diabetic Exchanges: 7 Meat (extra lean), 1 Bread, 1 Veg, 2¾ Fat

GRILLED MAHI-MAHI (DINNER MENU ONLY)

With white sweet corn and spinach, seabeans and citrus spice.

- ✓ CALORIES: Low (475)
- ✓ FAT: Low (14 g)
- CHOLESTEROL: Moderate (235 mg)
- ✓ SODIUM: Low (588 mg) **

Diabetic Exchanges: 7½ Meat (extra lean), 1¾ Bread, ¼ Veg, 2¼ Fat

PROVENCALE GARDEN PLATE (DINNER MENU ONLY)

Oven dried tomato, artichokes "Barigoule", potato and fennel puree, roasted bell pepper.

- ✓✓ CALORIES: Very Low (318)
- ✓ FAT: Low (19 g)
- ✓✓ CHOLESTEROL: Very Low (10 mg)
- ✓✓ SODIUM: Very Low (257 mg) **

Diabetic Exchanges: 3¾ Veg, ¾ Bread, 4 Fat

---

* Primarily unsaturated fat
** If you request no added salt

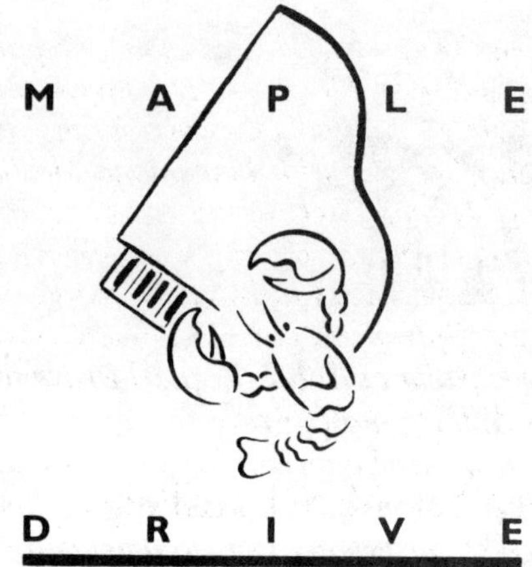

The menu at Maple Drive offers a counterbalance of simplicity and sophistication in its varied presentation of salads, pastas, risottos, seafood and grilled fowl. As well, it offers live jazz nightly to accompany the intelligent choices available to the health-minded diner. $$$

Maple Drive

345 N. Maple Drive
Beverly Hills, CA 90210   (310) 274-9800

GAZPACHO
(8 oz.)

✓✓ CALORIES: Very Low (145)   ✓✓ CHOLESTEROL: None (0 mg)
✓ FAT: Low* (11 g)   SODIUM: Moderate (818 mg)
Diabetic Exchanges: 1½ Veg, 2 Fat

CHARRED RARE HAWAIIAN TUNA - SPECIAL REQUEST
with Shittakes, Scallions and Japanese Vinaigrette. Request Vinaigrette on the side and use sparingly (not included in analysis).

✓ CALORIES: Low (498)   ✓✓ CHOLESTEROL: Very Low (64 mg)
✓ FAT: Low* (20 g)   ✓ SODIUM: Low (429 mg) **
Diabetic Exchanges: 5½ Meat (extra lean), 1¼ Bread, 1¾ Veg, 2¾ Fat

PENNE
with tomato, calamata olives, capers, basil and garlic.

✓ CALORIES: Low (517)   ✓✓ CHOLESTEROL: None (0 mg)
✓ FAT: Low* (19 g)   ✓ SODIUM: Low (356 mg) **
Diabetic Exchanges: 5 Bread, 1 Veg, 3½ Fat

MAPLE VEGGIES

✓ CALORIES: Low (543)   ✓✓ CHOLESTEROL: Very Low (10 mg)
✓✓ FAT: Very Low* (10 g)   ✓✓ SODIUM: Very Low (214 mg) **
Diabetic Exchanges: 5¼ Bread, 3½ Veg, 1½ Fat

GRILLED CHILEAN SEABASS - SPECIAL REQUEST
with artichokes, capers & French beans. Request light oil (1 Tbs.) and no butter.

✓ CALORIES: Low (392)   ✓✓ CHOLESTEROL: Very Low (70 mg)
✓ FAT: Low* (18 g)   ✓✓ SODIUM: Very Low (234 mg) **
Diabetic Exchanges: 4¼ Meat (extra lean), 3½ Veg, 2¾ Fat

✓ Low ✓✓ Very Low

     †Side dish guidelines are 1/3 of entree guidelines

Down-home Texas style Mexican food, prepared from scratch, and served in an upbeat, high-energy setting. "Sizzling" fajitas, chicken, shrimp and grilled "veggies," served with homemade tortillas, as well as our Mexican "light" food and vegetarian dishes (no lard or preservatives) - something for everyone! Full bar serving award-winning margaritas. Realistic prices. Open every day. MC, VISA, AMEX accepted. Valet parking. Banquets, parties, catering, take out and delivery available. $

Marix Tex Mex Locations:
Santa Monica: 118 Entrada Dr. (310) 459-8596
West Hollywood: 1108 N. Flores (213) 656-8800

SHRIMP AND VEGETABLE ENCHILADAS (LUNCH MENU ONLY)
Served with green rice and black beans (see analysis below).
✓✓ CALORIES: Very Low (247)   ✓✓ CHOLESTEROL: Very Low (55 mg)
✓✓ FAT: Very Low* (9 g)   SODIUM: Moderate (949 mg)
Diabetic Exchanges: ¾ Meat, 1¾ Bread, ½ Veg, 1¼ Fat

SUPER TACOS - CHICKEN
Three handmade corn tortillas with chicken, onions & peppers. Side dishes (rice & black beans) shown below.
✓ CALORIES: Low (476)   ✓ CHOLESTEROL: Low (120 mg)
✓✓ FAT: Very Low (10 g)   ✓ SODIUM: Low (488 mg)
Diabetic Exchanges: 6¼ Meat (extra lean), 2½ Bread, ¾ Veg, ½ Fat

SUPER TACOS - FISH
Fresh grilled fish served on three homemade corn tortillas with grilled pineapple salsa.
Served with 3 oz. rice and 4 oz. black beans (see analysis below).
✓ CALORIES: Low (334)   ✓✓ CHOLESTEROL: Very Low (77 mg)
✓✓ FAT: Very Low (8 g)   SODIUM: Moderate (638 mg) **
Diabetic Exchanges: 2½ Meat (extra lean), 2½ Bread, ¾ Veg, 1¼ Fat

PLATO PEPI
Grilled lime chicken breast, herb green rice, steamed veggies, & flour or corn tortillas. Fat free flour tortillas also available (subtract 4 g fat and 40 calories from analysis listed). Analysis for green rice shown separately below.
✓ CALORIES: Low (536)   ✓ CHOLESTEROL: Low (144 mg)
✓ FAT: Low (15 g)   ✓ SODIUM: Low (412 mg) **
Diabetic Exchanges: 7½ Meat (extra lean), 2 Bread, 1 Veg, 1¾ Fat

PLATO DE VERDURAS - SPECIAL REQUEST
Fresh steamed veggies with melted cheese and herb green rice (analysis for rice below). <u>Request fat-free cheese.</u>
✓✓ CALORIES: Very Low (129)   ✓✓ CHOLESTEROL: None (0 mg)
✓✓ FAT: Very Low* (1 g)   ✓ SODIUM: Low (407 mg) **
Diabetic Exchanges: ¾ Meat, 2½ Veg

GREEN RICE† *5 oz. prepared oil-free.*
✓ CALORIES: Low (150)   ✓✓ CHOLESTEROL: None (0 mg)
✓✓ FAT: Very Low (<1 g)   SODIUM: High (476 mg)
Diabetic Exchanges: 2 Bread, ¼ Veg

BLACK BEANS† *5 oz. prepared oil-free.*
✓ CALORIES: Low (143)   ✓✓ CHOLESTEROL: Very Low (3 mg)
✓✓ FAT: Very Low (2 g)   SODIUM: Moderate (359 mg)
Diabetic Exchanges: ½ Meat, 1½ Bread, ¼ Fat

* Primarily unsaturated fat
** If you request no added salt

Healthy Dining in Los Angeles **93**

McCORMICK&SCHMICK'S
SEAFOOD RESTAURANT

McCormick & Schmick's Seafood Restaurant is one of Los Angeles' most popular dining and gathering spots. Our menu features fresh seafood from the Pacific Northwest and other regional favorites. Salads, pastas, poultry and steak entrees are also available. Enjoy the timeless and traditional presentation and decor. Happy hour 3 - 7 pm Monday thru Friday. Dinner served daily from 5 pm. Reservations recommended. $$

McCormick & Schmick's Seafood Restaurant

111 N. Los Robles, Pasadena, CA 91101 (818) 405-0064
633 West 5th St. 4th Level, Los Angeles, CA 90071   (213) 629-1929
206 North Rodeo Drive, Beverly Hills, CA 90210 (310) 859-0434

DUNGENESS CRAB LOUIS SALAD - SPECIAL REQUEST
Request dressing on the side and use sparingly.
✓✓ CALORIES: Very Low (216)   ✓ CHOLESTEROL: Low (166 mg)
✓✓ FAT: Very Low (7 g)   SODIUM: High (1311 mg) **
Diabetic Exchanges: 4 Meat (extra lean), ½ Veg, 1 Fat

NICOISE SALAD WITH RARE TUNA - SPECIAL REQUEST
Request dressing on the side and use sparingly.
✓✓ CALORIES: Very Low (232)   ✓ CHOLESTEROL: Low (104 mg)
✓✓ FAT: Very Low (5 g)   ✓✓ SODIUM: Very Low (129 mg) **
Diabetic Exchanges: 3¾ Meat (extra lean), ¾ Bread, ¾ Veg, ¾ Fat

PACIFIC SEAFOOD STEW
with shellfish and tomato wine broth.
✓ CALORIES: Low (466)   CHOLESTEROL: Moderate (250 mg)
✓ FAT: Low* (12 g)   SODIUM: High (1556 mg) **
Diabetic Exchanges: 8 Meat (extra lean), 2 Veg, 1¼ Fat

GRILLED CHICKEN BREAST
with eggplant and tomato coulis. Served with steamed vegetables (included in analysis) and pasta (see analysis below).
✓ CALORIES: Low (468)   ✓ CHOLESTEROL: Low (144 mg)
✓ FAT: Low (20 g)   ✓✓ SODIUM: Very Low (253 mg) **
Diabetic Exchanges: 7½ Meat (extra lean), ¼ Bread, 1¼ Veg, 2¾ Fat

CEDAR PLANK SALMON - SPECIAL REQUEST
Request sauce on the side and use sparingly. Served with steamed vegetables (included in analysis) and pasta (see below).
✓ CALORIES: Low (436)   ✓ CHOLESTEROL: Low (144 mg)
✓ FAT: Low* (19 g)   ✓✓ SODIUM: Very Low (148 mg) **
Diabetic Exchanges: 8 Meat, ¾ Veg

PASTA† *(4 oz.)*
✓ CALORIES: Low (184)   ✓ CHOLESTEROL: Low (37 mg)
✓ FAT: Low* (5 g)   ✓✓ SODIUM: Very Low (7 mg) **
Diabetic Exchanges: 1¾ Bread, ¾ Fat

DESSERT: ### FRUIT COBBLER†
✓ CALORIES: Low (184)   ✓✓ CHOLESTEROL: Very Low (9 mg)
✓✓ FAT: Very Low (3 g)   ✓✓ SODIUM: Very Low (82 mg)
Diabetic Exchanges: 1½ Bread, 1¼ Fruit, ½ Fat

✓ Low ✓✓ Very Low

   †Side dish guidelines are 1/3 of entree guidelines

Mi PIACE

(Pia • ché)

Mi Piace means "I like it" in Italian. That is just how the owners Armen Shirvanian and Takis Markoutsis make you feel about their restaurant. From the warmest greeting at the door, to the friendliest servers at your table, and great food with moderate prices for your pocket. People walk out saying, "I like it." $$

Mi Piace   25 E. Colorado Boulevard, Pasadena, CA 91105   (818) 795-3131

INSALA DI CARCIOFI CON RUCOLA - SPECIAL REQUEST
Marinated artichokes with arugula salad and lemon rice wine vinaigrette. Request light oil (1 Tbs).

✓✓ CALORIES: Very Low (209)   ✓✓ CHOLESTEROL: None (0 mg)
✓ FAT: Low* (14 g)   ✓✓ SODIUM: Very Low (120 mg) **
Diabetic Exchanges: 2¾ Veg, ¼ Fruit, 2¾ Fat

CAPPELLINI POMODORO - SPECIAL REQUEST
Request light oil (1 Tbs).

✓ CALORIES: Low (598)   ✓✓ CHOLESTEROL: None (0 mg)
✓ FAT: Low* (16 g)   ✓ SODIUM: Low (396 mg) **
Diabetic Exchanges: 5½ Bread, 2½ Veg, 2¾ Fat

CAPPELLINI PRIMAVERA - SPECIAL REQUEST
Request light oil (1 Tbs).

✓ CALORIES: Low (506)   ✓✓ CHOLESTEROL: None (0 mg)
✓ FAT: Low* (16 g)   ✓ SODIUM: Low (395 mg) **
Diabetic Exchanges: 4¼ Bread, 3 Veg, 2¾ Fat

BRANZINO ALL GRILLA CON MELANZANE - SPECIAL REQUEST
Grilled Atlantic seabass with eggplant ratatouille. Request light oil (1 Tbs).

✓✓ CALORIES: Very Low (292)   ✓✓ CHOLESTEROL: Very Low (30 mg)
✓ FAT: Low* (16 g)   ✓✓ SODIUM: Very Low (66 mg) **
Diabetic Exchanges: 2 Meat (extra lean), ½ Bread, 1¼ Veg, 2¾ Fat

LINGUINI WITH GREEN LIP MUSSELS - SPECIAL REQUEST
in a white sauce. Request light oil (1 Tbs).

✓ CALORIES: Low (593)   ✓✓ CHOLESTEROL: Very Low (56 mg)
✓ FAT: Low (20 g)   SODIUM: Moderate (870 mg) **
Diabetic Exchanges: 2½ Meat (extra lean), 4¼ Bread, ¼ Veg, 3¼ Fat

---

* Primarily unsaturated fat
** If you request no added salt

MICHAEL'S

Now 40, Michael McCarty is still considered something of a boy wonder. At 18, he opened his first restaurant in Paris, where he graduated from the Ecole Hôtelière de Paris, the Cordon Bleu and the Academie du Vin. Back in the United States, he completed a business degree and opened Michael's in Santa Monica. He is now known as one of the pioneers of California cuisine. McCarty, one of the first restaurateurs to showcase modern art, believes that his clientele appreciates both great art and fine cuisine. $$$

Michael's   1147 Third Street, Santa Monica, CA 90403   (310) 451-0843

HAWAIIAN AHI CARPACCIO
with extra virgin olive oil, white mushrooms, reggiano parmesan and arugula.
✓✓ CALORIES: Very Low (282)   ✓✓ CHOLESTEROL: Very Low (73 mg)
✓ FAT: Low* (12 g)   ✓ SODIUM: Low (574 mg) **
Diabetic Exchanges: 5¼ Meat (extra lean), ¼ Veg, 1 Fat

PAPPARDELLE
with spinach, portobello mushrooms, pine nuts, garlic and olive oil.
✓ CALORIES: Low (587)   CHOLESTEROL: Moderate (213 mg)
✓ FAT: Low (15 g)   ✓✓ SODIUM: Very Low (58 mg) **
Diabetic Exchanges: 1 Meat, 5 Bread, 1 Veg, 2 Fat

OREGON STATE SHIITAKE AND TREE MUSHROOMS SALAD
with double blanched garlic, New Jersey pancetta, pine nuts, sherry wine vinegar and walnut oil on San Fernando Valley baby greens.
✓✓ CALORIES: Very Low (328)   ✓✓ CHOLESTEROL: Very Low (26 mg)
✓ FAT: Low (16 g)   ✓ SODIUM: Low (414 mg) **
Diabetic Exchanges: 1¾ Meat, 1 Bread, 1½ Veg, 2 Fat

MAINE LOBSTER SALAD
with Roma tomatoes, avocado and sweet grilled onions on San Fernando Valley baby greens with extra virgin olive oil and balsamic vinegar.
✓✓ CALORIES: Very Low (274)   ✓✓ CHOLESTEROL: Very Low (81 mg)
✓ FAT: Low* (16 g)   ✓ SODIUM: Low (452 mg) **
Diabetic Exchanges: 2¾ Meat (extra lean), ¾ Veg, 2¾ Fat

MIXED GRILL OF SEASONAL VEGETABLES
red and yellow peppers, baby red potatoes, asparagus and sweet onions with extra virgin olive oil and balsamic vinegar. Request light oil (½ oz).
✓✓ CALORIES: Very Low (329)   ✓✓ CHOLESTEROL: None (0 mg)
✓ FAT: Low* (19 g)   ✓✓ SODIUM: Very Low (52 mg) **
Diabetic Exchanges: 1 Bread, 2¾ Veg, 3½ Fat

ATLANTIC SALMON SALAD
with Roma tomato vinaigrette, roasted red and yellow sweet peppers and grilled sweet onions with balsamic vinegar and extra virgin olive oil.
✓ CALORIES: Low (391)   ✓ CHOLESTEROL: Low (108 mg)
✓ FAT: Low* (19 g)   ✓✓ SODIUM: Very Low (103 mg) **
Diabetic Exchanges: 6 Meat, 1 Veg, 1 Fat

✓ Low ✓✓ Very Low

   †Side dish guidelines are 1/3 of entree guidelines

Monroe's is romantically hidden away on one of the nicest beaches along the California coast line, with fabulous sunsets and moonglows over the ocean. The ambiance and service at Monroe's have no equal, and owners-hosts Richard and Donna are always on hand to ensure a perfect evening. The menu is very continental, using only the freshest ingredients available. Owner Richard Chesterfield makes many early morning trips to the produce, seafood and meat markets to purchase on a daily basis. Monroe's has also become one of L.A.'s premier catering companies, at your place or ours. No party too large or too small - no budget too low or too high! Open for dinner every evening from 5 pm 'till midnight. Reservations suggested. $$$

Monroe's of Malibu

6800 Westward Beach Road, Malibu, CA 90265 (310) 457-5521

SEARED SALMON WITH CUCUMBER DILL SALSA

✓ CALORIES: Low (563)　　✓ CHOLESTEROL: Low (126 mg)
✓ FAT: Low* (17 g)　　✓ SODIUM: Low (510 mg) **
Diabetic Exchanges: 7 Meat, 2½ Bread, ¼ Veg

GRILLED SWORDFISH WITH BLACK BEANS AND TOMATO LIME SALSA

✓ CALORIES: Low (563)　　✓✓ CHOLESTEROL: Very Low (77 mg)
✓ FAT: Low* (13 g)　　✓ SODIUM: Low (313 mg) **
Diabetic Exchanges: 5¼ Meat (extra lean), 2½ Bread, 1 Veg

GRILLED SEA BASS WITH BOK CHOY AND PINEAPPLE SOY GINGER SAUCE
Served with saffron rice (included in analysis).

✓ CALORIES: Low (484)　　✓✓ CHOLESTEROL: Very Low (97 mg)
✓ FAT: Low (11 g)　　SODIUM: High (2119 mg)
Diabetic Exchanges: 5 Meat (extra lean), 2 Bread, ¾ Fruit, 1¼ Fat

CAPPELINI WITH SHITAKE MUSHROOMS & SUNDRIED TOMATOES - SPECIAL REQUEST　*Request light oil (½ oz).*

✓ CALORIES: Low (559)　　✓✓ CHOLESTEROL: None (0 mg)
✓ FAT: Low* (15 g)　　✓✓ SODIUM: Very Low (73 mg) **
Diabetic Exchanges: 3¾ Bread, ½ Veg, 2¾ Fat

* Primarily unsaturated fat
** If you request no added salt

Eating at Mum's is an experience everyone can enjoy. You can watch as Chef Enrique Tinoco creates your every wish at our exposition line, or watch our pizza chef toss dough, or experience a wide variety of Grille items being prepared and pasta made to order. Everything we do at Mum's is fresh, from our fish, pastas, and desserts to our legendary spinach rolls. We are proud to be a part of the change and renaissance of the new downtown Long Beach. Come see us and share in the experience of Downtown. $$

Mum's   144 Pine Avenue, Long Beach, CA 90802   (310) 437-7700

VEGETARIAN PIZZA (½ WHOLE PIZZA)
Asparagus, mushrooms, artichoke hearts, goat cheese and tomatoes.

✓ CALORIES: Low (396) ✓✓ CHOLESTEROL: Very Low (13 mg)
✓✓ FAT: Very Low (10 g) SODIUM: Moderate (734 mg) **

Diabetic Exchanges: ¾ Meat, 3½ Bread, 1 Veg, 1¼ Fat

CAPELLINI CHECCA
Angel hair pasta with chopped roma tomatoes, basil and virgin olive oil.

✓ CALORIES: Low (458) ✓✓ CHOLESTEROL: None (0 mg)
✓ FAT: Low* (15 g) ✓ SODIUM: Low (547 mg) **

Diabetic Exchanges: 3¾ Bread, 1¼ Veg, 2¾ Fat

PENNE ALL'ARRABIATA
Tube pasta with spicy marinara sauce.

✓ CALORIES: Low (535) ✓ CHOLESTEROL: Low (110 mg)
✓ FAT: Low* (17 g) SODIUM: Moderate (682 mg) **

Diabetic Exchanges: 4¾ Bread, 1¾ Veg, 2½ Fat

SEAFOOD SPAGHETTI - REQUEST NO BUTTER
Spaghetti with scallops, shrimp and squid in light tomato herb sauce.

CALORIES: Moderate (700) ✓ CHOLESTEROL: Low (102 mg)
✓ FAT: Low (19 g) ✓ SODIUM: Low (571 mg)
Diabetic Exchanges: 1¾ Meat, 5¾ Bread, 1½ Veg, 3 Fat

✓ Low ✓✓ Very Low

    †Side dish guidelines are 1/3 of entree guidelines

Orleans Restaurant, the sole-surviving cajun eatery in the Los Angeles area, continues to serve up simply fine California cajun cuisine. Patrons can get their choices lightly or highly seasoned...or without hot-spice. "Fresh" is the key...no freezer on the premises! A consummate dining experience which leaves your taste sensations reeling for more! $$

Orleans Restaurant 11705 National Blvd. (at Barrington), Los Angeles (310) 479-4187

BRONZED SWORDFISH - SPECIAL REQUEST

with hot fanny sauce, mashed potatoes & vegetables (included in analysis). Request light butter (1 Tbs).
- ✓ CALORIES: Low (469)
- ✓ CHOLESTEROL: Low (109 mg)
- ✓ FAT: Low (20 g)
- ✓ SODIUM: Low (522 mg) ##

Diabetic Exchanges: 5 Meat, 1½ Bread, ¾ Veg, 2¼ Fat

BLACKENED FISH - SPECIAL REQUEST

Analysis for Ahi and also includes vegetables and potatoes. Request light butter (1 Tbs).
- ✓ CALORIES: Low (442)
- ✓ CHOLESTEROL: Low (120 mg)
- ✓ FAT: Low (14 g)
- ✓ SODIUM: Low (417 mg) ##

Diabetic Exchanges: 6½ Meat (extra lean), 1½ Bread, ¾ Veg, 2¼ Fat

PONY'S PASTA - SPECIAL REQUEST

Tomatoes, julienne vegetables, garlic & herbs over pasta. Request light oil (½ oz).
- ✓ CALORIES: Low (388)
- ✓✓ CHOLESTEROL: None (0 mg)
- ✓ FAT: Low* (15 g)
- SODIUM: Moderate (883 mg) ##

Diabetic Exchanges: 2¾ Bread, 2½ Veg, 3 Fat

ATCHAFALAYA PASTA - SPECIAL REQUEST

Shrimp, scallops & fresh fish over rotelli. Request light butter (1 Tbs).
- ✓ CALORIES: Low (464)
- ✓ CHOLESTEROL: Low (166 mg)
- ✓ FAT: Low (16 g)
- SODIUM: Moderate (676 mg) ##

Diabetic Exchanges: 3 Meat (extra lean), 2¾ Bread, ¾ Veg, 3 Fat

OVEN BAKED CHICKEN - SPECIAL REQUEST

Served with vegetables & potatoes (not included in analysis). Request light butter (1 Tbs).
- ✓ CALORIES: Low (431)
- ✓ CHOLESTEROL: Low (199 mg)
- ✓ FAT: Low (18 g)
- ✓ SODIUM: Low (475 mg) ##

Diabetic Exchanges: 8¾ Meat

Analysis shown on all items above assumes you special request "light seasoning" (1/3 tsp). Sodium can be reduced further if you request no cajun seasoning.

* Primarily unsaturated fat
** If you request no added salt

Papa Jon's

Welcome to Papa Jon's Natural Market & Cafe, a completely vegetarian restaurant founded in 1988 by Jon Quinn Jr. We attempt to accommodate as many dietary needs as possible, and do not add sugar or salt to most of our dishes. Dishes listed as vegan are completely without animal or animal by-products, and most other dishes are also available in vegan form upon request. $

5000 E. Second St., Long Beach, CA 90803 (310) 439-1059
11251 National Blvd., West Los Angeles, CA 90064 (310) 445-2541

STEAMED VEGGIES AND RICE (VEGAN)
Seasonal vegetables over our hearty short grain brown rice. Request veggies steamed rather than sauteed. Served with choice of soup, salad, or mashed potatoes. Analysis is for rice and veggies only.
- ✓✓ CALORIES: Very Low (306)
- ✓✓ CHOLESTEROL: None (0 mg)
- ✓✓ FAT: Very Low* (3 g)
- ✓✓ SODIUM: Very Low (55 mg)
- Diabetic Exchanges: 3¼ Bread, 2 Veg

SPINACH LASAGNA
A huge piece of dairy-free lasagne made with lasagne noodles, spinach, marinara sauce & tofu filling. Served with a whole wheat garlic roll & choice of soup, salad, rice or mashed potatoes. Analysis for lasagna only.
- ✓ CALORIES: Low (357)
- ✓✓ CHOLESTEROL: Very Low (6 mg)
- ✓ FAT: Low* (13 g)
- SODIUM: High (1503 mg)
- Diabetic Exchanges: 2¾ Meat, 3½ Bread, 4½ Veg, 1¾ Fat

TOMATO ZUCCHINI PASTA
Tomatoes and zucchini lightly fried in canola oil and spices over sesame pasta. Served with choice of soup, salad, rice or mashed potatoes. Analysis for pasta only.
- ✓ CALORIES: Low (558)
- ✓✓ CHOLESTEROL: None (0 mg)
- ✓ FAT: Low* (17 g)
- ✓ SODIUM: Low (447 mg)
- Diabetic Exchanges: 5 Bread, 1¾ Veg, 3 Fat

SHEPHERD'S PIE
A healthy pie with carrots, spinach, mushrooms, onions, peppers and mashed potatoes. Served with choice of soup, salad, rice or mashed potatoes. Analysis is for Shepherd's Pie only.
- ✓✓ CALORIES: Very Low (332)
- ✓✓ CHOLESTEROL: Very Low (8 mg)
- ✓✓ FAT: Very Low* (4 g)
- ✓ SODIUM: Low (412 mg)
- Diabetic Exchanges: 2 Bread, 6¾ Veg, ¼ Fat

VEGGIE BURGER (VEGAN)
A dairy-free version of the Garden Burger! Made with soybeans, mushrooms, brown rice, vegetables & spices. Served with lettuce, tomato, alfalfa sprouts, melted soycheese & mustard on a whole wheat bun. Served with choice of salad, soup, brown rice, fruit, or deli salad. Analysis for Veggie Burger only.
- ✓ CALORIES: Low (399)
- ✓✓ CHOLESTEROL: None (0 mg)
- ✓ FAT: Low* (16 g)
- SODIUM: High (1156 mg)
- Diabetic Exchanges: 2¼ Meat, 1¾ Bread, ¼ Veg, 2¾ Fat

CHILI BEAN SOUP† *(8 oz.)*
148 Calories, 3 g Fat*, 2 mg Cholesterol, 570 mg. Sodium; Diab. Ex: 1 Meat, 1½ Bread, 1¼ Veg, ¼ Fat

GARDEN VEGETABLE SOUP† (8 oz.)
65 Calories, <1 g Fat*, <1 mg Cholesterol, 57 mg Sodium; ½ Bread, 1¼ Veg

SPLIT PEA SOUP† *(8 oz.)*
52 Calories, <1 g Fat*, 0 Cholesterol, 32 mg Sodium; Diab. Ex: ¼ Bread, 1½ Veg

✓ Low ✓✓ Very Low
†Side dish guidelines are 1/3 of entree guidelines

Patina received Number 1 ratings for "most popular" and "best food" for the last 4 consecutive years in the Zagat guide of Los Angeles. Joachim Splichal, owner and chef, is an internationally renowned chef who brings a classic, yet unprecedented style, integrity and philosophy of food to Los Angeles. Patina's French-Californian cuisine uses only top quality ingredients, favoring fresh fish and vegetables. The lunch menu offers a fresh and basic "American" fare, designed to meet the needs of the business clientele. The dinner menu offers a more sophisticated and elaborate selection of innovative entrees. $$$

Patina   5955 Melrose Ave., Los Angeles, CA 90038   (213) 467-1108

PEPPERED TOURNEDOS OF TUNA
with Chinese vegetables and ponzu sauce. Analysis does not include wontons.

✓✓ CALORIES: Very Low (303)   ✓✓ CHOLESTEROL: Very Low (77 mg)
✓✓ FAT: Very Low* (9 g)   SODIUM: High (1120 mg) **
Diabetic Exchanges 5¾ Meat (extra lean), 1½ Veg, 1¼ Fat

SANTA BARBARA SHRIMP
with sundried tomato, leek and parsley juice.

✓✓ CALORIES: Very Low (341)   ✓ CHOLESTEROL: Low (146 mg)
✓ FAT: Low (14 g)   ✓✓ SODIUM: Very Low (269 mg) **
Diabetic Exchanges 1½ Meat (extra lean), 1½ Veg, 2½ Fat

BREAST OF FARM CHICKEN
with carrot rounds and thyme lemon sauce. Analysis does not include fried carrot strips.

✓ CALORIES: Low (592)   ✓ CHOLESTEROL: Low (175 mg)
✓ FAT: Low (18 g)   ✓ SODIUM: Low (322 mg) **
Diabetic Exchanges 7½ Meat (extra lean), 4½ Veg, 2½ Fat

FILLET OF SALMON - SPECIAL REQUEST
with stuffed cabbage and wild mushrooms. Request light butter (¼ Tbs).

✓ CALORIES: Low (458)   ✓✓ CHOLESTEROL: Very Low (91 mg)
✓ FAT: Low* (19 g)   ✓✓ SODIUM: Very Low (167 mg) **
Diabetic Exchanges 6¾ Meat (extra lean), ½ Bread, 2¾ Veg, 1 Fat

CHILLED SOUP OF CITRUS FRUIT†
with lemon gras and mango sherbet.

CALORIES: Moderate (222)   ✓✓ CHOLESTEROL: None (0 mg)
✓✓ FAT: Very Low* (1 g)   ✓✓ SODIUM: Very Low (4 mg)
Diabetic Exchanges 1¾ Fruit

* Primarily unsaturated fat
** If you request no added salt

PIAZZA RODEO

Like the great piazzas of Italy, Piazza Rodeo is where folks gather for the sights, scents, sounds and sumptuous cuisine of Italia. Situated in the marble splendor of Beverly Hills' newest Euro-village, Via Rodeo, Piazza Rodeo offers a concise menu in the Italian tradition - fine ingredients and skillful yet simple presentation. Menu items include specialty pastas, pleasing sandwich assortments and classic offerings such as Ceasar salad and bruschetta. $

Piazza Rodeo   208 Via Rodeo, Beverly Hills, CA 90210   (310) 275-2428

CHICKEN BREAST SANDWICH
Grilled whole chicken breast, lettuce, sliced tomato, served on a sesame roll.
Served with mixed greens tossed with raspberry dressing (included in analysis).

✓ CALORIES: Low (567)   ✓ CHOLESTEROL: Low (144 mg)
✓ FAT: Low (20 g)   ✓ SODIUM: Low (393 mg)
Diabetic Exchanges: 7½ Meat (extra lean), 1½ Bread, ¾ Veg, 2½ Fat

GRILLED SALMON - REQUEST SAUCE ON THE SIDE
Fresh grilled salmon served with steamed vegetables. Sauce and risotto not included in analysis.

✓ CALORIES: Low (475)   ✓ CHOLESTEROL: Low (162 mg)
✓ FAT: Low* (20 g)   ✓✓ SODIUM: Very Low (144 mg) **
Diabetic Exchanges: 9 Meat, ¾ Veg

SALAD NICOISE - REQUEST DRESSING ON THE SIDE
Blended tuna, tomatoes, green beans, black olives, capers, onions, chopped chervil
and tarragon with hard boiled egg. Request dressing on the side and
use sparingly (egg and dressing not included in analysis).

✓✓ CALORIES: Very Low (343)   ✓✓ CHOLESTEROL: Very Low (37 mg)
✓ FAT: Low* (16 g)   SODIUM: Moderate (853 mg) **
Diabetic Exchanges: 3 Meat (extra lean), ¾ Bread, 2 Veg, 4 Fat

ANGELHAIR PASTA
with fresh tomatoes, garlic and basil.

✓ CALORIES: Low (510)   ✓✓ CHOLESTEROL: Very Low (100 mg)
✓ FAT: Low* (20 g)   ✓✓ SODIUM: Very Low (225 mg)
Diabetic Exchanges: ½ Meat, 4 Bread, 1½ Veg, 3¾ Fat

PENNE
with marinara sauce.

✓ CALORIES: Low (403)   ✓✓ CHOLESTEROL: Very Low (100 mg)
✓✓ FAT: Very Low* (7 g)   ✓ SODIUM: Low (548 mg)
Diabetic Exchanges: ½ Meat, 4 Bread, 1½ Veg, 1¼ Fat

✓ Low ✓✓ Very Low

A fish is a fish is a fish, so they say. But Pine Avenue Fish House excels in resourcing only the freshest, highest quality fish and shellfish available. Located in downtown Long Beach, Pine Avenue Fish House provides the most extensive variety of daily changing seafood west of the Mississippi, serving more than 35 varieties of fresh seafood prepared in 10 different ways. The menu also offers expertly prepared chicken, steak, and pasta, all at prices guests from far and near find attractive. Lunch served 11:00 am to 4:00 pm; dinner until 10:00 pm Sunday through Thursday, until 11:00 pm Friday and Saturday. $$

Pine Avenue Fish House

100 West Broadway, Long Beach, CA 90802   (310) 432-7463
at Pine Square (corner of Pine and Broadway)

FRESH GRILLED HAWAIIAN SWORDFISH WITH PAPAYA SALSA

✓✓ CALORIES: Very Low (271)   ✓✓ CHOLESTEROL: Very Low (67 mg)
✓ FAT: Low* (11 g)   ✓ SODIUM: Low (541 mg) **
Diabetic Exchanges: 4¼ Meat (extra lean), ¼ Fruit, 1 Fat

FRESH GRILLED NEW ZEALAND YELLOWTAIL WITH THAI-CHILI SAUCE

✓✓ CALORIES: Very Low (306)   ✓✓ CHOLESTEROL: Very Low (83 mg)
✓ FAT: Low* (13 g)   ✓ SODIUM: Low (305 mg) **
Diabetic Exchanges: 5½ Meat (extra lean), 1 Fat

FRESH GRILLED HAWAIIAN AHI WITH LEMON-SCALLION SAUCE

✓✓ CALORIES: Very Low (318)   ✓✓ CHOLESTEROL: Very Low (77 mg)
✓ FAT: Low* (15 g)   SODIUM: Moderate (733 mg) **
Diabetic Exchanges: 5½ Meat (extra lean), 2½ Fat

GRILLED MARINATED CHICKEN BREAST WITH TWO SALSAS

✓✓ CALORIES: Very Low (335)   ✓ CHOLESTEROL: Low (144 mg)
✓ FAT: Low (12 g)   SODIUM: Moderate (775 mg)
Diabetic Exchanges: 7½ Meat (extra lean), 1¼ Fat

ANGEL HAIR WITH EASTERN SEA SCALLOPS
in a shrimp broth

✓ CALORIES: Low (469)   ✓✓ CHOLESTEROL: Very Low (67 mg)
✓ FAT: Low (14 g)   SODIUM: High (1060 mg)
Diabetic Exchanges: 4 Meat (extra lean), 2¾ Bread, 2¾ Fat

---

* Primarily unsaturated fat
** If you request no added salt

Rated #1 in the Valley by the Los Angeles Times, Pinot features classic French Bistro fare in a relaxed environment, where menu prices reflect the informality. "Our goal is to create a warm retreat where good friends, good talk and good food share equally in creating the good times," says proprietor and chef Joachim Splichal.

$$

Pinot Bistro

12969 Ventura Blvd.
Studio City, CA 91604   (818) 990-0500

POACHED ENGLISH SOLE WITH RAPINI
with broccoli and grain mustard yogurt sauce.

✓✓ CALORIES: Very Low (249)   ✓✓ CHOLESTEROL: Very Low (77 mg)
✓✓ FAT: Very Low* (5 g)   SODIUM: Moderate (821 mg) **
Diabetic Exchanges: 3¾ Meat (extra lean), 2¼ Veg, ½ Milk, ¼ Fat

BROILED PACIFIC SEABASS WITH CAPERS AND LEMON FILET

✓ CALORIES: Low (470)   ✓ CHOLESTEROL: Low (103 mg)
✓ FAT: Low (19 g)   ✓ SODIUM: Low (447 mg) **
Diabetic Exchanges: 4 Meat (extra lean), 2 Bread, 1¾ Veg, 3 Fat

CASARECCIA PASTA WITH BABY ARTICHOKES, OVEN DRIED TOMATOES AND BASIL

✓ CALORIES: Low (444)   ✓✓ CHOLESTEROL: Very Low (5 mg)
✓ FAT: Low* (17 g)   ✓✓ SODIUM: Very Low (212 mg) **
Diabetic Exchanges: ½ Meat, 3 Bread, 3½ Veg, 3 Fat

GRILLED AHI TUNA WITH PIPERADE SAUCE
(Analysis does not include onion rings.)

✓ CALORIES: Low (402)   ✓✓ CHOLESTEROL: Very Low (70 mg)
✓ FAT: Low* (16 g)   ✓✓ SODIUM: Very Low (75 mg) **
Diabetic Exchanges: 5¼ Meat (extra lean), 4½ Veg, 2¾ Fat

LINGUINI WITH CLAMS, SHRIMP AND BABY SCALLOPS - SPECIAL REQUEST
Request no added butter.

✓ CALORIES: Low (486)   ✓✓ CHOLESTEROL: Very Low (93 mg)
✓ FAT: Low* (16 g)   ✓✓ SODIUM: Very Low (202 mg) **
Diabetic Exchanges: 2¾ Meat (extra lean), 3¼ Bread, 1¼ Veg, 3 Fat

✓ Low ✓✓ Very Low
†Side dish guidelines are 1/3 of entree guidelines

CALIFORNIA GRILL

Conveniently located on East Green Street, Roxxi is a stylish restaurant with a contemporary western theme. An exhibition kitchen features a wood burning grill. Fresh seafood, prime Angus steaks, fowl and wild game are standard fare. Interesting pastas with intriguing ethnic touches, pizzas, premise made desserts, and an extensive California wine list balance the menu. Lunch Monday - Friday; dinner nightly. Free parking. $$

Roxxi   1065 East Green Street, Pasadena, CA 91106   (818) 449-4519

WOOD GRILLED THAI SHRIMP SALAD (LUNCH ONLY)
with select lettuces and crunchy peanut dressing.

✓✓ CALORIES: Very Low (191)   ✓ CHOLESTEROL: Low (138 mg)
✓✓ FAT: Very Low* (3 g)   ✓✓ SODIUM: Very Low (236 mg) **
Diabetic Exchanges: 2 Meat (extra lean), 1¾ Veg, ¼ Fat

CHOPSTIX CHICKEN SALAD (LUNCH ONLY) - SPECIAL REQUEST
Wood grilled with ginger and citrus rice wine vinaigrette. <u>Request dressing on the side</u> and use sparingly (dressing not included in analysis).

✓ CALORIES: Low (454)   ✓ CHOLESTEROL: Low (169 mg)
✓ FAT: Low (15 g)   ✓✓ SODIUM: Very Low (173 mg) **
Diabetic Exchanges: 8¾ Meat (extra lean), ¼ Bread, ½ Veg, 1½ Fat

WILD MUSHROOM AND EGGPLANT SALAD
with Parmesan crisp and balsamic-chili dressing.

✓ CALORIES: Low (399)   ✓✓ CHOLESTEROL: Very Low (10 mg)
✓✓ FAT: Very Low (6 g)   ✓✓ SODIUM: Very Low (270 mg) **
Diabetic Exchanges: ¾ Meat, 4 Bread, 1¾ Fruit, ¼ Fat

FRESH DUNGENESS CRAB ON CHILLED GAZPACHO
with ginger toast.

✓ CALORIES: Low (373)   ✓✓ CHOLESTEROL: Very Low (88 mg)
✓ FAT: Low (20 g)   SODIUM: Moderate (699 mg)
Diabetic Exchanges: 2 Meat (extra lean), 1 Bread, 1¾ Veg, 3½ Fat

RICOTTA CHEESE RAVIOLI
with spinach, tomatoes, and grilled onion sauce.

✓ CALORIES: Low (447)   ✓✓ CHOLESTEROL: Very Low (88 mg)
✓ FAT: Low (18 g)   SODIUM: High (1269 mg)
Diabetic Exchanges: ½ Meat, 3½ Bread, 1 Veg, 3½ Fat

---

* Primarily unsaturated fat
** If you request no added salt

Ruby's Diner with 5 Los Angeles area locations:

Glendale: 1322 Glendale Galeria   (818) 507-7829
Marina Del Rey: 13455 Maxella Ave.   (310) 574-7829
Palos Verdes: 550 Deep Valley Road   (310) 544-7829
Seal Beach Pier: 900 Ocean Blvd.   (310) 431-7829
Woodland Hills: 6100 Topanga Canyon Bl. (818) 340-7829
Additional locations in Orange and San Diego Counties

Ruby's Diner is the authentic 40's diner in Southern California! Step back in time to 40's memorabilia, gleaming red and white interiors and friendly, courteous service. We offer items to please every palate, including a variety of salads, sandwiches, and home style breakfasts. Swing by Ruby's today and experience great food and great service served up with a 40's flair. $

VEGGIE RUBYBURGER
with a tasty vegetable, rice, oats and wheat patty.
Request Ruby sauce on the side and use sparingly (not included in analysis).

✓ CALORIES: Low (404)   ✓✓ CHOLESTEROL: Very Low (8 mg)
✓✓ FAT: Very Low* (8 g)   SODIUM: Moderate (695 mg)
Diabetic Exchanges: ½ Meat, 4 Bread, ¼ Veg, 1¼ Fat

CHICKEN RUBYBURGER
with a tender, boneless, skinless chicken breast. Request no mayonnaise.

✓ CALORIES: Low (466)   ✓ CHOLESTEROL: Low (120 mg)
✓✓ FAT: Very Low (9 g)   SODIUM: Moderate (709 mg)
Diabetic Exchanges: 6¼ Meat (extra lean), 2½ Bread, ¼ Veg, ¾ Fat

TURKEY RUBYBURGER
with a full 1/3 lb. of lean ground turkey.
Request Ruby sauce on the side and use sparingly (not included in analysis).

✓ CALORIES: Low (420)   ✓✓ CHOLESTEROL: Very Low (56 mg)
✓ FAT: Low (15 g)   ✓ SODIUM: Low (519 mg)
Diabetic Exchanges: 5 Meat, 2½ Bread, ¼ Veg, 1¼ Fat

ROAST TURKEY BREAST SANDWICH
served with lettuce, cranberry sauce and mayo on a soft RubyRoll. Just like Thanksgiving!

✓ CALORIES: Low (591)   ✓ CHOLESTEROL: Low (126 mg)
✓ FAT: Low (15 g)   SODIUM: Moderate (642 mg)
Diabetic Exchanges: 6 Meat (extra lean), 2¾ Bread, 1½ Fruit, 2½ Fat

SKINNY LUNCH (CHICKEN BREAST)
Tender, boneless, skinless chicken breast with salsa, fresh fruit, and low-fat cottage cheese.

✓ CALORIES: Low (387)   ✓ CHOLESTEROL: Low (127 mg)
✓✓ FAT: Very Low (7 g)   SODIUM: Moderate (711 mg)
Diabetic Exchanges: 8 Meat (extra lean), 1 Fruit, ½ Veg

✓ Low ✓✓ Very Low
†Side dish guidelines are 1/3 of entree guidelines

SOUTHERN LATIN FLAVORS

It's creole... it's cajun... it's latin... it's...

"Top Latin/Caribbean restaurant in Los Angeles" - Zagat '94.

"The food at SABOR is just as jazzy as the ambience...The food itself is a lively mix of Southern and Latin cooking," - L.A. Times.

"Great food at moderate prices. Cross-cultural...with a menu offering a surprising blend of southern U.S. and Latin flavors...a delightful dinner out..." - Bon Appetit $$

Sabor   3221 Pico Blvd, Santa Monica, CA   (310) 829-3781

YUCATAN CHICKEN LIME SOUP - SPECIAL REQUEST

Grilled chicken breast, pasilla chilies, roasted tomato with crispy corn chips and fresh avocado.
<u>Request chicken without skin</u>.

✓ CALORIES: Low (393)   ✓✓ CHOLESTEROL: Very Low (99 mg)
✓ FAT: Low (15 g)   SODIUM: High (1750 mg) **
Diabetic Exchanges: 6½ Meat (extra lean), ½ Bread, ¼ Veg, 1¼ Fat

FRESH LOUISIANA CRAB CAKES

Served with baby cactus, tomato and cilantro salad with balsamic vinaigrette dressing (included in analysis).

✓✓ CALORIES: Very Low (252)   ✓✓ CHOLESTEROL: Very Low (77 mg)
✓ FAT: Low* (16 g)   SODIUM: High (1299 mg) **
Diabetic Exchanges: 2 Meat, ½ Veg, 2½ Fat

CHICKEN BREAST - SPECIAL REQUEST

Grilled and served on a bed of angel hair pasta with basil, tomatoes, pasilla chile, olive oil and anejo cheese. <u>Request light oil in sauce (1 Tbs.)</u> and <u>skinless chicken</u>.

✓ CALORIES: Low (564)   ✓ CHOLESTEROL: Low (123 mg)
✓ FAT: Low (20 g)   ✓✓ SODIUM: Very Low (169 mg) **
Diabetic Exchanges: 6¼ Meat (extra lean), 2 Bread, 1 Veg, 2¾ Fat

VEGETARIAN ROLL

Whole wheat tortilla filled with black beans, green leaves and roasted eggplant flavored with cilantro-tahini and topped with chipotle sauce. Garnish of creme fraiche and anejo cheese not included in analysis.

✓ CALORIES: Low (511)   ✓✓ CHOLESTEROL: None (0 mg)
✓ FAT: Low (19 g)   SODIUM: High (1816 mg) **
Diabetic Exchanges: 3½ Bread, 2½ Veg, ¼ Meat, 3 Fat

FRESH AHI TUNA - SPECIAL REQUEST

Blackened with cajun spices and served with a mustard, caper, tomato, cilantro and onion relish over lime-cilantro linguini. <u>Request light oil in sauce</u> (1 Tbs.) & <u>relish on the side</u>.
Relish not included in analysis (use sparingly).

✓ CALORIES: Low (600)   ✓✓ CHOLESTEROL: Very Low (89 mg)
✓ FAT: Low* (20 g)   ✓✓ SODIUM: Very Low (88 mg) **
Diabetic Exchanges: 6¼ Meat (extra lean), 2 Bread, 1 Veg, 3¼ Fat

* Primarily unsaturated fat
** If you request no added salt

Ours is not the only way to spend an evening, but it's one way to enjoy it. We make every effort to make your evening enjoyable by serving fresh fish, fine meats and seafood specialties, giving personal attention, and combining a warm and intimate atmosphere with surfside dining. We're located right on the sand on one of the prettiest beaches in California...where you can gaze out over the ocean while dining in comfort. Come spend an evening with us...and let us help you enjoy it! $$

Sand Castle   28128 Pacific Coast Highway, Malibu, CA 90265   (310) 457-2503

MARINE SALAD
With scallions, shrimp, crabmeat, tuna, asparagus, tomato and egg. <u>Request dressing on the side</u> and use sparingly (not included in analysis).
✓✓ CALORIES: Very Low (226)   CHOLESTEROL: Moderate (275 mg)
✓✓ FAT: Very Low (6 g)   ✓ SODIUM: Low (505 mg) **
Diabetic Exchanges: 4¼ Meat, ½ Veg, ½ Fat

CHARBROILED FILET OF TUNA
See analysis of side dishes below.
✓✓ CALORIES: Very Low (286)   ✓ CHOLESTEROL: Low (102 mg)
✓✓ FAT: Very Low* (7 g)   ✓✓ SODIUM: Very Low (83 mg) **
Diabetic Exchanges: 7¼ Meat, 1 Fat

FILET OF SHARK
Charbroiled to order. Analysis of side dishes below.
✓✓ CALORIES: Very Low (336)   ✓ CHOLESTEROL: Low (115 mg)
✓ FAT: Low* (15 g)   ✓✓ SODIUM: Very Low (179 mg) **
Diabetic Exchanges: 6½ Meat, 1 Fat

NORTHERN HALIBUT STEAK - REQUEST BROILED AND SAUCE ON SIDE
<u>*Request charbroiled with sauce served on the side*</u>*. Use sauce sparingly (not included in analysis).*
✓✓ CALORIES: Very Low (287)   ✓✓ CHOLESTEROL: Very Low (73 mg)
✓✓ FAT: Very Low* (10 g)   ✓✓ SODIUM: Very Low (123 mg) **
Diabetic Exchanges: 5 Meat, 1 Fat

BOUILLABAISSE MARSEILLAISE
The authentic bouillabaisse, with imported saffron. Prepared with lobster, shrimp, scallops, clams, crab meat and fresh fish.
✓ CALORIES: Low (550)   CHOLESTEROL: Moderate (262 mg)
✓ FAT: Low (20 g)   SODIUM: High (1549 mg) **
Diabetic Exchanges: 10 Meat, 1½ Veg, 2½ Fat

RICE PILAF† *(5 oz.)*
CALORIES: Moderate (226)   ✓✓ CHOLESTEROL: Very Low (3 mg)
✓✓ FAT: Very Low (2 g)   SODIUM: Moderate (215 mg)
Diabetic Exchanges: 3 Bread, ¼ Fat

VEGETABLES DU JOUR†
✓✓ CALORIES: Very Low (101)   ✓✓ CHOLESTEROL: None (0 mg)
✓ FAT: Low (7 g)   SODIUM: Moderate (230 mg)
Diabetic Exchanges: 1 Veg, 1½ Fat

✓ Low ✓✓ Very Low

Schatzi on Main is an inviting, comfortable and affordable neighborhood eatery tucked away on Main Street in Santa Monica, dishing up "Contemporary American Fare" for lunch and dinner seven days a week.

Founded in 1991 by Arnold Schwarzenegger and Maria Shriver, Schatzi (German for "little treasure") is a 3,000 square foot, 120-seat space featuring a casual, yet elegant indoor setting, as well as a lush outdoor garden patio.

Schatzi's executive chef Robert Cocca's creations are an intriguing blend of contemporary American selections and Austrian specialties, highlighted by their innovative presentations. Brunch: Saturday and Sunday 9 am - 3 pm. Lunch: 11:30 am - 3 pm Monday through Friday. Dinner: 6 - 10 pm Monday through Sunday. Dinner reservations suggested. $$

Schatzi on Main 3110 Main Street, Santa Monica, CA 90405 (310) 399-4800

AHI TUNA TARTARE
Chopped Asian salad and wasabe cilantro vinaigrette. Analysis does not include fried wontons.

✓ CALORIES: Low (360) ✓✓ CHOLESTEROL: Very Low (82 mg)
✓ FAT: Low* (20 g) ✓ SODIUM: Low (416 mg) **
Diabetic Exchanges: 3½ Meat, ¼ Veg, 3¾ Fat

SCHATZI VEGETABLE PLATE
Eight different vegetables. Sesame dressing served on the side (not included in analysis).

✓ CALORIES: Low (437) ✓✓ CHOLESTEROL: None (0 mg)
✓✓ FAT: Very Low* (6 g) ✓✓ SODIUM: Very Low (182 mg) **
Diabetic Exchanges: 3 Bread, 5½ Veg, 1 Fat

CAPELLINI TOSSED WITH FRESH TOMATO AND BASIL SAUCE

✓ CALORIES: Low (466) ✓✓ CHOLESTEROL: None (0 mg)
✓ FAT: Low* (15 g) ✓ SODIUM: Low (352 mg) **
Diabetic Exchanges: 3½ Bread, 1¾ Veg, 2½ Fat

ROASTED HALF CHICKEN - SPECIAL REQUEST
With warm corn and okra salad and basil essence. Rosemary mashed potatoes not included in analysis. <u>Request chicken without skin.</u>

✓ CALORIES: Low (498) ✓ CHOLESTEROL: Low (192 mg)
✓ FAT: Low (18 g) ✓✓ SODIUM: Very Low (203 mg) **
Diabetic Exchanges: 10 Meat (extra lean), ¼ Bread, ½ Veg, 1¾ Fat

* Primarily unsaturated fat
** If you request no added salt

The Shenandoah Cafe offers down-home "American" dishes like those your Grandmother used to prepare. Shenandoah Cafe strives to achieve the very best for you by constantly having only the freshest, best quality products available. Most items are cooked with original country style. Quality is never sacrificed. Come enjoy a wonderful meal and unlock the memories of a warm home, country living and family traditions. $$

Shenandoah Cafe

4722 East 2nd Street
Long Beach, CA 90803   (310) 434-3469

CRAB CAKES
Three crab cakes, served with choice of vegetables, soup or salad. Analysis for crab cakes only.
- ✓ CALORIES: Low (387)   CHOLESTEROL: Moderate (283 mg)
- ✓ FAT: Low (18 g)   SODIUM: High (2638 mg)

Diabetic Exchanges: 3½ Meat (extra lean), 1¼ Bread, 3 Fat

SAN FRANCISCO SWORDFISH (SAN FRANCISCO, CALIFORNIA)
Fresh fillet marinated in soy sauce, dijon mustard, fresh lemon & garlic and charbroiled.
- ✓ CALORIES: Low (398)   ✓ CHOLESTEROL: Low (112 mg)
- ✓ FAT: Low* (17 g)   ✓ SODIUM: Low (520 mg) **

Diabetic Exchanges: 7¼ Meat (extra lean), 1 Fat

FRESH STEAMED VEGETABLE PLATTER
Sauces not included in analysis.
- ✓✓ CALORIES: Very Low (224)   ✓✓ CHOLESTEROL: None (0 mg)
- ✓✓ FAT: Very Low* (2 g)   ✓✓ SODIUM: Very Low (96 mg) **

Diabetic Exchanges: 8½ Veg

DAILY FRESH CATCH
Prepared with artichoke hearts and mushrooms that are sauteed in a tangy lemon butter sauce. Analysis is for seabass - other fish similar.
- ✓ CALORIES: Low (422)   ✓ CHOLESTEROL: Low (124 mg)
- ✓ FAT: Low (16 g)   ✓ SODIUM: Low (344 mg) **

Diabetic Exchanges: 5¾ Meat (extra lean), 2 Veg, ½ Fruit, 2¼ Fat

BBQ STYLE CHICKEN (KERRVILLE, TEXAS) - SPECIAL REQUEST
A very large portion size. <u>Request preparation without skin</u>. Analysis includes ½ portion of sauce.
- ✓ CALORIES: Low (597)   CHOLESTEROL: Moderate (289 mg)
- ✓ FAT: Low (13 g)   SODIUM: Moderate (630 mg) **

Diabetic Exchanges: 15 Meat (extra lean), ¼ Fat

GOLD BEACH HALIBUT (GOLD COAST, FLORIDA)
Northern fillet topped with a creamy mushroom and herb sauce.
- ✓ CALORIES: Low (372)   ✓ CHOLESTEROL: Low (112 mg)
- ✓ FAT: Low (16 g)   ✓✓ SODIUM: Very Low (154 mg) **

Diabetic Exchanges: 5¼ Meat (extra lean), ¼ Veg, 2¼ Fat

✓ Low ✓✓ Very Low

          †Side dish guidelines are 1/3 of entree guidelines

A Japanese Restaurant & Sushi Bar

Tucked away within the Sheraton Long Beach Hotel, this new and intimate traditional Japanese restaurant and sushi bar provide ambiance and authenticity to a cuisine that cherishes its culture. Open for breakfast, lunch and dinner, Shioji also has a full compliment of sake, Japanese and domestic beer, and a diversified scotch list. Shioji - a healthy alternative to the all American dining experience! $$

Shioji Japanese Restaurant and Sushi Bar - Sheraton Long Beach Hotel

333 East Ocean Boulevard, Long Beach, CA 90802 (310) 436-3000

YAKITORI
Marinated skewered chicken, broiled.
✓✓ CALORIES: Very Low (288) ✓ CHOLESTEROL: Low (144 mg)
✓✓ FAT: Very Low (6 g) ✓ SODIUM: Low (442 mg) **
Diabetic Exchanges: 7½ Meat (extra lean)

MORIKOMI DINNER
California roll, fresh king salmon, and chicken breast teriyaki.
Analysis for miso soup below. Tempura and dessert not included in analysis.
✓ CALORIES: Low (527) ✓ CHOLESTEROL: Low (162 mg)
✓ FAT: Low (15 g) SODIUM: High (1079 mg) **
Diabetic Exchanges: 8½ Meat, 1½ Bread, ¼ Veg, ½ Fat

TERIYAKI DINNER - SALMON
with vegetables & teriyaki sauce. Tempura not included in analysis. Miso soup & rice shown below.
✓ CALORIES: Low (445) ✓ CHOLESTEROL: Low (144 mg)
✓ FAT: Low* (19 g) ✓ SODIUM: Low (465 mg) **
Diabetic Exchanges: 8 Meat, ¾ Veg

CHICKEN BREAST TERIYAKI DINNER
Broiled to perfection. Analysis includes tempura and sauces. See analysis for miso soup and rice below.
✓ CALORIES: Low (599) CHOLESTEROL: Moderate (255 mg)
✓ FAT: Low (16 g) SODIUM: High (2066 mg) **
Diabetic Exchanges: 11¾ Meat (extra lean), 1¼ Bread, ½ Fat

SUSHI DINNER
Assorted fresh fish sushi. Served with miso soup (see analysis below).
✓✓ CALORIES: Very Low (283) ✓✓ CHOLESTEROL: Very Low (82 mg)
✓✓ FAT: Very Low* (7 g) SODIUM: Moderate (745 mg) **
Diabetic Exchanges: 3½ Meat, 1½ Bread, ½ Fat

MISO SOUP† *(1 cup)*
✓✓ CALORIES: Very Low (77) ✓✓ CHOLESTEROL: None (0 mg)
✓✓ FAT: Very Low* (3 g) SODIUM: High (934 mg)
Diabetic Exchanges: ¾ Meat

STEAMED WHITE RICE† *(5½ oz.)*
CALORIES: Moderate (202) ✓✓ CHOLESTEROL: None (0 mg)
✓✓ FAT: Very Low (½ g) SODIUM: Information not available
Diabetic Exchanges: 3 Bread

---

* Primarily unsaturated fat
** If you request no added salt

Home-style cooking speaks to all who love to eat, and at Sisley Italian Kitchen you will find truly memorable food guaranteed to ignite even the most jaded palates. Sisley boasts of an enticing list of pastas, grilled chicken, eggplant, gourmet pizzas and more.
Come and experience the overwhelming attention we pay to every detail at Sisley Italian Kitchen! Sisley, creating magic. $

Sisley Italian Kitchen

10800 West Pico Boulevard, Los Angeles, CA 90064   (310) 466-3030
24201 West Valencia Boulevard, Valencia, CA 91355   (805) 287-4444

PASTA PRIMAVERA - SPECIAL REQUEST

Sauteed mushrooms, carrots, tomatoes, broccoli, pinenuts, white wine, basil, olive oil and fresh garlic tossed with penne pasta. Request light oil (½ oz).

✓ CALORIES: Low (463)   ✓✓ CHOLESTEROL: Very Low (47 mg)
✓ FAT: Low* (17 g)   ✓✓ SODIUM: Very Low (67 mg) **
Diabetic Exchanges: 2¾ Bread, 3¼ Veg, 2¾ Fat

DIJON MUSTARD BOWTIE PASTA - SPECIAL REQUEST

Chicken, garlic, mushrooms, and onions with a Dijon - white wine sauce over bowtie pasta. Request light oil (½ oz).

✓ CALORIES: Low (599)   ✓ CHOLESTEROL: Low (144 mg)
✓ FAT: Low (20 g)   SODIUM: Moderate (699 mg) **
Diabetic Exchanges: 5 Meat (extra lean), 2½ Bread, 3 Veg, 2¾ Fat

CHEESELESS PIZZA (½ PIZZA)

Broccoli, mushrooms, sundried tomatoes, onions and grilled eggplant. Analysis is for ½ pizza.

✓ CALORIES: Low (409)   ✓✓ CHOLESTEROL: None (0 mg)
✓ FAT: Low* (11 g)   SODIUM: Moderate (628 mg) **
Diabetic Exchanges: 2½ Bread, 1½ Veg, 2 Fat

COUNTRY HERB CHICKEN

Marinated chicken breast broiled with herbs and spices, served with vegetables (request steamed vegetables, included in analysis) and herb-roasted potatoes (not included in analysis).

✓ CALORIES: Low (556)   CHOLESTEROL: Moderate (241 mg)
✓ FAT: Low (15 g)   ✓✓ SODIUM: Very Low (244 mg) **
Diabetic Exchanges: 12½ Meat (extra lean), 1¾ Veg, 1 Fat

✓ Low ✓✓ Very Low

          †Side dish guidelines are 1/3 of entree guidelines

**At Sizzler locations in
the Los Angeles Area**

Sizzler is famous for affordable, delicious and comfortable family dining. Our grill menu features fresh, lean steaks that are hand cut daily, and boneless skinless breast of chicken that is marinated and grilled to perfection. Our salad bar offers even more variety. From fresh fruit, crisp vegetables and tasty salads to pasta with marinara sauce and hot, steaming soups, our salad bar offers an endless variety of delicious, healthy meals that you can select to suit your tastes and nutritional needs. At Sizzler, delicious healthy dining sounds good. $

LEMON-HERB CHICKEN# PLATTER
Two tender breasts of chicken marinated in lemon and herbs.

✓✓ CALORIES: Very Low (274)   ✓ CHOLESTEROL: Low (144 mg)
✓✓ FAT: Very Low (3 g)   ✓ SODIUM: Low (515 mg)
Diabetic Exch: 8 Meat (extra lean)

HIBACHI CHICKEN# PLATTER
Two delicious chicken breasts broiled and basted with Hibachi sauce.

✓✓ CALORIES: Very Low (318)   ✓ CHOLESTEROL: Low (144 mg)
✓✓ FAT: Very Low (4 g)   SODIUM: High (1770 mg)
Diabetic Exch: 8 Meat (extra lean)

TROUT - SPECIAL REQUEST
Request prepared <u>without buttery oil</u>.

✓✓ CALORIES: Very Low (317)   ✓ CHOLESTEROL: Low (123 mg)
✓ FAT: Low* (14 g)   ✓✓ SODIUM: Very Low (207 mg) **
Diabetic Exch: 6¼ Meat

BROILED SHRIMP PLATTER - SPECIAL REQUEST
Delicately seasoned broiled shrimp. Request prepared <u>without buttery oil</u>.

✓✓ CALORIES: Very Low (218)   CHOLESTEROL: Moderate (306 mg)
✓✓ FAT: Very Low* (4 g)   SODIUM: Moderate (686 mg)
Diabetic Exch: 5¾ Meat (extra lean)

SIZZLER'S FAMOUS SOUP AND SALAD BAR *(selections may vary)*

✓✓ **Very Low**
(Under 20 calories and 1 g fat per ¼ cup serving)

Alfalfa sprouts	Lemon wedges
Broccoli	Beets
Cucumbers	Jicama
Sliced onion	Lettuce
Mushrooms	Red cabbage
Tomatoes	Zucchini
Spinach	Red & green peppers
Seasonal fresh fruit	

✓ **Low**
(Under 70 calories and 2 g fat per ¼ cup serving)

Croutons
Garbanzo beans
Salsa
Kidney beans
Pasta (plain)
Cottage cheese (low-fat)
Chicken vegetable soup

Recommended Toppings: Low-cal Italian dressing, Low-cal French dressing, Salsa

Nutrition analysis for chicken supplied by Overhill Farms
* Primarily unsaturated fat
** If you request no added salt

California Cuisine

Opened in 1982, Spago is located on Sunset Boulevard in the heart of West Hollywood. Spago specializes in a variety of wonderfully-prepared pastas, pizzas, and signature entrees created by Wolfgang Puck. Barbara Lazaroff's "quintessential California Cafe", with its open dining area and exhibition kitchen, is one of the most popular restaurants in the world. $$$

Spago   1114 Horn Avenue, West Hollywood, CA 90069   (310) 652-4025

CHOPPED CHINO FARM VEGETABLE SALAD

✓✓ CALORIES: Very Low (229)   ✓✓ CHOLESTEROL: Very Low (2 mg)
✓ FAT: Low* (20 g)   ✓✓ SODIUM: Very Low (124 mg) **
Diabetic Exchanges: 2 Veg, 4 Fat

GRILLED LOUISIANA SHRIMP - SPECIAL REQUEST

with spicy fettucini and curried summer vegetables. Request light butter and oil (½ Tbs. each) and parmesan cheese served on the side (cheese not included in analysis).

CALORIES: Moderate (632)   CHOLESTEROL: Moderate (265 mg)
✓ FAT: Low (17 g)   ✓ SODIUM: Low (431 mg) **
Diabetic Exchanges: 2½ Meat (extra lean), 3 Bread, 4 Veg, ¼ Fruit, 3¼ Fat

GRILLED BIG-EYE TUNA - SPECIAL REQUEST

with roasted vegetable vinaigrette. Request light oil (½ oz).

✓ CALORIES: Low (483)   ✓✓ CHOLESTEROL: Very Low (89 mg)
✓ FAT: Low (16 g)   ✓✓ SODIUM: Very Low (156 mg) **
Diabetic Exchanges: 6½ Meat (extra lean), 4¼ Veg, 2¾ Fat

PIZZA WITH ARTICHOKES, SHIITAKE MUSHROOMS, EGGPLANT AND CARAMELIZED GARLIC (2/3 PIZZA) - SPECIAL REQUEST

Request light cheese (½ normal amount). Analysis is for 2/3 of a whole pizza.

✓ CALORIES: Low (515)   ✓✓ CHOLESTEROL: Very Low (54 mg)
✓ FAT: Low (20 g)   SODIUM: Moderate (769 mg) **
Diabetic Exchanges: 1¾ Meat, 3 Bread, 2¾ Veg, 3 Fat

✓ Low ✓✓ Very Low

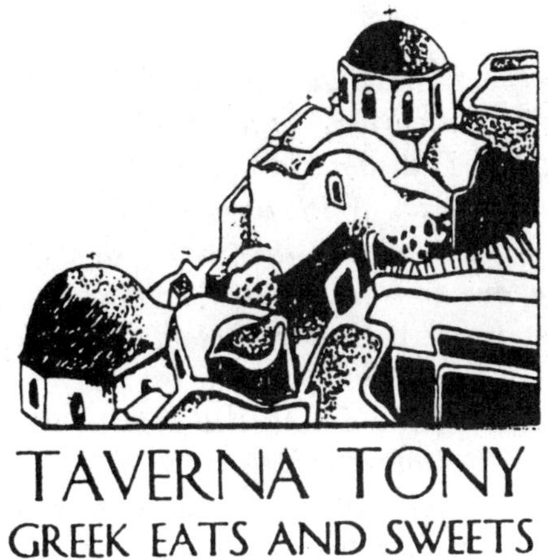

At long last, a Greek eatery in Malibu! "Award Winning on two continents, Chef Tony creates authentic Greek Cuisine for Malibu." Fabulous food, authentic Greek dancing, romantic ambiance and music. OPA! $$

Taverna Tony

GREEK EATS AND SWEETS
23410 Civic Center Way
Malibu, CA 90265
(310) 317-9667   FAX (310) 317-9991

LINGUINI ANIXIATIKO

Linguini topped with an array of spring vegetables, light tomato sauce, aromatic spices, and feta cheese. Request cheese on the side and use sparingly (not included in analysis).

✓ CALORIES: Low (600)   ✓✓ CHOLESTEROL: None (0 mg)
✓ FAT: Low* (16 g)   ✓✓ SODIUM: Very Low (39 mg) **
Diabetic Exchanges: 5¾ Bread, 2¼ Veg, 2¾ Fat

GRILLED CENTER-CUT SWORDFISH - REQUEST LIGHT OIL

with olive oil, lemon, garlic, and fresh oregano. Request light oil (½ Tbs).

✓ CALORIES: Low (371)   ✓✓ CHOLESTEROL: Very Low (99 mg)
✓ FAT: Low* (17 g)   ✓✓ SODIUM: Very Low (228 mg) **
Diabetic Exchanges: 7 Meat, 1¼ Fat

CHICKEN BREAST SOUVLAKI - REQUEST LIGHT OIL

Tender cubes of skinless, boneless chicken, flavored with a hint of garlic, oregano, and lemon. Request light oil (½ Tbs).

✓ CALORIES: Low (546)   CHOLESTEROL: Moderate (231 mg)
✓ FAT: Low (17 g)   ✓✓ SODIUM: Very Low (204 mg) **
Diabetic Exchanges: 12 Meat, 1½ Veg, 1¼ Fat

GRILLED VEGETABLE PLATTER - REQUEST LIGHT OIL

Eggplant, zucchini, bell peppers, tomatoes, mushrooms, spring onions and more! Brushed with olive oil and lemon. Request light oil (1 Tbs).

✓ CALORIES: Low (367)   ✓✓ CHOLESTEROL: None (0 mg)
✓ FAT: Low* (15 g)   ✓✓ SODIUM: Very Low (34 mg) **
Diabetic Exchanges: 1½ Bread, 4½ Veg, 2¾ Fat

Note: Main dishes are served with vegetables, roasted potatoes and rice pilaf which are not included in the analysis shown above.

* Primarily unsaturated fat
** If you request no added salt

Tower Restaurant

1150 South Olive Street, Los Angeles, CA 90015   (213) 746-1554

GAZPACHO (APPETIZER)†

✓✓ CALORIES: Very Low (91)   ✓✓ CHOLESTEROL: None (0 mg)
✓ FAT: Low* (5 g)   SODIUM: High (426 mg) **
Diabetic Exchanges: 2 Veg, 1 Fat

STEAMED ALASKAN HALIBUT WITH SPINACH
Served with rice (included in analysis).

✓ CALORIES: Low (423)   ✓✓ CHOLESTEROL: Very Low (54 mg)
✓ FAT: Low* (18 g)   ✓ SODIUM: Low (382 mg) **
Diabetic Exchanges: 5 Meat (extra lean), 1 Bread, 1½ Veg, 2¾ Fat

POACHED SALMON WITH A CUCUMBER DILL SAUCE
*Served with steamed asparagus (included in analysis) and steamed
red potatoes (additional 105 calories, no fat or cholesterol, 6 mg. sodium).*

✓ CALORIES: Low (558)   ✓ CHOLESTEROL: Low (112 mg)
✓ FAT: Low* (18 g)   ✓✓ SODIUM: Very Low (199 mg) **
Diabetic Exchanges: 8¾ Meat (extra lean), 3½ Veg, ½ Milk, ½ Fruit

POACHED BREAST OF CHICKEN
*stuffed with vegetables in a ginger herb broth, and served with steamed asparagus (included
in analysis) and white rice (additional 132 calories, no fat or cholesterol, 2 mg. sodium).*

✓ CALORIES: Low (560)   CHOLESTEROL: Moderate (241 mg)
✓ FAT: Low* (11 g)   ✓ SODIUM: Low (338 mg) **
Diabetic Exchanges: 13 Meat (extra lean), 3 Veg

✓ Low ✓✓ Very Low

     †Side dish guidelines are 1/3 of entree guidelines

TWIN  PALMS

Twin Palms is an enormous outdoor restaurant in Old Town Pasadena, surrounded by a white-washed wall and anchored by two century-old palm trees. Chef Michael Roberts' menu presents the simple, rustic foods of the Mediterranean countryside of Provence -- French home cooking, robust and abundant. Seating 400, the bustling place has the air of a village square in the south of France, complete with two bars, an open-air rotisserie and grill, and an outdoor bandstand featuring a cabaret of live entertainment. Open for lunch and dinner every day, Saturday afternoon tea, Sunday Brunch, and available for private parties. $$

Twin Palms 101 West Green Street, Pasadena, CA 91105 (818) 57-PALMS

ROTISSERIE ROSEMARY TURKEY - SPECIAL REQUEST

with warm escarole and bread salad. Analysis includes roasted potatoes.
Request sauce on the side and use sparingly (not included in analysis).

✓ CALORIES: Low (443) ✓✓ CHOLESTEROL: Very Low (94 mg)
✓ FAT: Low (18 g) SODIUM: High (1077 mg)
Diabetic Exchanges: 5 Meat (extra lean), 2 Bread, 3¼ Fat

ROTISSERIE CHICKEN - SPECIAL REQUEST

with wilted escarole and roasted garlic. Request chicken without skin and boiled potatoes instead of gratin potatoes (potatoes not included in analysis).

✓ CALORIES: Low (577) ✓ CHOLESTEROL: Low (168 mg)
✓ FAT: Low (20 g) SODIUM: High (2069 mg)
Diabetic Exchanges: 8¾ Meat (extra lean), ¼ Bread, ¾ Veg, 2½ Fat

GRAND VEGETABLE AIOLI WITH GRILLED SHRIMP - SPECIAL REQUEST

A platter of grilled seasonal vegetables served with a ramekin of intensely garlicky mayonnaise. Request light oil (1 Tbs). Analysis does not include sauce - use sparingly.

✓✓ CALORIES: Very Low (347) CHOLESTEROL: Moderate (221 mg)
✓ FAT: Low* (20 g) ✓✓ SODIUM: Very Low (292 mg)
Diabetic Exchanges: 3¼ Meat (extra lean), 2¾ Veg, 3½ Fat

BOUILLABAISSE

The famous fish stew from the south of France - rich with the flavors of tomato and saffron. Rouille garnish not included in analysis.

✓ CALORIES: Low (563) CHOLESTEROL: Moderate (209 mg)
✓ FAT: Low* (13 g) SODIUM: High (2084 mg)
Diabetic Exchanges: 8¾ Meat (extra lean), ½ Bread, 2 Veg, 1 Fat

* Primarily unsaturated fat
** If you request no added salt

Truly one of the unique dining landmarks in Southern California, this world-famous eatery has catered to the famous and the famished for over 25 years. Dine over the water, view the 6,000 private yachts, and enjoy the mouth-watering international menu with its fresh seafood, unique pastas, and dishes from the Mediterranean and Wine-Countries of California, all at moderate prices. The Warehouse is known as Marina del Rey's showplace where live entertainment is featured 7 days a week, and has received the Restaurant Critic's Award. Lunch and dinner daily, and enormous Saturday and Sunday champagne brunches. $$

The Warehouse   4499 Admiralty Way, Marina del Rey, CA 90292   (310) 823-5451

CHARBROILED SWORDFISH WITH PAPAYA SALSA

✓✓ CALORIES: Very Low (329)   ✓✓ CHOLESTEROL: Very Low (88 mg)
✓✓ FAT: Very Low* (10 g)   ✓✓ SODIUM: Very Low (237 mg) **
Diabetic Exchanges: 6 Meat (extra lean), 1¼ Veg

SEAFOOD BROCHETTE

Canadian scallops, Malaysian shrimp, Mako shark, bell peppers and sweet onions under a light Oriental glaze. Served with steamed vegetables (included in analysis) and rice (not included in analysis).

✓ CALORIES: Low (463)   CHOLESTEROL: Moderate (273 mg)
✓ FAT: Low (18 g)   SODIUM: High (1254 mg) **
Diabetic Exchanges: 7 Meat (extra lean), 1¾ Veg, 2¼ Fat

PASTA ROMA - SPECIAL REQUEST

Fresh scallops, shrimp, sauteed in olive oil, chardonnay, garlic, cilantro, tomatoes, and shitake mushrooms served over angel hair pasta. <u>Request light oil</u> (½ oz.).

✓ CALORIES: Low (509)   CHOLESTEROL: Moderate (204 mg)
✓ FAT: Low* (16 g)   ✓ SODIUM: Low (380 mg) **
Diabetic Exchanges: 5 Meat (extra lean), 2¼ Bread, ½ Veg, 2¾ Fat

SEAFOOD SERENADE - SPECIAL REQUEST

Medley of Gulf shrimp, Canadian snow crab and garden vegetables with raspberry vinaigrette. <u>Request dressing on the side and use sparingly</u> (not included in analysis).

✓✓ CALORIES: Very Low (230)   CHOLESTEROL: Moderate (297 mg)
✓✓ FAT: Very Low* (2 g)   SODIUM: Moderate (889 mg) **
Diabetic Exchanges: 4¾ Meat (extra lean), 1½ Veg

POACHED SALMON WITH PAPAYA SALSA

Served with steamed vegetables (included in analysis) and rice (not included).

✓ CALORIES: Low (486)   ✓ CHOLESTEROL: Low (144 mg)
✓ FAT: Low* (19 g)   ✓✓ SODIUM: Very Low (187 mg) **
Diabetic Exchanges: 8 Meat, 2¼ Veg

✓ Low   ✓✓ Very Low
†Side dish guidelines are 1/3 of entree guidelines

If you have a penchant for the finest quality seafood, in a chic non-pretentious atmosphere, the Water Grill is your E-ticket to paradise. Located in downtown Los Angeles next to the world famous Biltmore Hotel, the Water Grill is now the city's most decorated seafood emporium. Executive Chef Allyson Thurber masterfully blends the finest and freshest seafood and shellfish available with her own unique savoir-faire. Come join those who know, and have a meal worth remembering at the Water Grill. $$

Water Grill　　544 S. Grand, Los Angeles, CA 90071　　　　(213) 891-0900

BAJA CHOWDER
Hearty chowder with an assortment of fish, black beans and corn. (Bowl sized serving)

✓✓ CALORIES: Very Low (227)　✓✓ CHOLESTEROL: Very Low (55 mg)
✓✓ FAT: Very Low* (3 g)　　　✓ SODIUM: Low (419 mg)
Diabetic Exchanges: 2 Meat (extra lean), 1½ Bread, 2 Veg, ¼ Fat

PLANKED WHITEFISH WITH TOMATO BASIL SALSA

✓✓ CALORIES: Very Low (339)　✓✓ CHOLESTEROL: Very Low (46 mg)
✓✓ FAT: Very Low* (5 g)　　　✓✓ SODIUM: Very Low (231 mg)
Diabetic Exchanges: 3¼ Meat (extra lean), 1½ Bread, 3½ Veg

SEARED ONO
in an aromatic lemongrass-miso broth with soba noodles.

✓ CALORIES: Low (383)　　　✓✓ CHOLESTEROL: Very Low (76 mg)
✓✓ FAT: Very Low* (4 g)　　　SODIUM: Moderate (959 mg) **
Diabetic Exchanges: 5½ Meat (extra lean), ¾ Bread, 1 Veg, ¼ Fruit

GRILLED MAHI MAHI WITH TOMATO GINGER CHUTNEY
Served with Japanese jasmine rice (included in analysis).

✓✓ CALORIES: Very Low (282)　✓ CHOLESTEROL: Low (103 mg)
✓✓ FAT: Very Low* (7 g)　　　✓✓ SODIUM: Very Low (208 mg)
Diabetic Exchanges: 3½ Meat (extra lean), 1¼ Bread, ½ Veg, 1 Fat

ROASTED CANADIAN HALIBUT - REQUEST DRESSING ON THE SIDE
Request dressing on the side (not included in analysis).

✓✓ CALORIES: Very Low (259)　✓✓ CHOLESTEROL: Very Low (54 mg)
✓✓ FAT: Very Low* (4 g)　　　✓✓ SODIUM: Very Low (163 mg) **
Diabetic Exchanges: 5 Meat (extra lean), ¾ Bread, ½ Veg

PACIFIC NORTHWEST VEGETABLES†

✓ CALORIES: Low (165)　　　✓✓ CHOLESTEROL: None (0 mg)
FAT: Moderate* (14 g)　　　✓ SODIUM: Low (151 mg)
Diabetic Exchanges: 1 Veg, ¼ Bread, 2¾ Fat

---

* Primarily unsaturated fat
** If you request no added salt

THE FRESH CHINESE FOOD EXPERIENCE

Wok Spirit delivers contemporary Chinese food to your home or office. Our menu offers over 75 deliciously fresh, clean tasting dishes all prepared to order without MSG. All of our ingredients are gourmet quality, and you may request several of our dishes to be prepared WOK SMART ® (available without oil) for an even healthier approach to Chinese. $

WOK SPIRIT   1-800-477-4748
21917 Ventura Blvd., Woodland Hills, CA 91364

CHINESE GARDEN (½ SERVING) - REQUEST WOK SMART ®

Steamed fresh broccoli, carrots, peppers, mushrooms, pea pods, bok choy and water chestnuts. Request WOK SMART (prepared without oil). Analysis is for ½ serving (8 oz.) with 8 oz. steamed rice. Wok Spirit Peanut Sauce served on the side (see below).

- ✓ CALORIES: Low (364)
- ✓✓ FAT: Very Low* (1 g)
- ✓✓ CHOLESTEROL: None (0 mg)
- ✓✓ SODIUM: Very Low (40 mg)

Diabetic Exchanges: 4¼ Bread, 2 Veg

PEANUT SAUCE (1 TBS.): 30 calories, 2 g fat, 0 cholesterol, 220 mg sodium.

CHICKEN WITH CHINESE VEGETABLES (½ SERVING) - REQUEST WOK SMART ®

Sliced chicken breast with fresh broccoli, carrots, mushrooms, red bell peppers, and Oriental Vegetables, delicately flavored with chicken stock, garlic and ginger. Request WOK SMART (prepared without oil). Analysis is for ½ serving (8 oz.) with 8 oz. steamed rice.

- ✓ CALORIES: Low (489)
- ✓✓ FAT: Very Low (5 g)
- ✓✓ CHOLESTEROL: Very Low (48 mg)
- SODIUM: Moderate (691 mg)

Diabetic Exchanges: 2½ Meat (extra lean), 4¼ Bread, 1¾ Veg, ½ Fat

SPICY CHICKEN WITH BROCCOLI (½ SERVING) - REQUEST WOK SMART ®

Sliced chicken breast and fresh broccoli in our flavorful spicy garlic sauce. Request WOK SMART (prepared without oil). Analysis is for ½ serving (8 oz.) with 8 oz. steamed rice.

- ✓ CALORIES: Low (496)
- ✓✓ FAT: Very Low (5 g)
- ✓✓ CHOLESTEROL: Very Low (48 mg)
- SODIUM: Moderate (869 mg)

Diabetic Exchanges: 2½ Meat (extra lean), 4¼ Bread, 1¾ Veg, ½ Fat

KUNG PAO CHICKEN (½ SERVING)

Tender pieces of chicken wok-tossed with Szechuan chili peppers, carrots and bell peppers in a spicy chili sauce, sprinkled with crunchy roasted peanuts. Analysis is for ½ serving (8 oz.) with 8 oz. steamed rice.

- CALORIES: Moderate (665)
- ✓ FAT: Low (20 g)
- ✓✓ CHOLESTEROL: Very Low (48 mg)
- SODIUM: Moderate (888 mg)

Diabetic Exchanges: 2½ Meat (extra lean), 4¼ Bread, 1¾ Veg, 3½ Fat

VEGETABLE LO MEIN (½ SERVING)

Soft noodles wok-tossed with mixed Oriental Vegetables stir-fried in a light flavorful sauce. Analysis for ½ serving (8 oz.).

- ✓✓ CALORIES: Very Low (303)
- ✓✓ FAT: Very Low* (9 g)
- ✓✓ CHOLESTEROL: Very Low (<1 mg)
- SODIUM: Moderate (789 mg)

Diabetic Exchanges: 2 Bread, 1½ Veg, 1½ Fat

HOT & SOUR SOUP (½ SERVING, 8 OZ.)†

Spicy broth with chicken, vegetables, mushrooms, tofu and waterchestnuts, sprinkled with green onions.

- ✓✓ CALORIES: Very Low (97)
- ✓✓ FAT: Very Low (3 g)
- ✓✓ CHOLESTEROL: Very Low (23 mg)
- SODIUM: High (731 mg)

Diabetic Exchanges: ¾ Meat, ¾ Bread, ½ Veg, ¼ Fat

Nutrition information for sauces supplied by Wok Spirit Restaurant

✓ Low ✓✓ Very Low
†Side dish guidelines are 1/3 of entree guidelines

w o r l d   c a f e

• S A N T A   M O N I C A •

An expansive patio setting for al fresco dining welcomes guests to World Cafe, located on Santa Monica's popular Main Street. Only the freshest ingredients are used in creating the menu, which has something for all tastes. World Cafe is known for wood-fired pizzas, great pastas, excellent fish, chicken and meat items, an outstanding brunch on weekends, and lunch and dinner Tuesday through Sunday. Live entertainment every night and during weekend brunch. $$

World Cafe 2820 Main Street, Santa Monica, CA 90405   (310) 392-1661

GRILLED VEGETABLE PIZZA (CHEESELESS)

✓ CALORIES: Low (596)   ✓✓ CHOLESTEROL: None (0 mg)
✓ FAT: Low* (16 g)   SODIUM: High (1288 mg) **
Diabetic Exchanges: 5¼ Bread, 2 Veg, 2¾ Fat

SEARED PEPPER CRUSTED TUNA

with lemon ginger sauce. Served with rice (included in analysis).

✓ CALORIES: Low (539)   ✓ CHOLESTEROL: Low (102 mg)
✓ FAT: Low* (11 g)   SODIUM: Moderate (910 mg) **
Diabetic Exchanges: 7¼ Meat (extra lean), 3 Bread, 1½ Fat

STEAMED VEGETABLE PLATE WITH TOFU

✓✓ CALORIES: Very Low (265)   ✓✓ CHOLESTEROL: None (0 mg)
✓ FAT: Low* (17 g)   ✓✓ SODIUM: Very Low (77 mg) **
Diabetic Exchanges: 1¾ Meat, 1¾ Bread, 3 Veg, 2¾ Fat

SPICY VEGETABLE BOWTIE PASTA (HALF-ORDER SIZE)

Request Parmesan cheese on the side (not included in analysis).
Analysis is for the ½-order size (9 oz).

✓ CALORIES: Low (527)   ✓✓ CHOLESTEROL: Very Low (85 mg)
✓ FAT: Low* (16 g)   ✓✓ SODIUM: Very Low (243 mg) **
Diabetic Exchanges: 4½ Bread, 1 Veg, 2¼ Fat

GRILLED SWORDFISH - SPECIAL REQUEST

with sesame vegetable stir fry. Request light oil (½ Tbs).

✓ CALORIES: Low (462)   ✓✓ CHOLESTEROL: Very Low (89 mg)
✓ FAT: Low* (18 g)   ✓ SODIUM: Low (575 mg) **
Diabetic Exchanges: 5½ Meat (extra lean), 2½ Veg, 1½ Fat

* Primarily unsaturated fat
** If you request no added salt

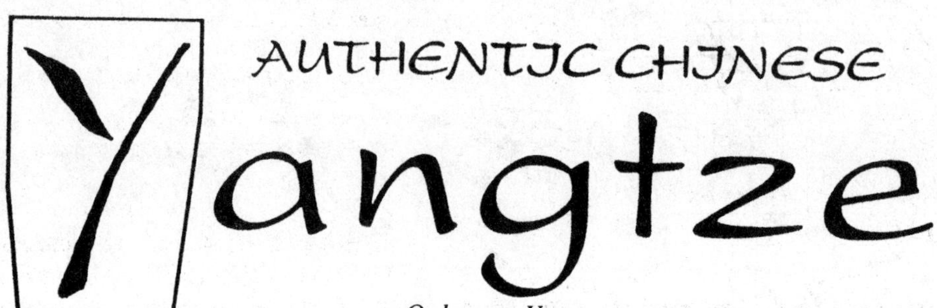

Only at Yangtze can you enjoy the diversity of *Chinese, Thai, Korean, and Japanese foods. All orders are made upon request with the finest gourmet ingredients possible. International wines and beers complement Yangtze's myriad of foods. Please inquire about our daily sushi bar specials. All dishes are available for pick-up or free delivery. Yangtze is a total handcrafted environment designed by the Santa Monica architecture firm of Coscia Day. $*

Yangtze 1333 3rd Street, Promenade, Santa Monica, CA 90401 (310) 260-1994

Please visit our new location: 58 East Colorado Blvd., Old Town, Pasadena (818) 405-1994

BANGKOK INFERNO WITH SHRIMP
A spicy combination of red bell peppers, onions, chilis, basil and garlic. Chicken also available.

✓✓ CALORIES: Very Low (190)   ✓ CHOLESTEROL: Low (174 mg)
✓✓ FAT: Very Low* (8 g)   SODIUM: Moderate (934 mg) **
Diabetic Exchanges: 2½ Meat (extra lean), ¼ Bread, ½ Veg, 1¼ Fat

JINGMEN HARVEST
A vegetarian delight of assorted sauteed Chinese vegetables in a regional brown sauce.

✓✓ CALORIES: Very Low (267)   ✓✓ CHOLESTEROL: Very Low (2 mg)
✓✓ FAT: Very Low* (8 g)   SODIUM: High (1659 mg) **
Diabetic Exchanges: 1½ Bread, 2¼ Veg, 1¼ Fat

BLACK BUTTERFLIES
Black mushrooms served on a field of Chinese cabbage in a white garlic sauce.

✓✓ CALORIES: Very Low (181)   ✓✓ CHOLESTEROL: Very Low (3 mg)
✓✓ FAT: Very Low* (8 g)   ✓✓ SODIUM: Very Low (204 mg) **
Diabetic Exchanges: 1½ Veg, 1¼ Fat

JINSHI PEPPERS WITH CHICKEN
A combination of red and green bell peppers sauteed in a garlic black bean sauce. Shrimp also available.

✓ CALORIES: Low (491)   ✓ CHOLESTEROL: Low (170 mg)
✓ FAT: Low (15 g)   SODIUM: Moderate (782 mg) **
Diabetic Exchanges: 8¾ Meat (extra lean), 1 Bread, 1 Veg, 1½ Fat

SUSHI OMAKASE (20 PIECES)

✓ CALORIES: Low (522)   ✓✓ CHOLESTEROL: Very Low (74 mg)
✓✓ FAT: Very Low* (8 g)   ✓ SODIUM: Low (354 mg) **
Diabetic Exchanges: 3 Meat (extra lean), 4¾ Bread, ½ Fat

✓ Low ✓✓ Very Low

 †Side dish guidelines are 1/3 of entree guidelines

For 9 years Zach's Italian Cafe has been <u>The</u> Neighborhood Italian Restaurant. Our food is fresh and tasty, our service is fast and friendly, and our atmosphere is comfortable. The menu offers a large variety of fresh salads, pastas, pizzas as well as seafood, chicken and other Italian specialties. Open for lunch & dinner Mon-Sat at 11:30 am and Sundays at 4 pm. Delivery, take-out and catering also available. All major credit cards accepted. Give us a try; you'll be happy you did! $

Zach's Italian Cafe

11056 Ventura Blvd., Studio City, CA 91604 (818) 762-4225

PIZZA ALTOBELLO - REQUEST EASY CHEESE (½ PIZZA)

Extra thin crusted. Mushrooms, eggplant, basil, cilantro with mozzarella, white cheddar
* *and parmesan. <u>Request easy cheese</u> (½ portion of cheese). Analysis is for ½ pizza.*

✓ CALORIES: Low (584)	✓✓ CHOLESTEROL: Very Low (44 mg)
✓ FAT: Low (20 g)	SODIUM: High (1443 mg) **

Diabetic Exchanges: 1½ Meat, 4¼ Bread, ¾ Veg, 2½ Fat

PASTA PRIMAVERA - REQUEST STEAMED

A medley of fresh broccoli, mushrooms, carrots, and snow peas - <u>request steamed</u>. Topped with diced red peppers and served with choice of pasta. Analysis is for regular sized serving.

✓ CALORIES: Low (398)	✓✓ CHOLESTEROL: Very Low (76 mg)
✓✓ FAT: Very Low* (3 g)	✓✓ SODIUM: Very Low (182 mg) **

Diabetic Exchanges: 4¼ Bread, 2¼ Veg

PASTA MARINARA

Tomatoes, garlic and Italian spices, masterfully combined to create this robust Italian classic. Analysis is for regular sized serving.

✓✓ CALORIES: Very Low (312)	✓✓ CHOLESTEROL: None (0 mg)
✓✓ FAT: Very Low* (3 g)	✓ SODIUM: Low (503 mg) **

Diabetic Exchanges: 4 Bread, 1 Veg

PASTA POMODORO - REQUEST LIGHT OIL

The classic dish made better - tomatoes, garlic, basil and extra virgin olive oil with just of touch of our marinara sauce. <u>Request light oil</u> (½ oz). Analysis is for a regular serving.

✓ CALORIES: Low (454)	✓✓ CHOLESTEROL: None (0 mg)
✓ FAT: Low* (17 g)	✓ SODIUM: Low (345 mg) **

Diabetic Exchanges: 4 Bread, 2 Veg, 2¾ Fat

CHINESE CHICKEN SALAD (DINNER SIZE) - REQUEST DRESSING ON THE SIDE

A California favorite. Fresh lettuce, sliced water chestnuts, mandarin oranges, chicken, rice noodles, cashews, and our homemade pineapple sesame dressing. <u>Request dressing on the side</u> and use sparingly (not included in analysis).

✓ CALORIES: Low (528)	✓✓ CHOLESTEROL: Very Low (48 mg)
✓ FAT: Low (20 g)	SODIUM: Moderate (655 mg) **

Diabetic Exchanges: 2½ Meat (extra lean), 2¼ Bread, ¼ Veg, ¼ Fruit, 3¾ Fat

---

* Primarily unsaturated fat
** If you request no added salt

Zenzero, located a stone's throw from the Pacific Ocean in Santa Monica, has been applauded by the country's foremost food critics for its delicious Cal-Asian cuisine. Renowned chef Kazuto Matsusaka uses only the finest quality ingredients to create an exotic, health-conscious menu where "East meets West." Sit in our architecturally award-winning main room or grab a little fresh air and dine "al fresco" on either of two terraces. The Zenzero experience is further enhanced by unparalleled service and a wine list recognized by Wine Spectator *with a 1994 Award of Excellence for its thoughtful offerings. $$$*

Zenzero 1535 Ocean Ave, Santa Monica, CA 90401 (310) 451-4455

CILANTRO CURED SALMON

accompanied by warm potato salad and salmon roe vinaigrette (included in analysis).

✓✓ CALORIES: Very Low (314)　　✓✓ CHOLESTEROL: Very Low (95 mg)
✓ FAT: Low* (14 g)　　✓✓ SODIUM: Very Low (242 mg) **
Diabetic Exchanges: 3¼ Meat, 1¼ Bread, 1¼ Fat

GLAZED LEMON PEPPER CHICKEN - REQUEST NO SKIN

Served with grilled vegetables and goat cheese potatoes (included in analysis).

✓ CALORIES: Low (600)　　✓ CHOLESTEROL: Low (179 mg)
✓ FAT: Low (20 g)　　✓ SODIUM: Low (514 mg) **
Diabetic Exchanges: 9 Meat (extra lean), 1 Bread, 2 Veg, 2½ Fat

GRILLED AHI TUNA

with tomato-corn salsa and grilled vegetables.

✓ CALORIES: Low (401)　　✓✓ CHOLESTEROL: Very Low (76 mg)
✓ FAT: Low* (18 g)　　✓✓ SODIUM: Very Low (121 mg) **
Diabetic Exchanges: 5½ Meat (extra lean), ½ Bread, 1 Veg, 3¼ Fat

CHILEAN SEABASS WITH BLACK BEAN CRUST - REQUEST SALSA ON THE SIDE

Request tomato salsa on the side and use sparingly (not included in analysis).

✓ CALORIES: Low (405)　　✓✓ CHOLESTEROL: Very Low (72 mg)
✓ FAT: Low* (14 g)　　　SODIUM: Moderate (921 mg) **
Diabetic Exchanges: 3½ Meat (extra lean), 1¼ Bread, ¾ Veg, 2 Fat

GRILLED SALMON

with sauteed shiitake and shimeji mushrooms, deglazed with Ponzu.

✓ CALORIES: Low (384)　　✓✓ CHOLESTEROL: Very Low (99 mg)
✓ FAT: Low* (18 g)　　　SODIUM: Moderate (802 mg) **
Diabetic Exchanges: 5½ Meat, ½ Bread, 1 Fat

✓ Low　✓✓ Very Low
†Side dish guidelines are 1/3 of entree guidelines

Fast Food,

Markets and Delis

Andree's Oven and Catering Company specializes in healthy and hearty gourmet foods, with many low-fat and fat-free items to choose from. Our goal is to provide great tasting food that is healthy, fast and affordable. Come in and try our unique house specialties. Something new is always cooking! $

Andree's Oven and Catering

23410 Civic Center Way #C-2, Malibu, CA 90265 (310) 456-8533

GARBANZO SPREAD AND PITA BREAD TRIANGLES (½ ORDER)
✓✓ CALORIES: Very Low (245) ✓✓ CHOLESTEROL: None (0 mg)
✓✓ FAT: Very Low* (3 g) SODIUM: Moderate (921 mg) **
Diabetic Exchanges: 3 Bread, ¼ Fat

LOW FAT CAESAR SALAD
Served on hearts of romaine, with Andree's special low-fat Caesar dressing and homemade croutons.
✓✓ CALORIES: Very Low (171) ✓✓ CHOLESTEROL: Very Low (<1 mg)
✓✓ FAT: Very Low* (7 g) SODIUM: Moderate (892 mg) **
Diabetic Exchanges: 1 Bread, ½ Veg, 1¼ Fat

LOW FAT CHICKEN BAJA ROLLS (2 ROLLS)
Flour tortilla, herb cream cheese, chicken breast, cheddar cheese, red bell pepper, green onion, celery, cilantro and mild Ortega chilies.
✓✓ CALORIES: Very Low (283) ✓✓ CHOLESTEROL: Very Low (24 mg)
✓✓ FAT: Very Low (10 g) SODIUM: Moderate (706 mg) **
Diabetic Exchanges: 1½ Meat (extra lean), 1½ Bread, ¼ Milk, 2¼ Fat

WILD MUSHROOM ALFREDO
With fat free cream, wild mushrooms and Reggiano parmesan.
✓ CALORIES: Low (600) ✓✓ CHOLESTEROL: Very Low (30 mg)
✓ FAT: Low (14 g) SODIUM: Moderate (798 mg) **
Diabetic Exchanges: 2 Meat, 4½ Bread, ½ Veg, 1½ Milk, 1½ Fat

TURKEY MEATLOAF
Served with fat free mashed potatoes and country gravy (included in analysis).
✓ CALORIES: Low (453) ✓✓ CHOLESTEROL: Very Low (57 mg)
✓ FAT: Low (13 g) SODIUM: High (1387 mg) **
Diabetic Exchanges: 3¼ Meat, 2½ Bread, 1 Veg, ½ Fat

DESSERT: ### PEACH AND BLUEBERRY COBBLER†
✓ CALORIES: Low (190) ✓✓ CHOLESTEROL: Very Low (1 mg)
✓✓ FAT: Very Low (1 g) SODIUM: Moderate (215 mg)
Diabetic Exchanges: 1¾ Bread, ¾ Fruit, ½ Fat

✓ Low ✓✓ Very Low

  †Side dish guidelines are 1/3 of entree guidelines

BRISTOL FARMS

Healthy eating is easy and pleasurable with the many fine foods available at Bristol Farms Markets. We offer the freshest, highest quality fruits and vegetables, delivered six days a week, fresh poultry and seafood, freshly baked whole gain breads and muffins, specially formulated Heart Healthy deli salads and entrees, tofu, low-fat yogurts, granolas and much more. $

Bristol Farms locations:

1570 Rosecrans Ave, Manhattan Beach, CA 90266 (310) 643-5229
837 Silver Spur Rd, Rolling Hills Estates, CA 90274 (310) 541-9157
606 Fair Oaks Avenue, Pasadena, CA 91031 (818) 441-5450

Items below are available in the deli:

ORZO SALAD *(6 oz.)*

✓ CALORIES: Low (440) ✓✓ CHOLESTEROL: None (0 mg)
✓✓ FAT: Very Low (8 g) ✓✓ SODIUM: Very Low (250 mg)

CHEESE AND BASIL RICE *(6 oz.)*

✓✓ CALORIES: Very Low (180) ✓✓ CHOLESTEROL: Very Low (10 mg)
✓✓ FAT: Very Low (4 g) SODIUM: Moderate (720 mg)

SKINNY CHICKEN CHILI *(6 oz.)*

✓✓ CALORIES: Very Low (140) ✓✓ CHOLESTEROL: Very Low (10 mg)
✓✓ FAT: Very Low (4 g) ✓ SODIUM: Low (400 mg)

BY ALL BEANS *(6 oz.)*

✓✓ CALORIES: Very Low (300) ✓✓ CHOLESTEROL: None (0 mg)
✓✓ FAT: Very Low* (10 g) ✓ SODIUM: Low (320 mg)

CHICKEN POTATO SALAD *(6 oz.)*

✓✓ CALORIES: Very Low (200) ✓✓ CHOLESTEROL: Very Low (30 mg)
✓✓ FAT: Very Low (10 g) ✓✓ SODIUM: Very Low (280 mg)

Nutrition information supplied by Bristol Farms.

* Primarily unsaturated fat
** If you request no added salt

Years before the trend toward "nutritious" fast food, El Pollo Loco provided health-conscious consumers a variety of menu choices, including, of course, our one and only flame-broiled chicken. Today we are still the nutrition leader in fast food and have an entire menu dedicated to selections that are health-consciously prepared. $

El Pollo Loco

with hundreds of Southern California locations!

CHICKEN COMBO MEAL
Information is for 2 pieces of chicken.
✓✓ CALORIES: Very Low (310)   ✓✓ CHOLESTEROL: Very Low (80 mg)
✓ FAT: Low (18 g)   ✓ SODIUM: Low (460 mg) **
Diabetic Exchanges: 5¼ Meat, ½ Fat

RECOMMENDED SIDE DISHES
Very Low in calories, fat and cholesterol:
Salsa *(very low sodium)*   Rice *(moderate sodium)*
Corn Tortillas *(very low sodium)*   Corn *(low sodium)*
Beans *(not advised for low salt diets)*

FLAME-BROILED CHICKEN SALAD
Analysis does not include dressing; use sparingly.
✓✓ CALORIES: Very Low (200)   ✓✓ CHOLESTEROL: Very Low (approx. 50 mg)
✓✓ FAT: Very Low (3 g)   ✓ SODIUM: Low (375 mg) **
Diabetic Exchanges: 3½ Meat (extra lean), ¾ Bread

CHICKEN TACO
✓✓ CALORIES: Very Low (170)   ✓✓ CHOLESTEROL: Very Low (25 mg)
✓✓ FAT: Very Low (5 g)   ✓ SODIUM: Low (400 mg) **
Diabetic Exchanges: 1½ Meat, 1 Bread

CLASSIC CHICKEN BURRITO
✓ CALORIES: Low (480)   ✓✓ CHOLESTEROL: Very Low (50 mg)
✓ FAT: Low (12 g)   SODIUM: High (1275 mg)
Diabetic Exchanges: 2½ Meat, 4¼ Bread, 1 Fat

BEANS, RICE & CHEESE BURRITO
✓ CALORIES: Low (530)   ✓✓ CHOLESTEROL: Very Low (15 mg)
✓ FAT: Low (13 g)   SODIUM: Moderate (730 mg)
Diabetic Exchanges: 1½ Meat, 3½ Bread, 1 Fat

✓ Low ✓✓ Very Low
†Side dish guidelines are 1/3 of entree guidelines

JACK IN THE BOX® prepares food that not only tastes great, but also provides the nutritional balance that people are looking for. We cook with only 100% cholesterol-free vegetable oil, a soybean/cottonseed blend that contains no tropical oils, and is low in saturated fat. And we're looking out for you with lowfat milk, farm fresh vegetables in our sandwiches and salads, and reduced calorie dressing. JACK IN THE BOX® has only one mission: to continually create the most exciting, best tasting fast food anywhere. $

CHICKEN TERIYAKI BOWL

Strips of teriyaki-marinated chicken breast, broccoli florets, carrots and teriyaki sauce, all served on a bed of steamed white rice.

✓ CALORIES: Low (580) ✓✓ CHOLESTEROL: Very Low (30 mg)
✓✓ FAT: Very Low (1½ g) SODIUM: High (1220 mg)
Diabetic Exch: ½+ Meat, 6 Bread, 2½ Veg

CHICKEN FAJITA PITA

Tender chunks of all white meat chicken, natural cheddar cheese, tomatoes & lettuce. All in a pita pocket and all less than 300 calories. Served with guacamole (use sparingly) or salsa on the side (not included in analysis).

✓✓ CALORIES: Very Low (290) ✓✓ CHOLESTEROL: Very Low (35 mg)
✓✓ FAT: Very Low (8 g) SODIUM: Moderate (700 mg)
Diabetic Exch: 2 Meat, 2 Bread

GRILLED CHICKEN FILLET

Tender, boneless breast of chicken, lightly seasoned and grilled. Topped with cheese, tomatoes, lettuce and sauce on a toasted wheat bun.

✓ CALORIES: Low (430) ✓✓ CHOLESTEROL: Very Low (65 mg)
✓ FAT: Low (19 g) SODIUM: High (1070 mg)
Diabetic Exch: 3 Meat, 2 Bread, 1 Fat

GARDEN CHICKEN SALAD

Iceberg & Romaine lettuce with strips of marinated chicken breast, natural cheddar cheese, fresh carrots and tomatoes. Served with choice of dressing and croutons (not included in analysis).

✓✓ CALORIES: Very Low (200) ✓✓ CHOLESTEROL: Very Low (65 mg)
✓✓ FAT: Very Low (9 g) ✓ SODIUM: Low (420 mg)
Diabetic Exchanges: 3 Meat, 1 Veg, 1 Fat

Nutrition information supplied by JACK IN THE BOX®

* Primarily unsaturated fat
** If you request no added salt

Inspired by the famous street taquerias of Mexico City, La Salsa has grown to be Southern California's favorite family of Mexican restaurants. We serve only the freshest, healthiest gourmet food that is truly authentic. All of our meat is 95% fat-free and we use only canola or peanut oils. We make over 1 ton of fresh salsa daily and can accommodate most vegetarian requests. Customize your dish with the unique flavors found in our fresh salsa bar. Every La Salsa restaurant also features an enthusiastic staff that wants to share with you the wonderful Mexican tradition of food and hospitality. $

La Salsa - Los Angeles County Locations:

Beverly Hills: 9631 Little Santa Monica	(310) 276-2373	Northridge: 9084 Tampa Avenue	(818) 772-8530
Brentwood: 11740 San Vicente Blvd.	(310) 826-7337	Pasadena: 44 N. Fair Oaks	(818) 793-0732
Canoga Park: 6600 Topanga Cyn. Blvd.	(818) 716-7012	Redondo Beach:	
Glendale: 1144 Glendale Galleria	(818) 548-5341	2790 Manhattan Beach Blvd.	(310) 793-9444
Long Beach: 245 Pine Avenue	(310) 491-1104	Santa Monica: 1401 3rd Street	(310) 587-0755
Los Angeles: Beverly Center	(310) 854-3987	Studio City: 12048 Ventura Blvd.	(818) 760-0797
727 West 7th Street	(213) 892-8227	Torrance: 24223 Crenshaw Blvd.	(310) 326-1444
3460 Wilshire Blvd.	(213) 487-4210	West Los Angeles: 11075 W. Pico Bl.	(310) 479-0919
Malibu: 22800 Pacific Coast Hwy.	(310) 456-6299	11901 Santa Monica Blvd.	(310) 473-7880
Montebello: 1604 Montebello Town Ctr.	(213) 722-7172	Westwood: 1154 Westwood Blvd.	(310) 208-7083

Chips not included in analyses below.

FISH TACO (SONORA STYLE)

✓✓ CALORIES: Very Low (236)   ✓✓ CHOLESTEROL: Very Low (36 mg)
✓✓ FAT: Very Low* (8 g)   ✓ SODIUM: Low (484 mg)
Diabetic Exchanges: 1¼ Meat, 1½ Bread, 1 Fat

VEGETARIAN TACO

✓✓ CALORIES: Very Low (292)   ✓✓ CHOLESTEROL: Very Low (7 mg)
✓✓ FAT: Very Low (8 g)   ✓ SODIUM: Low (402 mg)
Diabetic Exchanges: ¼ Meat, 2½ Bread, ½ Veg, 1½ Fat

THE ORIGINAL GOURMET BURRITO

✓ CALORIES: Low (509)   ✓✓ CHOLESTEROL: Very Low (62 mg)
✓ FAT: Low (16 g)   SODIUM: Moderate (937 mg)
Diabetic Exchanges: 3 Bread, 4 Meat, 3¼ Fat

CALIFORNIA BURRITO
Request without avocado.

✓ CALORIES: Low (516)   ✓✓ CHOLESTEROL: Very Low (7 mg)
✓ FAT: Low (15 g)   SODIUM: High (1071 mg)
Diabetic Exchanges: 1 Meat, 5 Bread, ½ Veg, 2½ Fat

#1 COMBO: 2 TACO COMBO
Includes 2 chicken tacos, beans, rice and salad.

CALORIES: Moderate (694)   ✓✓ CHOLESTEROL: Very Low (68 mg)
✓ FAT: Low (13 g)   SODIUM: Moderate (854 mg)
Diabetic Exchanges: 4 Meat, 6¾ Bread, 1¼ Fat

Nutrition information supplied by La Salsa.

✓ Low ✓✓ Very Low

Mrs. Gooch's Whole Foods Market is dedicated to supplying the finest, most natural, wholesome foods available, including an ever-increasing selection of organically grown produce and products with organically grown ingredients. Our savory salads, delectable dressings, steamy soups, enticing entrees and many of our delicious baked goods are prepared in our own kitchen, using time honored recipes with no artificial flavors, artificial colors, artificial sweeteners or preservatives. $

Mrs. Gooch's Whole Foods Markets

Beverly Hills: 239 N. Crescent Drive, Beverly Hills, CA 90210 (310) 274-3360
Glendale: 826 N. Glendale Avenue, Glendale, CA 91206 (818) 240-9350
Northridge: 9350 Reseda Boulevard, Northridge, CA 91324 (818) 701-5122
Redondo Beach: 405 N. Pacific Coast Highway, Redondo Beach, CA 90277 (310) 376-6931
Sherman Oaks: 12905 Riverside Drive, Sherman Oaks, CA 91423 (818) 762-5548
Thousand Oaks: 451 Avenida de los Arboles, Thousand Oaks, CA 91360 (805) 492-5340
West Los Angeles: 3476 Centinela Avenue, Los Angeles, CA 90066 (310) 391-5209

Items below are available in the deli:

QUINOA AND BLACK BEANS *(½ lb. serving)*

✓✓ CALORIES: Very Low (302)   ✓✓ CHOLESTEROL: None (0 mg)
✓✓ FAT: Very Low* (7 g)   ✓ SODIUM: Low (560 mg) **
Diabetic Exchanges: 3¼ Bread, ¼ Veg, ¾ Fat

MEXICAN TUNA *(½ lb. serving)*

✓✓ CALORIES: Very Low (184)   ✓✓ CHOLESTEROL: Very Low (25 mg)
✓✓ FAT: Very Low* (3 g)   ✓✓ SODIUM: Very Low (118 mg) **
Diabetic Exchanges: 4¾ Meat (extra lean), ½ Veg

CARROT AND RAISIN SALAD *(½ lb. serving)*

✓ CALORIES: Low (381)   ✓✓ CHOLESTEROL: None (0 mg)
✓✓ FAT: Very Low (9 g)   ✓✓ SODIUM: Very Low (118 mg) **
Diabetic Exchanges: 2¾ Veg, 3¼ Fruit, 1½ Fat

LEMON HERB CHICKEN *(1 chicken breast)*

✓ CALORIES: Low (377)   ✓ CHOLESTEROL: Low (192 mg)
✓✓ FAT: Very Low (8 g)   ✓✓ SODIUM: Very Low (166 mg) **
Diabetic Exchanges: 10 Meat (extra lean)

BLACK BEAN CHILE *(½ lb. serving)*

✓✓ CALORIES: Very Low (223)   ✓✓ CHOLESTEROL: None (0 mg)
✓✓ FAT: Very Low* (8 g)   ✓✓ SODIUM: Very Low (236 mg) **
Diabetic Exchanges: 1 Bread, 1¼ Veg, 1 Fat

BLACK BEAN AND CORN RELISH *(½ lb. serving)*

✓✓ CALORIES: Very Low (142)   ✓✓ CHOLESTEROL: None (0 mg)
✓✓ FAT: Very Low* (1 g)   SODIUM: Moderate (617 mg) **
Diabetic Exchanges: 1½ Bread, ½ Veg

* Primarily unsaturated fat
** If you request no added salt

Ralphs Chef Express is pleased to provide nutrition information for those entrees, salads, and side dishes which serve as healthy, delicious choices for consumers concerned with their intake of calories, fat, cholesterol and/or sodium. Chef Express offers the highest quality foods available, at reasonable prices. All menu items are made fresh daily without preservatives, artificial ingredients or MSG. (Chef Express departments are not available at all Ralphs stores. For locations contact store management. Not all items available at all times). $

Ralphs at over 70 locations in the Los Angeles area.

GARLIC ROASTED CHICKEN *(6 oz. portion)*
✓✓ CALORIES: Very Low (197) ✓✓ CHOLESTEROL: Very Low (83 mg)
✓✓ FAT: Very Low (7 g) ✓✓ SODIUM: Very Low (70 mg)

VEGETARIAN LASAGNA *(6 oz. portion)*
✓✓ CALORIES: Very Low (199) ✓✓ CHOLESTEROL: Very Low (42 mg)
✓✓ FAT: Very Low (5 g) ✓ SODIUM: Low (416 mg)

SPICY MEXICAN CHICKEN SALAD *(6 oz. portion)*
✓✓ CALORIES: Very Low (209) ✓✓ CHOLESTEROL: Very Low (42 mg)
✓ FAT: Low (11 g) ✓✓ SODIUM: Very Low (140 mg)

FETTUCCINI WITH VEGETABLES† *(4 oz. portion)*
✓✓ CALORIES: Very Low (107) ✓✓ CHOLESTEROL: None (0 mg)
✓ FAT: Low (5 g) ✓ SODIUM: Low (104 mg)

FRESH FRUIT SALAD† *(4 oz. portion)*
✓✓ CALORIES: Very Low (96) ✓✓ CHOLESTEROL: None (0 mg)
✓✓ FAT: None (0 g) ✓✓ SODIUM: Very Low (9 mg)

GARLIC ROASTED POTATOES† *(4 oz. portion)*
✓✓ CALORIES: Very Low (94) ✓✓ CHOLESTEROL: None (0 mg)
✓✓ FAT: Very Low (2 g) ✓✓ SODIUM: Very Low (4 mg)

DILL POTATO SALAD† *(4 oz. portion)*
✓ CALORIES: Low (165) ✓✓ CHOLESTEROL: Very Low (5 mg)
✓ FAT: Low (7 g) ✓✓ SODIUM: Very Low (59 mg)

Nutrition information supplied by Ralphs Grocery.

✓ Low ✓✓ Very Low
†Side dish guidelines are 1/3 of entree guidelines

Index

By Location

By Type of Cuisine

Alphabetical

Index by Location

Alphabetical Index

Coupons,

Questionnaire

and Order Form

<table>
<tr><td>Coupon</td><td>Healthy Dining in Los Angeles</td><td>Coupon</td></tr>
</table>

$5.00 OFF

Buy one meal, get $5.00 off
the price of a second meal.
Not valid with any other special offer.

BeauRivage

26025 W. Pacific Coast Hwy, Malibu
(310) 456-5733

<table>
<tr><td>Coupon</td><td>Healthy Dining in Los Angeles</td><td>Coupon</td></tr>
</table>

10% OFF
Entire Meal

Alcoholic beverages included.
Up to 4 in party.
Not valid with any other offer.

Bristol's Café

Bristol's Cafe

1570 Rosecrans Ave.
Manhattan Beach, CA
(213) 643-5229

<table>
<tr><td>Coupon</td><td>Healthy Dining in Los Angeles</td><td>Coupon</td></tr>
</table>

25% OFF
Entire Meal

Alcoholic beverages excluded.   Up to 4 in party.
Not valid with any other offer.

Chommanade

5009 E. 2nd St., Belmont Shore
(310) 433-1037

<table>
<tr><td>Coupon</td><td>Healthy Dining in Los Angeles</td><td>Coupon</td></tr>
</table>

Free Meal

With purchase of one meal
of equal or greater value.
Not valid with any other special offers.
Offer expires 12/31/95.

Cutters

At MGM Plaza
2425 Colorado Ave.
Santa Monica, CA 90404
(310) 453-3588

<table>
<tr><td>Coupon</td><td>Healthy Dining in Los Angeles</td><td>Coupon</td></tr>
</table>

50% OFF DINNER
Buy one dinner and get
50% off second dinner
Up to 4 in party.
Not valid with any other offer.

Dante's
Italian Cuisine

1611 S. Catalina Ave.
Redondo Beach, CA 90277
(310) 792-1972

Markets, Delis and Fast Food Coupons

Coupon   *Healthy Dining in Los Angeles*   Coupon

15% OFF
Entire Meal
With minimum food purchase of $10.⁰⁰

Andree's
Oven & Catering
23410 Civic Center Way #C-2
Malibu, CA   (310) 456-8533

Coupon   *Healthy Dining in Los Angeles*   Coupon

10% OFF
deli items
With minimum purchase of $10.⁰⁰

BRISTOL FARMS

the Food Place

1570 Rosecrans Ave., Manhattan Beach (310) 643-5229
837 Silver Spur Rd., Rolling Hills Estates (310) 541-9157
606 Fair Oaks Avenue, Pasadena (818) 441-5450

Coupon   *Healthy Dining in Los Angeles*   Coupon

20% OFF
any item in our full-service deli department. Expires 4/1/96
Not valid with any other offer.

MRS. GOOCH'S
WHOLE FOODS MARKET

Locations in Beverly Hills, Glendale, Northridge,
Redondo Beach, Sherman Oaks, Thousand Oaks & West LA

Coupon   *Healthy Dining in Los Angeles*   Coupon

Ralphs

Any Service Deli Salad or Entree
1 lb. or More–Cannot Exceed Value of Item
Limit One Item and One Coupon Per Customer. Coupon Effective thru December 27, 1995.

100 OFF with coupon

61749

$3.00 OFF
your next purchase of *Healthy Dining*

We want to know more about you and your thoughts about ***Healthy Dining***. So we'll give you $3.00 off your next copy of ***Healthy Dining*** if you'll return this questionnaire (information is confidential). To thank you, we will contact you when new editions are published and offer $3.00 off the retail price. You may also order now at the discount price (see reverse side).

1. How did you learn about ***Healthy Dining in Los Angeles***?

    ____ Newspaper   ____ Family or friend   ____ Dietitian

    ____ Radio   ____ Restaurant   ____ Personal Trainer

    ____ Television   ____ Health Organization   ____ Fitness Center

    ____ Store __________   ____ Physician   ____ Other __________

2. Are you on any of these special diets?

    ____ weight loss   ____ low-cholesterol   ____ diabetic   ____ vegetarian

    ____ low-fat   ____ low-sodium   ____ general health-conscious

3. Please rate the following features of the book:

	Very helpful	Moderately helpful	Not needed
Chapters on general nutrition	____	____	____
List of restaurants offering healthier items	____	____	____
Specific menu items available at these restaurants	____	____	____
Numerical values of fat, calories, cholesterol, etc.	____	____	____
Categories for "✓ low" and "✓✓ very low"	____	____	____
Discount coupons	____	____	____

4. Please list your favorite restaurants from this book:

5. What other restaurants would you like to see in the next edition?

6. What other food or health-related publications do you read? (American Health Magazine, Berkeley Wellness, Nutrition Action Healthletter, Eating Well, Cooking Light, etc.)

7. On average, how many times <u>per month</u> do you dine out? ______

8. Is this book primarily used by: ___ female   ___ male   ___ both

9. What is the age of the primary user of this book?

    ____ Under 30   ____ 30 to 45   ____ 45 to 60   ____ over 60

10. Would you or any of your personal contacts like more information about: ____ fundraising ____ seminars or community events ____ wholesale prices for ***Healthy Dining***?

Other Comments?

Fold on lines with address on outside.

Name _________________________________

Address _________________________________

____

Phone (   ) _____________

Stamp

Hill & Hill Publishing
P. O. Box 927215
San Diego, CA 92192-7215

Special $3.00 OFF any *Healthy Dining* books.

Order as many as you want at the special discount! It's our thank-you for answering our questionnaire.
You will also receive the $3.00 discount on future editions. Orders normally processed within 1 week.

Quantity		Price
_____ *Healthy Dining in Los Angeles*	$14.95 - $3.00 discount = $11.95	_________
_____ *Healthy Dining in Orange County*	$14.95 - $3.00 discount = $11.95	_________
_____ *Healthy Dining in San Diego*	$14.95 - $3.00 discount = $11.95	_________
	Subtotal	_________
	Tax (8¼% in Los Angeles)	_________
	Postage ($1.25 for 1st book + 50¢ each for additional books)	_________
	Total	_________

_____ Check enclosed

_____ VISA/Mastercard # _____________________________ exp._____ Signature _________________

Please fill out questionnaire on reverse and your name & address above. If sending check, make to
Hill & Hill Publishing and fasten your check securely to this sheet or use a separate envelope. Thanks.